FILM 70/71

An Anthology by the
National Society
of Film Critics

edited by
DAVID DENBY

Simon and Schuster   New York

The reviews and articles in this book originally appeared, for the most part, in the publications for which the contributors regularly write. Thanks are hereby given by the contributors as follows:

Hollis Alpert, reviews of *Soldier Blue, Catch-22, The Boys in the Band,* and *Ryan's Daughter,* reprinted by permission of *Saturday Review,* copyright © 1970 by Saturday Review, Inc.

Gary Arnold, reviews of *Joe, Tora! Tora! Tora!, Airport, The Owl and the Pussycat, Love Story,* and *Mississippi Mermaid,* reprinted by permission of the Washington *Post,* copyright © 1970 by The Washington Post Company, Inc.

Jacob Brackman, reviews of *Five Easy Pieces, Husbands, Getting Straight,* and *Catch-22,* reprinted by permission from *Esquire,* copyright © 1970, 1971 by Esquire, Inc.

Harold Clurman, reviews of *Tristana* and *Five Easy Pieces* from article "The New York Film Festival," reprinted by permission of *The Nation,* copyright © 1970 by The Nation, Inc.

Jay Cocks, reviews of *The Revolutionary, Woodstock, Performance, Scrooge,* and *Sympathy for the Devil,* reprinted by permission from *Time,* copyright © 1970 by Time Inc.

Brad Darrach, reviews of *M*A*S*H* and *The Damned,* reprinted by permission from *Movie,* copyright © 1970 by Time Inc.

David Denby, reviews of *Little Big Man, M*A*S*H, The Wild Child, The Strawberry Statement* and *Getting Straight,* reprinted by permission of *The Atlantic,* copyright © 1970, 1971 by The Atlantic Monthly Company.

Penelope Gilliatt, reviews of *Joe, The Virgin and the Gypsy, My Night at Maud's, The Passion of Anna, Two or Three Things I Know About Her,* and the article "Buster Keaton," reprinted by permission of *The New Yorker,* copyright © 1970 by The New Yorker Magazine, Inc.

CONTENTS

                                                                   7

III: ADAPTATIONS

IV: MUSICALS

V: SPECTACLES

VI: REFLECTIONS

AN EDITORIAL NOTE

In recent years The National Society of Film Critics has become a larger and broader group; there are now twenty-two members, as against the original twelve of 1966. The intentions of this fourth volume of Society criticism, however, remain the same as ever: to present a cross section of critical opinion on the most interesting films of the year, reflections on certain emerging trends, genres, and moods, and a sampling of the work of individual critics. Once again editorial exigencies—both for the authors and the editor of this volume—have forced an underrepresentation of several contributors. The editor readily admits that the situation is unfair and hopes that future editors will redress the imbalance.

DAVID DENBY

THE AWARDS

THE NATIONAL SOCIETY OF FILM CRITICS, in its fifth annual awards, voted *M*A*S*H* as the best picture of 1970. The Society named Ingmar Bergman as the best director of the year for *The Passion of Anna*, while Glenda Jackson, who appears in *Women in Love*, was honored for her performance. Miss Jackson won the best actress award. The award for the best actor went to George C. Scott in recognition of his performance in *Patton*.

Other awards voted by the Society named Chief Dan George as the best supporting actor for his performance in *Little Big Man*, and Lois Smith as the best supporting actress for her role in *Five Easy Pieces*.

The best cinematographer award was given to Nestor Almendros, who was responsible for the photography in *The Wild Child* and *My Night at Maud's*.

Eric Rohmer received the best screenplay of the year citation from the Society for *My Night at Maud's*.

Two special awards were given: to Donald Richie and the Film Department of the Museum of Modern Art for the three-month Retrospective of Japanese Films which they held in 1970; and to Daniel Talbot of the New Yorker theater for the contribution he has made to the cinema by showing films that might not otherwise have been available to the public.

Participants in the voting included Hollis Alpert of *Saturday Review*; Gary Arnold of the Washington *Post*; Harold Clurman of *The Nation*; Jay Cocks of *Time*; David Denby of *The Atlantic*; Penelope Gilliatt of *The New Yorker*; Philip T. Hartung of *Commonweal*; Pauline Kael of *The New Yorker*; Stefan Kanfer of *Time*; Stanley Kauffmann of *The New Republic*; Arthur Knight of *Saturday Review*; Robert Kotlowitz of *Harper's Magazine*; Joseph Morgenstern of *Newsweek*; Andrew Sarris of *The Village Voice*; Richard Schickel of *Life*; Arthur Schlesinger, Jr., of *Vogue*; John Simon of *The New Leader*; Bruce Williamson of *Playboy*; and Paul D. Zimmerman of *Newsweek*.

VOTING FOR 1970 AWARDS—
THE NATIONAL SOCIETY
OF FILM CRITICS

Each critic was asked to vote for three candidates in each category. The first choice was worth three points, the second two, the third one, and a simple plurality established the winner.

BEST PICTURE

HOLLIS ALPERT:	M*A*S*H; Investigation of a Citizen Above Suspicion; Husbands
GARY ARNOLD:	The Wild Child; M*A*S*H; Burn!
HAROLD CLURMAN:	The Passion of Anna; Tristana; The Wild Child
JAY COCKS:	The Passion of Anna; Husbands; My Night at Maud's
DAVID DENBY:	The Wild Child; My Night at Maud's; M*A*S*H
PENELOPE GILLIATT:	The Passion of Anna; The Wild Child; M*A*S*H
PHILIP T. HARTUNG:	My Night at Maud's; The Passion of Anna; Five Easy Pieces
PAULINE KAEL:	M*A*S*H; The Wild Child; The Confession
STEFAN KANFER:	The Passion of Anna; M*A*S*H; My Night at Maud's
STANLEY KAUFFMANN:	The Passion of Anna; The Milky Way; Five Easy Pieces

ARTHUR KNIGHT:	*The Wild Child; Five Easy Pieces; My Night at Maud's*
ROBERT KOTLOWITZ:	*Five Easy Pieces; M*A*S*H; The Confession*
JOSEPH MORGENSTERN:	*M*A*S*H; The Passion of Anna; The Wild Child*
ANDREW SARRIS:	*M*A*S*H; My Night at Maud's; Tristana*
RICHARD SCHICKEL:	*My Night at Maud's; Five Easy Pieces; The Wild Child*
ARTHUR SCHLESINGER, JR.:	*M*A*S*H; The Passion of Anna; Five Easy Pieces*
JOHN SIMON:	*The Passion of Anna; Investigation of a Citizen Above Suspicion; M*A*S*H*
BRUCE WILLIAMSON:	*M*A*S*H; Fellini Satyricon; The Passion of Anna*
PAUL D. ZIMMERMAN:	*My Night at Maud's; The Wild Child; The Rise of Louis XIV*

BEST DIRECTOR

HOLLIS ALPERT:	Federico Fellini (*Fellini Satyricon*); Elio Petri (*Investigation of a Citizen Above Suspicion*); Robert Altman (*M*A*S*H*)
GARY ARNOLD:	François Truffaut (*The Wild Child*); Robert Altman (*M*A*S*H*); Gillo Pontecorvo (*Burn!*)
HAROLD CLURMAN:	Ingmar Bergman (*The Passion of Anna*); Luis Buñuel (*Tristana*); François Truffaut (*The Wild Child*)
JAY COCKS:	Ingmar Bergman (*The Passion of Anna*); John Cassavetes (*Husbands*); François Truffaut (*The Wild Child*)
DAVID DENBY:	François Truffaut (*The Wild Child*); Robert Altman (*M*A*S*H*); Costa-Gavras (*The Confession*)
PENELOPE GILLIATT:	Ingmar Bergman (*The Passion of Anna*); François Truffaut (*The Wild Child*); Luis Buñuel (*Tristana*)
PHILIP T. HARTUNG:	Elio Petri (*Investigation of a Citizen Above Suspicion*); Eric Rohmer (*My*

Night at Maud's); Arthur Penn (*Little Big Man*)

PAULINE KAEL: François Truffaut (*The Wild Child*); Robert Altman (*M*A*S*H*); Irvin Kershner (*Loving*)

STEFAN KANFER: Ingmar Bergman (*The Passion of Anna*); Robert Altman (*M*A*S*H*); Luis Buñuel (*Tristana*)

STANLEY KAUFFMANN: Ingmar Bergman (*The Passion of Anna*); Luis Buñuel (*The Milky Way*); Bob Rafelson (*Five Easy Pieces*)

ARTHUR KNIGHT: François Truffaut (*The Wild Child*); Bob Rafelson (*Five Easy Pieces*); Robert Altman (*M*A*S*H*)

ROBERT KOTLOWITZ: Bob Rafelson (*Five Easy Pieces*); Costa-Gavras (*The Confession*); Roberto Rossellini (*The Rise of Louis XIV*)

JOSEPH MORGENSTERN: Robert Altman (*M*A*S*H*); Ingmar Bergman (*The Passion of Anna*); François Truffaut (*The Wild Child*)

ANDREW SARRIS: Luis Buñuel (*Tristana*); Eric Rohmer (*My Night at Maud's*); Robert Bresson (*Au Hasard, Balthazar*)

RICHARD SCHICKEL: Bob Rafelson (*Five Easy Pieces*); François Truffaut (*The Wild Child*); Luis Buñuel (*Tristana*)

ARTHUR SCHLESINGER, JR.: Robert Altman (*M*A*S*H*); Irvin Kershner (*Loving*); Ingmar Bergman (*The Passion of Anna*)

JOHN SIMON: Ingmar Bergman (*The Passion of Anna*); Yasushiro Ozu (*Late Summer*); Elio Petri (*Investigation of a Citizen Above Suspicion*)

BRUCE WILLIAMSON: Ingmar Bergman (*The Passion of Anna*); John Cassavetes (*Husbands*); Federico Fellini (*Fellini Satyricon*)

PAUL D. ZIMMERMAN: Robert Altman (*M*A*S*H*); Eric Rohmer (*My Night at Maud's*); François Truffaut (*The Wild Child*)

BEST ACTOR

HOLLIS ALPERT:
Robert Redford (*Little Fauss and Big Halsy*); George C. Scott (*Patton*); Ben Gazzara (*Husbands*)

GARY ARNOLD:
George Segal (*Loving; The Owl and the Pussycat; Where's Poppa?*); Peter Boyle (*Joe*); George C. Scott (*Patton*)

HAROLD CLURMAN:
Dustin Hoffman (*Little Big Man*); Alan Arkin (*Catch-22*); George Segal (*Loving*)

JAY COCKS:
Ben Gazzara (*Husbands*); Jason Robards (*The Ballad of Cable Hogue*); Peter Falk (*Husbands*)

DAVID DENBY:
George Segal (*Loving; The Owl and the Pussycat; Where's Poppa?*); George C. Scott (*Patton*); Dustin Hoffman (*Little Big Man*)

PENELOPE GILLIATT:
François Truffaut (*The Wild Child*); Max von Sydow (*The Passion of Anna*); Jean-Louis Trintignant (*My Night at Maud's*)

PHILIP T. HARTUNG:
Jean-Louis Trintignant (*My Night at Maud's*); Gian Maria Volonte (*Investigation of a Citizen Above Suspicion*); Dustin Hoffman (*Little Big Man*)

PAULINE KAEL:
George Segal (*Loving; The Owl and the Pussycat; Where's Poppa?*); Marcello Mastroianni (*The Pizza Triangle*) (no third choice)

STEFAN KANFER:
Alan Arkin (*Catch-22*); George C. Scott (*Patton*); Dustin Hoffman (*Little Big Man*)

STANLEY KAUFFMANN:
Peter O'Toole (*Brotherly Love*); George C. Scott (*Patton*); Jack Nicholson (*Five Easy Pieces*)

ARTHUR KNIGHT:
George C. Scott (*Patton*); James Earl Jones (*The Great White Hope*); Jack Nicholson (*Five Easy Pieces*)

ROBERT KOTLOWITZ:
Jack Nicholson (*Five Easy Pieces*); Marcello Mastroianni (*The Pizza Triangle*); Jean-Pierre Cargol (*The Wild Child*)

JOSEPH MORGENSTERN: George Segal (*Loving; The Owl and the Pussycat*); Jack Nicholson (*Five Easy Pieces*); Alan Arkin (*Catch-22*)

ANDREW SARRIS: Jean-Louis Trintignant (*My Night at Maud's*); Marcello Mastroianni (*The Pizza Triangle*); George Segal (*Loving; Where's Poppa?*)

RICHARD SCHICKEL: Jean-Louis Trintignant (*My Night at Maud's*); Jack Nicholson (*Five Easy Pieces*); Peter O'Toole (*Brotherly Love*)

ARTHUR SCHLESINGER, JR.: George C. Scott (*Patton*); Melvyn Douglas (*I Never Sang for My Father*); James Earl Jones (*The Great White Hope*)

JOHN SIMON: Gian Maria Volonte (*Investigation of a Citizen Above Suspicion*); Peter Boyle (*Joe*); Fernando Rey (*Tristana*)

BRUCE WILLIAMSON: George C. Scott (*Patton*); Jean-Louis Trintignant (*My Night at Maud's*); Alan Bates (*Women in Love*)

PAUL D. ZIMMERMAN: Alan Arkin (*Catch-22*); Jack Nicholson (*Five Easy Pieces*); Dustin Hoffman (*Little Big Man*)

BEST ACTRESS

HOLLIS ALPERT: Glenda Jackson (*Women in Love*); Karen Black (*Five Easy Pieces*); Tina Chen (*The Hawaiians*)

GARY ARNOLD: Barbra Streisand (*The Owl and the Pussycat*); Eva Marie Saint (*Loving*); Karen Black (*Five Easy Pieces*)

HAROLD CLURMAN: Glenda Jackson (*Women in Love*); Liv Ullmann (*The Passion of Anna*); Karen Black (*Five Easy Pieces*)

JAY COCKS: Stella Stevens (*The Ballad of Cable Hogue*); Liv Ullmann (*The Passion of Anna*); Françoise Fabian (*My Night at Maud's*)

DAVID DENBY: Françoise Fabian (*My Night at Maud's*); Glenda Jackson (*Women in Love*);

Barbra Streisand (*The Owl and the Pussycat*)

PENELOPE GILLIATT: Glenda Jackson (*Women in Love*); Liv Ullmann (*The Passion of Anna*); Françoise Fabian (*My Night at Maud's*)

PHILIP T. HARTUNG: Carrie Snodgress (*Diary of a Mad Housewife*); Catherine Deneuve (*Tristana*); Françoise Fabian (*My Night at Maud's*)

PAULINE KAEL: Barbra Streisand (*The Owl and the Pussycat*); Glenda Jackson (*Women in Love*); Monica Vitti (*The Pizza Triangle*)

STEFAN KANFER: Stella Stevens (*The Ballad of Cable Hogue*); Glenda Jackson (*Women in Love*); Joanna Shimkus (*The Virgin and the Gypsy*)

STANLEY KAUFFMANN: Liv Ullmann (*The Passion of Anna*); Bibi Andersson (*The Passion of Anna*); Glenda Jackson (*Women in Love*)

ARTHUR KNIGHT: Carrie Snodgress (*Diary of a Mad Housewife*); Glenda Jackson (*Women in Love*); Karen Black (*Five Easy Pieces*)

ROBERT KOTLOWITZ: Monica Vitti (*The Pizza Triangle*); Glenda Jackson (*Women in Love*); Liv Ullmann (*The Passion of Anna*)

JOSEPH MORGENSTERN: Liv Ullmann (*The Passion of Anna*); Barbra Streisand (*The Owl and the Pussycat*); Françoise Fabian (*My Night at Maud's*)

ANDREW SARRIS: Françoise Fabian (*My Night at Maud's*); Tuesday Weld (*I Walk the Line*); Annie Girardot (*Love Is a Funny Thing*)

RICHARD SCHICKEL: Monica Vitti (*The Pizza Triangle*); Françoise Fabian (*My Night at Maud's*); Stella Stevens (*The Ballad of Cable Hogue*)

ARTHUR SCHLESINGER, JR.: Glenda Jackson (*Women in Love*); Carrie Snodgress (*Diary of a Mad House-*

	wife); Liv Ullmann (*The Passion of Anna*)
JOHN SIMON:	Françoise Fabian (*My Night at Maud's*); Dorothy Tristan (*End of the Road*); Liv Ullmann (*The Passion of Anna*)
BRUCE WILLIAMSON:	Glenda Jackson (*Women in Love*); Françoise Fabian (*My Night at Maud's*); Jane Alexander (*The Great White Hope*)
PAUL D. ZIMMERMAN:	Françoise Fabian (*My Night at Maud's*); Karen Black (*Five Easy Pieces*); Glenda Jackson (*Women in Love*)

BEST SUPPORTING ACTOR

HOLLIS ALPERT:	Frank Langella (*Diary of a Mad Housewife*); Paul Mazursky (*Alex in Wonderland*); Peter Boyle (*Joe*)
GARY ARNOLD:	Richard Castellano (*Lovers and Other Strangers*); Anthony Perkins (*WUSA; Catch-22*); Michael Greer (*The Magic Garden of Stanley Sweetheart*)
HAROLD CLURMAN:	Chief Dan George (*Little Big Man*); Jacques Rispal (*The Confession*); Oliver Reed (*Women in Love*)
JAY COCKS:	David Warner (*The Ballad of Cable Hogue; Perfect Friday*); Jack Palance (*Monte Walsh*); Colin Blakely (*The Private Life of Sherlock Holmes*)
DAVID DENBY:	Paul Mazursky (*Alex in Wonderland*); Richard Castellano (*Lovers and Other Strangers*); Chief Dan George (*Little Big Man*)
PENELOPE GILLIATT:	Antoine Vitez (*My Night at Maud's*); Anthony Perkins (*Catch-22*); Paul Mazursky (*Alex in Wonderland*)
PHILIP T. HARTUNG:	Chief Dan George (*Little Big Man*); Anthony Perkins (*Catch-22*); Orson Welles (*Catch-22*)
PAULINE KAEL:	Anthony Perkins (*Catch-22; WUSA*); Paul Mazursky (*Alex in Wonderland*); Jacques Rispal (*The Confession*)
STEFAN KANFER:	Chief Dan George (*Little Big Man*);

Peter Boyle (*Joe*); David Warner (*The Ballad of Cable Hogue*)

STANLEY KAUFFMANN: Frank Langella (*Diary of a Mad House-wife*); Victor Jory (*Flap*); Hume Cronyn (*There Was a Crooked Man*)

ARTHUR KNIGHT: Peter Boyle (*Joe*); Melvyn Douglas (*I Never Sang for My Father*); Chief Dan George (*Little Big Man*)

ROBERT KOTLOWITZ: Richard Castellano (*Lovers and Other Strangers*); Chief Dan George (*Little Big Man*); Donald Sutherland (*M*A*S*H*)

JOSEPH MORGENSTERN: Robert Duvall (*M*A*S*H*); Anthony Perkins (*Catch-22*); François Truffaut (*The Wild Child*)

ANDREW SARRIS: Hume Cronyn (*There Was a Crooked Man*); George Sanders (*The Kremlin Letter*); Ralph Meeker (*I Walk the Line*)

RICHARD SCHICKEL: Anthony Perkins (*Catch-22*; *WUSA*); Fernando Rey (*Tristana*); Chief Dan George (*Little Big Man*)

ARTHUR SCHLESINGER, JR.: Melvyn Douglas (*I Never Sang for My Father*); Peter Boyle (*Joe*); Jacques Rispal (*The Confession*)

JOHN SIMON: Chief Dan George (*Little Big Man*); Trevor Howard (*Ryan's Daughter*); George Macready (*Tora! Tora! Tora!*)

BRUCE WILLIAMSON: Richard Castellano (*Lovers and Other Strangers*); Anthony Perkins (*Catch-22*); Chief Dan George (*Little Big Man*)

PAUL D. ZIMMERMAN: Chief Dan George (*Little Big Man*); Billy Bush Green (*Five Easy Pieces*) (no third choice)

BEST SUPPORTING ACTRESS

HOLLIS ALPERT: Trish van Devere (*Where's Poppa?*); Sally Kellerman (*M*A*S*H*); Lois Smith (*Five Easy Pieces*)

GARY ARNOLD:	Trish van Devere (*Where's Poppa?*); Karen Black (*Five Easy Pieces*); Lee Grant (*The Landlord*)
HAROLD CLURMAN:	Lois Smith (*Five Easy Pieces*); Karen Black (*Five Easy Pieces*); Marie-Christine Barrault (*My Night at Maud's*)
JAY COCKS:	Sally Kellerman (*M*A*S*H; Brewster McCloud*); Lois Smith (*Five Easy Pieces*); Dorothy Tristan (*End of the Road*)
DAVID DENBY:	Lois Smith (*Five Easy Pieces*); Jenny Runacre (*Husbands*); Trish van Devere (*Where's Poppa?*)
PENELOPE GILLIATT:	Karen Black (*Five Easy Pieces*); Marie-Christine Barrault (*My Night at Maud's*); Bibi Andersson (*The Passion of Anna*)
PHILIP T. HARTUNG:	Lois Smith (*Five Easy Pieces*); Marie Marc (*Me*); Stella Stevens (*The Ballad of Cable Hogue*)
PAULINE KAEL:	Eva Marie Saint (*Loving*); Sally Kellerman (*M*A*S*H*); Trish van Devere (*Where's Poppa?*)
STEFAN KANFER:	Lois Smith (*Five Easy Pieces*); Sally Kellerman (*M*A*S*H*); Stella Stevens (*The Ballad of Cable Hogue*)
STANLEY KAUFFMANN:	Lois Smith (*Five Easy Pieces*); Dorothy Tristan (*End of the Road*); Caroline Cellier (*This Man Must Die*)
ARTHUR KNIGHT:	Tuesday Weld (*I Walk the Line*); Jane Alexander (*The Great White Hope*); Helena Kallianiotes (*Five Easy Pieces*)
ROBERT KOTLOWITZ:	Lois Smith (*Five Easy Pieces*); Eva Marie Saint (*Loving*); Karen Black (*Five Easy Pieces*)
JOSEPH MORGENSTERN:	Stella Stevens (*The Ballad of Cable Hogue*); Eva Marie Saint (*Loving*); Sally Kellerman (*M*A*S*H*)
ANDREW SARRIS:	Jenny Runacre (*Husbands*); Ellen Burstyn (*Alex in Wonderland*); Candy Barr (*The History of the Blue Movie*)

RICHARD SCHICKEL:	Ellen Burstyn (*Alex in Wonderland*); Jenny Runacre (*Husbands*); Trish van Devere (*Where's Poppa?*)
ARTHUR SCHLESINGER, JR.:	Eva Marie Saint (*Loving*); Simone Signoret (*The Confession*); Jane Alexander (*The Great White Hope*)
JOHN SIMON:	Lois Smith (*Five Easy Pieces*); Marie Marc (*Me*); Bibi Andersson (*The Passion of Anna*)
BRUCE WILLIAMSON:	Lois Smith (*Five Easy Pieces*); Sally Kellerman (*M*A*S*H*); Stella Stevens (*The Ballad of Cable Hogue*)
PAUL D. ZIMMERMAN:	Françoise Fabian (*My Night at Maud's*); Lois Smith (*Five Easy Pieces*); Karen Black (*Five Easy Pieces*)

BEST SCREENPLAY

HOLLIS ALPERT:	Eric Rohmer (*My Night at Maud's*); Charles Eastman (*Little Fauss and Big Halsy*); Adrien Joyce (*Five Easy Pieces*)
GARY ARNOLD:	Eric Rohmer (*My Night at Maud's*); François Truffaut and Jean Gruault (*The Wild Child*); Alan Plater (*The Virgin and the Gypsy*)
HAROLD CLURMAN:	Ingmar Bergman (*The Passion of Anna*); Luis Buñuel and Julio Alejandro (*Tristana*); Elio Petri and Ugo Pirro (*Investigation of a Citizen Above Suspicion*)
JAY COCKS:	Walter Bernstein (*The Molly Maguires*); François Truffaut and Jean-Louis Richard (*Mississippi Mermaid*); Ingmar Bergman (*The Passion of Anna*)
DAVID DENBY:	Eric Rohmer (*My Night at Maud's*); Jorge Semprun (*The Confession*); Ring Lardner, Jr. (*M*A*S*H*)
PENELOPE GILLIATT:	François Truffaut and Jean Gruault (*The Wild Child*); Eric Rohmer (*My Night at Maud's*); Ingmar Bergman (*The Passion of Anna*)
PHILIP T. HARTUNG:	Eric Rohmer (*My Night at Maud's*); Adrien Joyce (*Five Easy Pieces*); Cal-

der Willingham (*Little Big Man*)

PAULINE KAEL: François Truffaut and Jean Gruault (*The Wild Child*); Jorge Semprun (*The Confession*) (no third choice)

STEFAN KANFER: Ingmar Bergman (*The Passion of Anna*); Ring Lardner, Jr. (*M*A*S*H*); Eric Rohmer (*My Night at Maud's*)

STANLEY KAUFFMANN: Ingmar Bergman (*The Passion of Anna*); Luis Buñuel and Jean-Claude Carriere (*The Milky Way*); Adrien Joyce (*Five Easy Pieces*)

ARTHUR KNIGHT: Eric Rohmer (*My Night at Maud's*); François Truffaut and Jean Gruault (*The Wild Child*); Jorge Semprun (*The Confession*)

ROBERT KOTLOWITZ: Adrien Joyce (*Five Easy Pieces*); Jorge Semprun (*The Confession*); Philippe Erlanger (*The Rise of Louis XIV*)

JOSEPH MORGENSTERN: Ingmar Bergman (*The Passion of Anna*); François Truffaut and Jean Gruault (*The Wild Child*); Adrien Joyce (*Five Easy Pieces*)

ANDREW SARRIS: Eric Rohmer (*My Night at Maud's*); (no second and third choice)

RICHARD SCHICKEL: Eric Rohmer (*My Night at Maud's*); Adrien Joyce (*Five Easy Pieces*); François Truffaut and Jean Gruault (*The Wild Child*)

ARTHUR SCHLESINGER, JR.: Jorge Semprun (*The Confession*); Ring Lardner, Jr. (*M*A*S*H*) (no third choice)

JOHN SIMON: Ingmar Bergman (*The Passion of Anna*); Elio Petri and Ugo Pirro (*Investigation of a Citizen Above Suspicion*); Ring Lardner, Jr. (*M*A*S*H*)

BRUCE WILLIAMSON: Adrien Joyce (*Five Easy Pieces*); Ring Lardner, Jr. (*M*A*S*H*); Eric Rohmer (*My Night at Maud's*)

PAUL D. ZIMMERMAN: Eric Rohmer (*My Night at Maud's*); Adrien Joyce (*Five Easy Pieces*) (no third choice)

BEST
CINEMATOGRAPHY

HOLLIS ALPERT: Billy Williams (*Women in Love*); Sven Nykvist (*First Love*); Giuseppe Rotunno (*Fellini Satyricon*)

GARY ARNOLD: Nestor Almendros (*The Wild Child; My Night at Maud's*); James Wong Howe (*The Molly Maguires*); Gordon Willis (*Loving; The Landlord; End of the Road*)

HAROLD CLURMAN: Sven Nykvist (*The Passion of Anna; First Love*); Nestor Almendros (*My Night at Maud's; The Wild Child*); (no third choice)

JAY COCKS: Laszlo Kovacs (*Alex in Wonderland*); Michael Wadleigh (*Woodstock*).; Peter Suschitzky (*Leo the Last*)

DAVID DENBY: Nestor Almendros (*The Wild Child; My Night at Maud's*); Billy Williams (*Women in Love*); Marcello Gatti (*Burn!*)

PENELOPE GILLIATT: Sven Nykvist (*The Passion of Anna; First Love*); Billy Williams (*Women in Love*); Nestor Almendros (*The Wild Child; My Night at Maud's*)

PHILIP T. HARTUNG: Billy Williams (*Women in Love*); Giuseppe Rotunno (*Fellini Satyricon*); Nestor Almendros (*My Night at Maud's*)

PAULINE KAEL: Nestor Almendros (*The Wild Child*); Harold Stine (*M*A*S*H*); Gordon Willis (*Loving; End of the Road*)

STEFAN KANFER: Sven Nykvist (*The Passion of Anna; First Love*); Fred Koenekamp (*Patton*); Nestor Almendros (*The Wild Child*)

STANLEY KAUFFMANN: (Abstained)

ARTHUR KNIGHT: Billy Williams (*Women in Love*); James Wong Howe (*The Molly Maguires*); Fred Young (*Ryan's Daughter*)

ROBERT KOTLOWITZ: Billy Williams (*Women in Love*); Nes-

	tor Almendros (*The Wild Child*) (no third choice)
JOSEPH MORGENSTERN:	Gordon Willis (*Loving; The Landlord; End of the Road*) (no second and third choice)
ANDREW SARRIS:	Nestor Almendros (*My Night at Maud's; The Wild Child*) (no second and third choice)
RICHARD SCHICKEL:	Harold Stine (*M*A*S*H*); Nestor Almendros (*My Night at Maud's; The Wild Child*); Sven Nykvist (*The Passion of Anna*)
ARTHUR SCHLESINGER, JR.:	Fred Koenekamp (*Patton*); Giuseppe Rotunno (*Fellini Satyricon*); Fred Young (*Ryan's Daughter*)
JOHN SIMON:	Sven Nykvist (*The Passion of Anna; First Love*); Jose Aguayo (*Tristana*); Jean Boffety (*The Things of Life; Act of the Heart*)
BRUCE WILLIAMSON:	Sven Nykvist (*The Passion of Anna; First Love*); Giuseppe Rotunno (*Fellini Satyricon*); Fred Koenekamp (*Patton*)
PAUL D. ZIMMERMAN:	Nestor Almendros (*The Wild Child; My Night at Maud's*); Georges LeClerc (*The Rise of Louis XIV*) (no third choice)

Voting Tabulation (1st choice = 3 points, 2nd choice = 2 points, 3rd choice = 1 point)

BEST PICTURE

27 POINTS	*M*A*S*H*
25 POINTS	*The Passion of Anna*
18 POINTS	*The Wild Child*
16 POINTS	*My Night at Maud's*
10 POINTS	*Five Easy Pieces*

BEST DIRECTOR

24 POINTS	Ingmar Bergman (*The Passion of Anna*)
20 POINTS	François Truffaut (*The Wild Child*)
19 POINTS	Robert Altman (*M*A*S*H*)
10 POINTS	Luis Buñuel (*Tristana*)
9 POINTS	Bob Rafelson (*Five Easy Pieces*)

BEST ACTOR

18 POINTS	George C. Scott (*Patton*)
14 POINTS	George Segal (*Loving; The Owl and the Pussycat; Where's Poppa?*)
12 POINTS	Jean-Louis Trintignant (*My Night at Maud's*)
11 POINTS	Jack Nicholson (*Five Easy Pieces*)
9 POINTS	Alan Arkin (*Catch-22*)

BEST ACTRESS

27 POINTS	Glenda Jackson (*Women in Love*)
20 POINTS	Françoise Fabian (*My Night at Maud's*)
15 POINTS	Liv Ullmann (*The Passion of Anna*)
9 POINTS	Barbra Streisand (*The Owl and the Pussycat*)
8 POINTS	Carrie Snodgress (*Diary of a Mad Housewife*)

BEST SUPPORTING ACTOR

21 POINTS	Chief Dan George (*Little Big Man*)
16 POINTS	Anthony Perkins (*Catch-22; WUSA*)
11 POINTS	Richard Castellano (*Lovers and Other Strangers*)
8 POINTS	Peter Boyle (*Joe*)
8 POINTS	Paul Mazursky (*Alex in Wonderland*)

BEST SUPPORTING ACTRESS

29 POINTS	Lois Smith (*Five Easy Pieces*)
12 POINTS	Sally Kellerman (*M*A*S*H*)

10 POINTS	Eva Marie Saint (*Loving*)
9 POINTS	Karen Black (*Five Easy Pieces*)
9 POINTS	Trish van Devere (*Where's Poppa?*)

BEST SCREENPLAY

23 POINTS	Eric Rohmer (*My Night at Maud's*)
17 POINTS	Ingmar Bergman (*The Passion of Anna*)
15 POINTS	Adrien Joyce (*Five Easy Pieces*)
13 POINTS	François Truffaut and Jean Gruault (*The Wild Child*)
10 POINTS	Jorge Semprun (*The Confession*)

BEST CINEMATOGRAPHY

24 POINTS	Nestor Almendros (*The Wild Child; My Night at Maud's*)
18 POINTS	Sven Nykvist (*The Passion of Anna; First Love*)
16 POINTS	Billy Williams (*Women in Love*)
7 POINTS	Giuseppe Rotunno (*Fellini Satyricon*)

SPECIAL AWARD TO DONALD RICHIE AND THE FILM DEPARTMENT OF THE MUSEUM OF MODERN ART— by majority vote

SPECIAL AWARD TO DANIEL TALBOT OF THE NEW YORKER THEATER—by majority vote

I:

IN OUR TIME

I
ANTI-HEROES

FIVE EASY PIECES

Jacob Brackman

Jack Nicholson played the alcoholic Southern lawyer who biked along with Fonda and Hopper toward New Orleans, until cracker night riders beat him to death while he slept. On the strength of that supporting performance (*Easy Rider* was a third over when he came on, and had a third left to run when they killed him off) Nicholson joined the several important movie "finds" who surfaced at the decade's end. Like Hoffman, Voight, Wilder, Gould, Sutherland or Arkin, he seems spectacularly intelligent, and a *person*, relative to the stars we grew up with.

In *Five Easy Pieces*, Nicholson's on screen practically from beginning to end. We meet him in a Southern California oil field: hard-hatted, grease-covered. Working the rigs, collecting his pay in a dank trailer locker room, boozing. Cleaning up at poker, diddling a couple pickups, flush with simple pleasures. Or stuck with Rayette, his tacky, lachrymose girl friend, on a treadmill of neglect, tears, and making up.

His mate on the rigs is a wild-eyed peckerwood named Elton, with an unpredictable, hebephrenic laugh and an overweight, TV-addicted, henna-rinse, mobile-home wife named Stoney, who, like the boys, bowls a mean string. Rayette can do no better than gutter the ball. Nicholson sulks. Hurt, she waits in the car. They inhabit a world in which romantic anguish gets thrashed out in parking lots behind bowling alleys, in the glare of burger-stand neon, to the rumble of passing engines. On the track, the sleazy country syrup

of Tammy Wynette. Dimly, one senses Nicholson's "superiority"
to his scene. He seems to dissemble in his moods. Restless irony
plays beneath his smiles.

One fine morning, having reported for work hung over and been
sent home, he and Elton get stuck bumper to bumper on the freeway. Everybody's honking. Nicholson gets madder and madder at
the absurdity of their predicament. Finally he climbs out of his car,
starts yelling at the other motorists. Clambers aboard a moving van
in line ahead of him to get a long view of the traffic. Still hollering
and clowning, he discovers an old upright piano on the truck, pulls
off the dropcloth, seats himself before it with an elaborate flourish.
Elton whoops uncertain encouragement. Nicholson launches into
Chopin's "Fantasy in F. Minor." The old upright is tinny, with
broken notes, out of tune—but he's a terrific pianist! As the truck
pulls off onto an exit, his discordant sonata swells above the honking.

It's the first in a series of astonishing fake-outs that leave you
suddenly adrift, with no presuppositions about what lies ahead. To
this juncture, the movie promised to be a funny, scrupulously observed slice of oil town. As the truck pulls off the freeway with
Nicholson pummeling out Chopin, all bets, for a moment, are off.
He hops off in a strange town, wanders the streets until nightfall.
Then he's back. Slips into the luncheonette around closing time.
Rayette and another waitress are cleaning up. Nicholson sits sullen
at one end of the counter. At the other, a man holds a baby in his
lap. It wails miserably throughout the scene.

During lunch break in the field, Elton, sober with a sense of
responsibility, confides to Nicholson that Rayette is pregnant,
scared to tell him. He'll find himself getting used to the idea, Elton
reassures, even liking it. Elton inhabits a world where marriage
simply begins that way, inauspiciously. "Hell," he recalls, "when
Stoney first told *me*, I coulda s - - - !"

"It's ridiculous," Nicholson fumes at last. "I'm sitting here listening to some cracker asshole who lives in a trailer park compare
his life to mine."

They quarrel. Nicholson stalks off toward the foreground. Elton,
from behind a rig, not quite comprehending *how* he's been betrayed, hurls a beer can toward his back.

There follows another sequence which gives you the excited feeling that this film may go absolutely anywhere. Nicholson slams his gear into his car and ambles over to the foreman, perhaps hoping to create something dramatic out of quitting. But he can't even get the foreman's attention. Finally, distractedly, the foreman says, "I don't give a damn what you do." Nicholson turns to head out. Meanwhile, way back, near the top of the frame, in extremely deep focus, an ominous cat-and-mouse ballet has been shaping up in silhouette: Elton stalked by two men in suits. As they close in on him, the camera approaches. Nicholson's voice comes booming from offscreen, "Hey! What's going on here?" Then he's running at them, raising dust, leaping onto Elton's tormentors for a losing roughhouse. One of them prepares to clap handcuffs on Nicholson. Elton had stood "accused of robbing a filling station up in the Indian nation . . . got wild and jumped bail." Now, a year later, the law comes after him. As the officers shove him into their car, he calls matter-of-factly, "Tell Stoney for me, ya hear?" It seems the natural conclusion to his homily on the fulfillments of stable family life. How could we guess at this point that Elton has gone from the movie for good, or that Rayette's pregnancy will never again be mentioned?

Nicholson, in shades, a coat and tie, driving on the freeway into Los Angeles. Then in a recording-studio control booth. The engineer patiently copes, via microphone, with an intense woman pianist who can't desist warbling off-key with Bach's "Chromatic Fantasy and Fugue." We quickly learn that the pianist, Partita, is Nicholson's sister. She lives with his family on an island off the coast of Washington. They haven't seen or heard from him in a long time. Carl Fidelio, their older brother, recently sprained his neck in an absurd bicycle accident, cutting short his career as a fiddler. No longer able to tuck the violin beneath his chin, he's been coaching a young woman in piano. Brother and sister laugh together. She must tell him: father has had two serious strokes. She tries to persuade him to come home with her that very evening. Visibly agonized at the prospect of returning, he nonetheless promises to drive up soon.

His oil-town life now appears to have run out. But just as we've lost all sense of where the movie may be preparing to take us, we're whirling around a room with Nicholson and a girl from the bowl-

ing alley, her moaning accelerating toward climax. Wearing a Triumph T-shirt, he gyres in absolute silence. Hand-held camera.
Maelstrom fornication, equilibrium and geography lapsed, the universe swung wide and topsy-turvy, so one does not know or care
where one body leaves off and the other begins. Her cry reaches its
peak, abates into a whimper. Nicholson stands back from his work,
grinning, still unbalanced by sexual rhythms. The whole sequence
lasts perhaps a minute.

He returns to Rayette's apartment to pick up his things. On the
sound track, Tammy Wynette laments D-I-V-O-R-C-E. Packing,
he tells Rayette his father is sick. He's going away for a few weeks.
Crumpled in a heap beneath the bedclothes, her cheeks shiny with
tears, Rayette knows better: "You're going away, period."

Nicholson heaves his suitcase in the back window of his car.
Slides in behind the wheel. Slams the door behind him. Turns on
the ignition. Explodes, thrashing, cursing. After a moment's stillness, he goes back inside and invites Rayette along.

Looking back, one can say the first half of *Five Easy Pieces* ends
here. Before the second half proper commences, there's a long interlude on the road—a limbo between the film's two insular
worlds. In the world behind and the world ahead, Nicholson seems
half stranger, half prisoner. But here, between stoppings, lapping
the miles, he seems loosest, caught up in the illusion of progress
and Clean Starts.

Much of this northward drive concerns two young women of
questionable sexuality, whose car has overturned en route to
Alaska. They foist themselves on Nicholson and Rayette. (Though
he may be relieved at diversion.) Their spokesman, a Charles Ad-
damsish, filth-obsessed girl who calls herself Palm Apodaca, spews
out hostility disguised as ecological angst, offending Rayette with
her language and negative attitudes. After dropping off Palm and
her companion, Terry Grouse, Nicholson stashes Rayette in a
motel on the mainland, promising to telephone in a few days, after
he feels out his family. Grim shots of him on the ferry, crossing
through fog to the island where he grew up.

The remainder deals with three weeks—between lives—that
Nicholson spends "home." Home is more oppressive a mausoleum
than when he ran away from it, three years earlier. Reduced to a

nearly vegetable condition by the strokes, his father is attended, spoon-fed, by a swaggering, ex-sailor muscleman named Spicer. Tita believes father to be alert and conscious behind the mask of his paralysis. Love-starved, high-strung as an overbred race horse, she's fascinated by Spicer's physicality. Brother Carl is mannered, cheery with a bitchy underside, oblivious to the interactions seething around him. Nicholson fascinates, and is fascinated by, Carl's student, Catherine Van Ost, a cool and beautiful divorcée. How could he, with so exceptional a gift and background, forsake his musical career without a second thought?

"I gave it a second thought," Nicholson says.

On the day Carl goes to the mainland for his hydrotherapy, she asks him to play for her, as a special favor, and he does. As he plays a Chopin Prelude, the camera trails around the room, over the Steinway, over Carl's violin, over all the artifacts of forty years' family music, portraits of the immortals, youthful photographs of Partita and Nicholson, of their bearded father at the height of his powers, electric with potency. When Catherine appears visibly moved, Nicholson's quick to tell her the Prelude's the easiest piece he knows, he played it better at age eight, he felt nothing in the playing. She acts repelled, as if by his self-loathing, but he storms her. After they make it, relaxed and smiling, she glistens with sweat.

Unable to believe she could choose to sequester herself in this island rest home, he fastens upon her, single-mindedly, as the means to change his life—as *prerequisite* to changing it, to making some place for himself. But his sudden hopes become unhinged. Having run out of motel money, Rayette shows up in a taxi. He learns Catherine and Carl are engaged to be married. In his frenzy to straighten things out with her, he upsets a party of their friends, then breaks in on Spicer rubbing down Tita in a bedroom; flails at him, held helpless in a headlock. Catherine finally brings him to understand that she has sealed certain treaties with life; they cannot accommodate him. She leaves him standing by the water. It was the first time we saw him want anything. Now he looks raw and vulnerable, almost frightened. "Okay," he whispers.

He wheels his father into a meadow, against an expanse of horizon at dawn. Leaning forward on his haunches, he tries to sustain a one-way conversation about essentials with that impassive hulk until tears choke him off. Lamely, he tries to brush aside his having messed up so. "Anyway, we both know I was never that good at it." (The piano? Is that all?) He sets off with Rayette and later, at a gas station, impulsively abandons her, his car, his wallet.

If I've not described the characters and progress too crudely, you may share my conviction, straight off, that *Five Easy Pieces* would be exciting even if it contained a hundred things that didn't work. (One felt that way about *Easy Rider, Alice's Restaurant, Zabriskie Point, Catch-22*. They reached for something more and, for that, one would gladly allow them their falling short.) But astoundingly, *Five Easy Pieces*, stretching out into thematic territory virtually uncharted in American film, is rich with a hundred things that *do* work: small authenticities which synopsis can't hint at. Surely Nicholson's a great new star, charming and complicated; yet surrounded here with actors as strong or stronger, he becomes simply the pivot for the evenest, most beautiful ensemble playing I've seen outside of Bergman. The film making is at once modest and masterful, rhythmical, tasteful. You laugh at each of its three segments in completely new ways, and at last get swept away by despair, which lay beneath the laughter all along. It is the opposite of a genre film: What you least expected and therefore most hoped to see. Many critics have been using the word *auteur* to draw attention to tiny "individual" touches with which directors flavor "standard fare." By that measure, *Five Easy Pieces* is too original, too artful even to register on the meter.

Listen. I've waited here nearly two years for an American picture I could full-out get behind, no hemming and hawing, no qualms that matter. So far this is it. *Five Easy Pieces*. Not some quotable aside fished from a mire of misgivings. I'm pressing you to check this one out.

Bob Rafelson directed one previous film (which he wrote, incidentally, along with Nicholson), a manic distillation of decades of clichés from American popular culture. *Head* turned out to star The Monkees, whose Dr. Frankenstein Rafelson was. By late 1968, when it was released, The Monkees (who for a couple years grossed almost as much as The Beatles) had become an anathema to anyone past puberty. Feeling itself suckered, the public's affection for them froze. In one of the most radical reversals of show-biz fortune ever, they were dead within months. They couldn't get a concert date. The pre-release promotion for *Head* concealed its stars' identities, and as soon as that further shuck transpired, the picture was dead too: neither critics nor moviegoers were prepared to see past The Monkees to its brilliance. "Manufactured!" "*Plastic!*" For once, the annoying rejoinder, "But that's exactly the *point*," seemed apt.

HAROLD CLURMAN

The films now coming from the Hollywood studios—*Getting Straight, Diary of a Mad Housewife* and the like—and often hailed by reviewers as tremendously important, reveal how much slackness of judgment, sloppiness of feeling and fundamental conventionality is to be found in both the makers and publicists of these films.

Take Bob Rafelson's *Five Easy Pieces*. It is certainly superior to most of the local high-cost products. It is well photographed (excellence in camera work is becoming the rule rather than the exception), its acting and direction are also of good quality. Karen Black, Lois Smith, Helena Kallianiotes are outstanding in a well-chosen cast. But at the heart of the matter there is a fatal flaw.

The picture presents one Robert Eroica Dupea, seen first as an oil worker. We later learn that he was once a pianist, a member of a family devoted entirely to music. He gave up the piano and practically everything else except boozing and promiscuous fornication. In a word, he is totally disaffected. Such types have already become commonplace in novels, plays, pictures. They do of course exist. The trouble in *Five Easy Pieces* is that one is supposed to take for granted that (*a*) our society must perforce produce such types (they are a new sort of "elite"); and (*b*) that they are worthy of special sympathy, that they are interesting and somehow endearing.

Dupea (adequately played by Jack Nicholson, who was more effective in *Easy Rider*) weeps as he kneels before his paralyzed father and confesses contrition for not having become the sort of person the old man must have hoped for. The viewer is expected to be touched, but it is difficult to feel compassion for the erring son: his relation to women is coarse; he is basically impervious to the

general environment, against which his unruliness is supposed to
represent an oblique protest. Irresponsibility is not a winning trait.
Yes, he tries to defend his buddy who is being arrested for theft; he
leaves his wallet with his girl friend before he abandons her (is she
or is she not pregnant by him, as momentarily suggested?). But all
this is patchwork, intended to complete a studio pattern; it does
not create a central character who arouses the sense of personal
concordance one can experience with the minor figures of, let us
say, Ray's *Days and Nights in the Forest* or Truffaut's *Wild Child*.

To the picture's credit there are such entertaining sequences as
Dupea's attempt to get two pieces of toast with his meal at a roadside eating place, an even funnier episode in which a lesbian tramp
goes on and on about the prevalence of filth everywhere so bad she
"doesn't even want to talk about it." These and other such bits
make the film of more than passable grade.

JOHN SIMON

Five Easy Pieces, also shown at the late lamentable New
York Film Festival, is an attempt at making an American film
adult and artistic as well as commercial. As a program, this is admirable; as a finished film, rather less so. The opening reveals an oil
rigger, Bobby Dupea, living with a waitress, Rayette, in a Southern
California oil town. Everything seems ordinary enough: the dis-
pleasure with one's work; restlessness in one's rented mobile-home
quarters; resentment of one's pregnant and nagging girl friend with
her dreams of becoming a pop singer; drinking and wenching forays with one's married buddy. But this series of typicalities is im-
pinged on by another series of sprouting signs pointing toward
Bobby's being really a displaced person, a refugee from upper-
middle-class musical circles, and himself a not unskilled pianist.

When he learns that his father, paralyzed and struck mute, is
close to death, Bobby decides to drive up to the family house in the
woods of northern Washington. Rayette emotionally blackmails
him into taking her along, and the journey is full of colorful little
incidents—a pair of lesbian hitchhikers fleeing pollution and
headed for Alaska; a roadside café waitress as domineering as she is
obtuse—until they reach a motel near the Dupea house. There

Bobby dumps his girl while, as he says, he investigates the situation at home. He meets again his patronizing concert-artist brother, Carl; Carl's newly acquired student concert-artist fiancée, Catherine; his dowdy, scatterbrained, kindly concert-artist sister, Tita; the mute, motionless father, a former concert artist and teacher; and an almost equally mute, uniformed male nurse. Promptly he starts seducing the ethereal yet sexy Catherine, and for her sake even sits down at the piano again, to serenade her with a little Chopin. When she praises his playing, he poohspoohs her paean.

For Bobby, whose full name is Robert Eroica Dupea (Tita is really Partita, Carl is Carl Fidelio), seems never to be satisfied. And in the end he rejects, or is rejected by, both his worlds, only to run off north (Alaska, alas!) to escape the pollution that seems to be as much inside as around him. Yet Bobby's two worlds are seen only superficially, in images approaching and often achieving caricature, and his apostasy from his cultivated background is neither shown nor sufficiently explained. We do not even get to appreciate his human potential with whose waste we would have to commiserate if the film were to have serious merit.

Though Bobby says and does things that indicate his rootlessness and discontent, there is no real getting inside him; we never know whether we are watching a soul in torment or a set of jangling nerves. Bob Rafelson, the director and co-scenarist with Adrien Joyce, tends to do things by doubles or by halves. Thus there are two traffic-jam scenes, two overlong sequences with a psychotic lesbian hitchhiker (played unsubtly albeit to great critical acclaim by Helena Kallianiotes), but almost nothing about what drew Bobby to Rayette in the first place, or how he discovers that things, as he puts it, have a way of going bad on him. Why does his brother's fiancée tumble into bed with him so readily? Why should this rather mannered, affected creature even begin to seem the *summum bonum* to him?

Other flaws include obvious transitions, like that from a couple about to have intercourse to a ball in a bowling alley racing toward an orgasmic scattering of pins; and grandiosely flashy shots such as those of the inactive machinery of the oil field looking, at nightfall, like a combination petrified forest and Calvary. Or take the scene that is supposed to explain Bobby's flight from home. At a gathering in the Dupea home, an arrogant neighbor woman is spouting

intellectual slogans and, at the same time, being offensively condescending to Rayette. The scene is vulgarly written and grossly over-
directed and overacted (by Irene Dailey). When Bobby gives it to
her, we are clearly meant to side with him against these smug, superior upper-crust eggheads. Bobby's friend at the oil field, though
apparently an escaped robber, presents the lower-class concept of
the good life in similarly oversimplified terms, and, though Bobby
rejects it, we are asked to feel a basic sympathy for his buddy's
position.

Along with oversimplification, we get pretentiousness. The very
title, *Five Easy Pieces*, strikes me as a bit of attitudinizing. It refers
primarily to the five pieces of piano music performed at various
times in the film (two Chopins, two Mozarts, one Bach), although
I cannot affirm that they are really easy pieces. A parallel is presumably intended with the five women with whom we see Bobby
making out: Rayette, two small-town hookers, one pickup in Los
Angeles, and Catherine. Yet what is this analogy saying? Something about a parallel between music and sex, art and life? Something about everything in life being, or seeming, too easy for the disaffected person? Bobby himself does not play more than two of
those piano pieces, however, and Tita finds one of the others anything but easy going. We are meant to feel some grand assertion or
irony lurking in the title, if we could only seize it; but here as elsewhere the film fails to deliver.

Pretentious, too, is the color cinematography by Laszlo Kovacs,
frame after frame looking like something destined for the covers of
the photography annuals. Take Bobby leaving the oil field at sunset: a low-angle shot with an elaborate cloud formation (cumulo-
stratus, if I remember correctly), filters for greater color contrast,
and the solitary hard-hatted figure jutting into the sky. Surely this
is meant to be Tired, Suffering Man Against the August, Uncaring
Heavens, a nobly capitalizable commonplace.

What, more than anything, saves *Five Easy Pieces* from triviality
is the acting. Almost all the performances are good; a few, excellent. I particularly liked Lois Smith as the well-meaning but fuzzy
Tita, Karen Black as the banal but pitiable Rayette, and Billy
"Green" Bush as the hero's buddy; all of them resisted the script's
and director's nudging toward obviousness. Jack Nicholson, as
Bobby, has some searing moments, but though I can believe him as

a tough worker, he (or at least his voice and accent) cannot convince me as belonging to an intellectual and artistic milieu. I certainly can't see him playing any piece less easy than "Chopsticks." Susan Anspach, an actress I have found thoroughly irritating on stage, is well used here in the role of the elusive Catherine; perhaps Rafelson does know how to handle some actors. The film generally keeps our senses occupied as we watch and listen. I only wish it could also make a deeper kind of sense.

JOE

GARY ARNOLD

A year ago today Dennis Hopper's *Easy Rider* opened in Washington and settled in for a very profitable run of four months. There's every reason to believe that John Avildsen's *Joe* is going to be just as successful.

Like *Easy Rider*, *Joe* is a low-budget sleeper, an independent production that was shot in New York last winter on a budget of about $300,000. And like *Easy Rider*, it's a fascinating, tendentious picture—a topical murder melodrama and social parable, done in that vivid, loaded, paranoid style which seems to have become a tradition in record time but remains exciting to watch, even if you question the drift and outcome of the parable.

Joe is more or less equal portions of crime story, character study, class and situation comedy, and political and generational Rorschach test. The film was originally called *The Gap*, and its protagonist was probably supposed to be the character played by Dennis Patrick—Bill Compton, a respectable, prosperous upper-middle-class man who becomes a murderer.

Compton's victim is his daughter's boy friend, a scurrilous young drug pusher and addict named Frank Russo (Patrick McDermott). The girl (Susan Sarandon) has been taken to Bellevue in an amphetamine daze, and Compton goes to retrieve her belongings from Russo's East Village apartment. There he meets the boy, is taunted by him and kills him. Immediately afterward Compton enters a bar where a voluble, bigoted factory worker named Joe Curran (Peter Boyle) is elaborating on his favorite themes—"The niggers and hippies are screwing up the country. . . . Forty-two per cent of the liberals are queer, and that's a fact: the Wallace people took a poll." Etc., etc.

Curran announces that he'd like to "kill one of 'em—just one," and Compton mutters, "I just did." At the time he manages to pass off the remark as a joke, and Curran assumes he's being kidded. Later, following news accounts of the crime, Curran plays an intuitive hunch and traces Compton. The latter assumes that the motive is blackmail, but what Curran really wants is to congratulate Compton and to cultivate his friendship. The two men become oddly mismatched pals and eventually mass murderers: in the course of looking for Compton's daughter, who runs away from home after learning of his crime, they massacre the residents of a hippie commune. (Among the victims is the daughter, and if you think this sounds a little pat, you're absolutely right.)

The writer, Norman Wexler (evidently no kin to Haskell Wexler), is a playwright whose work happens to be unknown to me, but I think it's safe to assume that he's been around off-Broadway and revue comedy. The central relationship is reminiscent of *The Zoo Story*, and the most entertaining scenes—Joe's harangues and the disastrous, funny-ghastly socializing between the Comptons and Currans—would play just as well as cabaret sketches or one-acters.

Wexler is undeniably talented. He writes very good comic dialogue, particularly for lower-middle-class characters like Joe Curran, whose specialty is opinionated stupidity, and Curran's wife (K. Callan), whose specialty is prattle. At the same time, he often lets his wit and facility lead him astray, particularly in a dinner-party scene which is climaxed by a dumb gag: the Currans, playing host to the much more affluent Comptons, have dinner delivered from "the best Chinese restaurant in Astoria." It's a good example of the limitations of revue humor—you play a joker instead of thinking the situation through. If anything, a woman like poor, well-meaning Mrs. Curran would go overboard preparing a meal for better-off and more genteel company.

There are several errors of this kind throughout the film. In addition, the plotting is rather embarrassing for a man of Wexler's obvious sophistication. The story is advanced through clumsy, arbitrary devices. The daughter eavesdrops in the next room while her father talks about killing her lover. Joe *entertains* us by being dense and vulgar but gets intuitive and subtle and Machiavellian whenever the story needs a push.

Structurally, the film is sort of the antithesis of Hal Ashby's *The Landlord*, which began awkwardly and then found itself. *Joe* is unusually taut and compelling for the first reel or so, but it becomes less convincing, although still sharply directed and acted from scene to scene, as the plot complications multiply.

The basic problem seems unavoidable: although the character of Joe shouldn't dominate the story, there's no way to stop him. The role is simply too fat and juicy and photogenic, and Peter Boyle plays it brilliantly. It's a traditional crowd-pleaser: vulgarians are always great fun on the screen, and Boyle, belching and ranting and probably ad-libbing as well, is as irresistibly uncouth as the early Brando. Moreover, he gets to attack both the jugular and the funny bone of liberal audiences, venting every reactionary prejudice currently in vogue.

Still, the element responsible for most of the film's verve and probable popular success is precisely the element that undermines it thematically. If anything, Joe should function as a kind of ironic avenging conscience, a torment to Compton, who knows that he did not commit murder for Joe's reasons, to justify Joe's point of view. As it is, Wexler is not successful at establishing a feeling of complicity between the two men: virtually every detail tends to stress what separates them in terms of class and taste and temperament.

The opening sequences, which establish the decidedly harrowing relationship between the daughter and the boy friend (a deglamorized hippie, by the way, and played by McDermott as a disturbingly casual, self-centered brute) and then the murder, lead us to expect a contemporary variant on *Crime and Punishment*. Compton's dilemma—first as a responsible, protective family man, then as a murderer and finally as a *venerated* murderer—taps some common anxieties and has rather interesting tragic possibilities.

The movie takes another tack, but its chances of commercial

success have been increased by Joe's emergence to center stage. For better and worse, he's a fabulous character, and he forces Wexler and Avildsen into a tight, expedient corner: they play their reactionary middle-aged hero at the prejudices of young and liberal audiences. The violent ending, in which both Joe and Compton become bloody moral monsters, tends to reinforce the prejudices and absolve us of understanding. Both Peter Boyle, in an interview in *The New York Times*, and Penelope Gilliatt, reviewing *Joe* in *The New Yorker*, have recorded incidents of kids shouting "We'll get you, Joe!" at the screen. I don't know if the film makers would be prepared to dramatize this sort of irrationality, but I think the anecdotes illustrate why this striking and slanted film will be a hit and why it seems dramatically meretricious.

PENELOPE GILLIATT

Joe, it seems, is a hot-weather picture. People want to *see* it, for God's sake, because it's about what's *happening*.

The "o" of *Joe* on some of the poster material is a design of Stars and Stripes. The slogan—Joe's slogan—says "Keep America Beautiful." I saw a mild-spoken young wit outside the theater carefully changing that to "Make America Beautiful."

Well, maybe people will want to see the film here, but I don't think they'll give much for it outside this country, except insofar as it throws a piece of putrid fish to people who want anti-American nourishment.

I can believe that the idea started off as one that, though fabricated, was intellectually interesting. (Norman Wexler wrote it; John G. Avildsen directed it.) A loudmouthed blue-collar worker called Joe, an arsenal of every prejudice in New York, happens to cotton on to the fact that a high-class, weak-natured ad man has murdered his own daughter's dope-pushing boy friend in an uncharacteristic (and unexplored) moment of passion for her. From then on, the two men are joined in an unholy alliance. They are alike in hating hippies, and the ad man doesn't balk at Joe's other bigotries as much as he might. There is no blackmail between them —only a dank brotherhood. Their wives meet, awkwardly; the men go on a binge together, smoking grass and having girls and getting

their pockets ransacked during a search of Greenwich Village for
the now lost daughter. At the end, there is a colossal shoot-up by
both the men in which they kill every single person in a hippie
commune, including the daughter, who is shot unwittingly by her
father. The plot goes a bit overboard now and again.

Obviously, the premise of two socially alienated men uneasily
conjoined is an interesting one, and it could have prospered if film
makers gifted with greater lucidity and a more charitable sense of
character had done it. *Joe* has one of the very few film plots to
recognize that class is deep-bitten in white American life, and there
is a whip sting in its observation that bigotry, like the love of
music, transcends all barriers. Joe (he is played by Peter Boyle)
earns a hundred and sixty dollars a week. The ad man, Bill Compton (Dennis Patrick), earns sixty thousand dollars a year. Their
wives are practically from different species—Joe's a cheerful chat-
terer who gossips blithely to him about the latest dire crises in their
favorite soap operas, Compton's a rich bitch in a little black dress
who rolls exhausted eyes to her husband about getting through the
evening at Joe's place. The trouble is that every point is shoved
home with such crassness that the film becomes immeasurably
coarse and vicious. It is typical that when Joe burps he burps on
camera every time. It is typical that Joe, the blue-collar worker,
actually *wears* a blue collar through the picture. The character
points are dropped on your toes like bags of cement. We hear Joe
bashing into queers and liberals and hippies and blacks and people
on welfare—watch him being endowed with such manic and depressing energies that the film begins to partake in his thrashing
about. It revels in his outrageousness, and audiences respond by
guffawing; thick wits are catching, and it is hard and rare for any
audience to do better than reply in kind. At the end of the melodrama, after the caricatured hippies on the screen had been picked
off and killed one by one, a group of youngish people at a midnight
Broadway showing got up and yelled, "We'll get you, Joe!"

If it is true, as I believe it to be, that there is a sort of grace or
manners in the verbal arts that can be raised to the pitch of meta-
physics—a matter to do with paying heed to characters' spirits and
leaving room for them—*Joe* is both graceless and rude. The meeting between the two couples could be Chekhovian. In the movie as
it is, Joe suddenly sees something about his wife that he doesn't

want to see. The scene could be like Andrei's terrible acknowledgment to himself of Natasha's vulgarity in *The Three Sisters* ("A
wife is a wife"). Instead, it is stereotyped and harsh, with Joe's
wife made to look physically ridiculous. And then, in the hippie-
orgy scene, the reluctantly naked Joe is derided in his turn. He
wants to make love with his clothes on, which is believable, but
once he has agreed to take them off, at the bidding of his calm,
beautiful date, he wouldn't stand about looking daft in just his
socks. In some curious way, the picture, because of its attitude toward Joe, is made to seem racist. He is traduced and patronized as
the type of the hard-hat worker as thoroughly as any Negro character was ever traduced and patronized in older movies. We learn
about him generically, not idiosyncratically. We learn that his kind
hate welfare, keep guns in the cellar, abuse the out-of-step, salute
the flag, and make love as though manhood depended on getting it
over with in two minutes. This seems about as true, and as untrue,
as a study of a black that tells us he has a sense of rhythm and
laughs a lot.

Oddly, in spite of the title, the rightful central character of the
story is not Joe but Bill Compton. Something went wrong in the
dialogue writing, though. Bill Compton becomes an interesting
character only in one fleeting good scene with his secretary. Something went even more wrong in the casting. Peter Boyle as Joe is
strong meat, so the character acquires a quite spurious heroic
energy during his rantings. Bill Compton should have been played
by, ideally, Henry Fonda, given another order of script. It would
have been wonderful to see the type-cast saint as this honeyed,
mannerly murderer. Instead, we have a performance by an actor
without much technique or depth. The brow of Dennis Patrick's
handsome face furrows, but it isn't the furrowing of guilt or of
thought; it is more like the puckering of a male model's face in a
commercial about pills for expense-account indigestion. In every
sense, *Joe* sells us short. It shows us clashing archetypes, promises
us something of large mind, and then stammers platitudes that
lead theatrically every which way. In the end, baffled, and bumping
its nose against the idea that it needs a cathartic scene where none
has been made apt by any ethical conflict, it does an about-face of
moral logic and turns on the villainous Joe's own enemies—the
hippies—to make them the mythic bad guys, so that they can be

shot down in a climax of blood that is really a welter of muddle-headedness. After all, goes the chaotic evidence of the narrative, Joe may be a bigot, but he's a good friend (to a murderer), and the murderer is quite a decent man (apart from the murder); so the film, in sudden want of a through-and-through-fink type, forgets that it has established two of the girl hippies as loyal and nice, and haplessly fixes on the whole commune as something possible to slaughter, remembering only the members of it who pushed dope to schoolgirls or ran out on their chums. As a story idea suggested to moneymen, I daresay *Joe* sounded brilliant. But the idea never grew, perhaps because it had its origins in simple pursuit of the current, and the end of the matter is a bad film disfigured by brute strokes of tendentiousness.

LOVING

Recognizable Human Behavior

Pauline Kael

Loving is an unusual movie—compassionate but unsentimental. It looks at the failures of middle-class life without despising the people; it understands that they already despise themselves. Although it doesn't try to spare the characters, and it is sometimes rather wry in its humor, there's a decency—almost a tenderness—in the way that the director, Irvin Kershner, is fair to everyone. He shows the lives of mediocre people for what they are, but he never allows us to feel superior to them.

Kershner is a director who has been on the verge of broad recognition for over a decade. Among Hollywood legends are the stories that people tell of seeing Kershner's *The Hoodlum Priest* before the studio re-edited it, and of how Jack Warner suddenly got the point of *A Fine Madness*, discovered that it was "anti-social," and ordered it recut. Despite everything, Kershner generally managed to bring some intelligence to the screen in at least a few sequences of each film, and traces of his original intentions would also shine through now and then. There was the ravenous energy of Sean Connery as the artist-hero of A *Fine Madness*, walking across a bridge in a way that told us the world was his; and the friendless young ex-convict of Keir Dullea in *The Hoodlum Priest*, so tense and pale that his fear of society was a justified neurosis. And in the film that Kershner made in Canada, *The Luck of Ginger Coffey*, Robert Shaw and Mary Ure, skilled professionals in other films, were suddenly—maybe for their only time on the screen—believable human beings. *The Luck of Ginger Coffey* was a picture that one knew—even while watching it and admiring the love and craftsmanship that had gone into it—wouldn't be a commercial success, no matter how much reviewers praised it. Not only was it the story of a loser but structurally and dramatically it ran downhill, and further down than the material really warranted. Though *Loving* is emotionally very similar, it doesn't drag one down that way; it's a more playful film, and the time may now be right for Kershner's temperament and talent. In 1964, concern for the lives of losers like Ginger Coffey was considered depressing, but, the way the world has changed, what seemed too downbeat five years ago may seem hopeful now. And movies have been on such a crash course of shock and depersonalization that concern for people, whether they're winners or losers, may in itself be inspiriting—almost healing. Back then, Kershner's subtleties and his balanced approach to character didn't stand much chance with the mass movie audience, which wanted entertainment that was easier to respond to. In most big movies, responses were built into the product; you were signaled when to be afraid, when to swallow the lump in your throat, when to be awed, as clearly as if cue cards were being held up for you. In essence, they were. But it is no longer true that no one ever went broke underestimating the intelligence of the American public; look at the figures on *Doctor Dolittle*. The European moviemakers who became popular at the art houses helped to break down the acceptance of predigested entertainment, and during the last year talented Americans who in the past were frustrated and crushed by the studio heads have finally been making contact with audiences who are willing to work out their own responses.

The company releasing *Loving* has been publicizing it as if it were for the older audience; I think the young audience will respond, too, because it's a good movie: not a great movie but a good one—better than one expects, and different from other movies. It isn't callous, and it isn't bitter; though more sophisticated in its comedy, it resembles the Czech movies that have been giving American audiences the pleasure of seeing recognizable human behavior. I think the young audience will discover it; unlike the movie companies, the young don't all swallow the mass-media line about youth's being interested only in youth. *Loving* may be a key film, even a turning point in films, because it assumes (I hope rightly) that we will care about its characters although they are just the kind of people it is currently so easy to treat with contempt—the people from whom the educated young audience that now talks of reverence for life sprang.

Kershner is fortunate in having as his middle-class anti-hero George Segal, an actor with a core of humor and a loose, informal sense of irony, and one who radiates human decency and likable human weakness. He has perhaps the warmest presence of any current screen actor. I don't know anyone who doesn't like Segal—not just Segal the actor but Segal the person who comes through in the actor—and this is an immense advantage to the movie, because even though he plays a mediocre, failed artist, we like him to start with and can't dismiss him without dismissing almost all of humanity. Segal gives what I think is his best performance. The story is of the artist's dissatisfaction with his life. He's a free-lance illustrator, plodding along from one grubby job he hates to the next, making good money but never making enough money, fighting off decisions until they're made for him. There's no word for the defeats of a limited man; one can't quite call *Loving* a tragicomedy, any more than one could quite call *L'Avventura* a tragedy. Segal's hero never rises high enough for a classic fall, but he's aware of his stumbling. He's a bit of a clown, but he's not a fool; he's a poor bastard trying to make a living, do right by his wife and children, and keep the possibility open that he could yet be a dashing, gifted artist. The new girl he longs to run away with is not very different from his wife—only younger, and not bound down by his children. As the wife, Eva Marie Saint gives a stunning performance in what might have been a cliché role (and what she herself has played in the past as a cliché role). It's wonderful to see what reserves of

talent performers can sometimes draw upon when they get the
chance. Miss Saint lets us see that the wife doesn't have many
illusions about her husband or herself. She knows what will happen
to her if he leaves; there's not much she can do except try to hang
on, and it's a humiliating position. But she's not just a hanger-on;
she's a tough, gallant woman who will somehow manage to take
care of her children whatever her husband does. As for the hero,
his life is a mess, but it's not a tragic, austere mess, and, unlike
Antonioni's hero-failures, he manages to blot out his troubles and
have a pretty good time. The movie keeps a sane—often funny—
perspective on his wriggling this way and that.

The script, by Don Devlin, is somewhat sparse, and this seems
rather negligent, since in the novel it's based on—*Brooks Wilson
Ltd.*, by J. M. Ryan—there is material that might have given the
movie a richer substance and more of the resonances of American
middle-income life. Because the script isn't full enough, we become
too mindful of every action and vocal inflection; we get the feeling
that the director is trying to stretch the material and make it count
for more than it's worth. Nevertheless, *Loving* is Kershner's best-
sustained film. From start to finish, it's a demonstration of his
sensibility and his superb craftsmanship. It's a relief to see such a
harmonious, beautifully rhythmed piece of moviemaking, and a special pleasure to see an American movie that's so quietly detailed.
The score, by Bernardo Segall (who also scored *Ginger Coffey*), is
unusually delicate for an American movie score, and Gordon Willis' camera work serves the conception gracefully and unostenta-
tiously. This is a modest and somewhat obviously controlled picture. It doesn't reveal the exuberance or the liberated, explosive
intelligence that has sometimes broken through in bits of Kershner's other films, but there are remarkably fine moments: domestic
scenes between Eva Marie Saint and the children; Segal just standing and looking at his two daughters through the window of a dress
shop—exceptionally unsentimentalized children, who are simulta-
neously alien to their father's life and at the center of it.

Sensibility has become so rare in movies that to see people on
the screen whom one can relate to is a gift of feeling. The characters in *Loving* seem to have believable human reactions and conversations, for a change. Kershner doesn't strike attitudes; he opens
up these people's lives to the camera and reveals that they don't

really mean to hurt each other, that they do it out of carelessness—
or, sometimes, when they do what they want, it just goes wrong for
other people and they can't help it. After so many movies that
come on strong with big, flamboyant truths, a movie that doesn't
pretend to know more than it does but comes up with some small
truths about the way the middle class sweats gives us something we
can respond to; it gives us something we desperately need from the
movies now—an extension of understanding.

THE BALLAD OF CABLE HOGUE

Desert Rat

JOSEPH MORGENSTERN

From the very same desert that spawned the deathly *Zabriskie Point* comes Sam Peckinpah's *The Ballad of Cable Hogue,*
a vital and jubilant tale of a desert rat who stumbles on a water
hole. Life floods through this movie, life as its own nutty reason for
reproduction, life seen with its warts, belches, bare asses and
mean motives, but seen also with its grace, good cheer, and its on-
again-off-again joys of love.

Peckinpah starts with the violent death of a Gila monster, evok-
ing his opening shots of the tortured scorpions in *The Wild
Bunch.* But the director is only having fun at his own expense
(and the Gila monster's). This is no sequel to *The Wild Bunch,*
except for its similar concern with aging loners at a similar time in
history, when the Old West was retreating fast in the face of a
little law, a bit of order and a very few horseless carriages.

Hogue himself, played splendidly by Jason Robards, is a perfect
primitive prototype of the American capitalist. He starts with nothing but his own thirst in a land of Biblical barrenness. He duns the
good Lord for water, and the Lord finally pays up with a mudhole.
With the sweat of his own brow and the moisture of the mud,
Hogue develops his little find into a flourishing oasis on the stage-

coach line between Gila and Deaddog, a filling station for horses and people. Soon he's talking about "*my* land, *my* water," perverting his legitimate need and original gumption into possessiveness.

This is, in a way, a ballad of free enterprise, of rapacity, of man's determination to make his own that which can never be his. In a more important and rewarding way, though, it's a ballad of man's funny, free, even sweet determination to live and love as long as he possibly can, and one man's efforts to trick himself into thinking that revenge, rather than love, gives him the will to go on. Hogue is an unprincipled bastard but a delightful one, and all the more so in the presence of a whore named Hildy who comes to live with him for a while.

Stella Stevens does magical things with the part—it's surely the best performance she's ever given and an enormous asset to the movie. One of the most concentrated doses of pleasure comes when Hogue and Hildy sing an exquisite new song called "Butterfly Mornings." They sing it while they bathe in the God-given water that Hogue now insists is his own, and the song tells us what they might be, ageless spirits in the early hours of nature's perfect day, while the scene shows us what they are, briefly clean bodies that are bound to get cruddy again.

The Ballad of Cable Hogue isn't a musical and doesn't need to be. It does most of its balladeering with Peckinpah's lyrical direction, a strong script by John Crawford and Edmund Penney, Lucien Ballard's photography in that nostalgic kind of Technicolor where the grass was always goldener, and a remarkable set of performances: David Warner's bogus priest, hilarious and fiendishly energetic, who collars every nubile girl he can find and conducts private services in bed; Strother Martin's Bowen, who starts everything by leaving Hogue to his own devices on the desert and becomes the target of his revenge.

It is Peckinpah's movie in the final analysis, zestful and virile and delicate too, as in a fine small scene with Hogue and a bank president (Peter Whitney) exchanging tacit understandings about the profit motive. The director is clearly in a mood to please, which is a good mood for him to be in. He's a little overplayful with fast emotion, and he lets some unclothed artifice poke through a few lines of dialogue. But the main thing about the movie is pleasure, and it's even a great pleasure to watch Peckinpah play with his ending and go farther and farther into fantasy as he gets deeper and deeper into the literal problems of a resolution. Endings bother us all, after all. This one leaves a sharp aftertaste of life.

LITTLE BIG MAN

The Red and The White

STEFAN KANFER

Jack Crabb is 121 years old. His eyes are agate chips; senility seeps through the cracks in his voice. But Crabb is not your average superannuated former Indian fighter, former Indian, intimate of Wild Bill Hickok and General George Armstrong Custer, ex-gunslinger, scalawag and drunkard. No sir. He is *Little Big Man*, sole survivor of the Battle of Little Bighorn. He may tell a stretcher or two, but when he reminisces, graduate students listen. A budding anthropologist starts a tape recorder, Crabb opens his toothless yawp and the saga unfurls.

And unfurls. And unfurls. For two and a half hours *Little Big Man* turns the tableaux on nearly every aspect of Western man. Thomas Berger's panoramic novel owed its salinity to an immediate relative, *Huckleberry Finn,* from which it ransacked idiom and hyperbole by the chapterful. Like Huck, young Jack had no social insight; he accepted violence and duplicity the way he regarded sleet and fire—as aspects of earthly life. The film happily preserves the chronicle's innocence, if not its exact text.

Crabb knows Americana as he knows an old penny; from the Indian side and the In God We Trust side. He first appears as a boy whose family has been massacred by redskins. The Cheyennes who carry him off seem a mere mob to begin with, but they soon separate into individuals who refer to one another (in English translation) as "Human Beings." The boy becomes an adopted brave, Little Big Man.

In the title role, shuttling incessantly from the red to the white side, Dustin Hoffman adopts precisely the right attitude of bewildered reality lost in myth, a photograph projected on a Frederic Remington painting. Unhappily, not all the cast is as comfortable in their roles. Some of the whites, such as Faye Dunaway as a preacher's oestrous wife, and Martin Balsam as a bunco artist, play like fugitives from a road company of *The Drunkard*, with galvanic gestures and frozen speech patterns. The Human Beings, by contrast, are a people of dignity and variety. Among them are the homosexual Little Horse; the contrary Younger Bear, who says "hello" for "goodbye" and bathes in dirt instead of water; and the true lodestar of the film, Old Lodge Skins (played by Chief Dan George).

Director Arthur Penn has been alternately shrewd and loco with *Little Big Man*, but mainly he has been plumb lucky. In the book, Crabb complains about western movies that show Indians played by Caucasians "with 5 o'clock shadows and lumpy arms." Perversely, Penn sought Sir Laurence Olivier and Paul Scofield for the chieftain's role. When they refused, he awarded the part to Richard Boone, who resigned shortly before filming. It was only then that Penn chose a hereditary leader of Canada's Salish tribe, Chief George, to play the old man. It was a momentous decision. Dan George's stoicism and grace give him an almost Biblical presence. Sometimes, standing to one side, the chief seems to be the essence of the Cheyenne, waiting for some unnamed event—perhaps the time when the white man uses up all the firewood and moves on forever. He is no less memorable uttering an occasional phrase. When Little Big Man announces that he has a wife, Old Lodge Skins inquires: "Does she show a pleasant enthusiasm when you mount her?" The question seems not lascivious, but full of paternal concern. When he prepares to die, the ancient Human Being chants a prayer and stretches supine before his Maker. Result: nothing. His answer, "Sometimes the magic works, sometimes it doesn't," gives new credence to the speculation that the Indians are one of the lost tribes of Israel.

Would that the film makers had Chief George's ingenuousness or Hoffman's technique. For Calder Willingham (*End as a Man*) has provided a scenario that begins with robust rawhide humor, turns to profundity—and then collapses into petulant editorial. In the era of occupied Alcatraz, surely it is no news that the white

man spoke with forked tongue, that the first Americans were mal-
treated as the last savages. The Battle of Little Bighorn, which
should be the film's climax, is its weakest point. General Custer is
pure Pig on the Prairie, babbling insanely as the consummate racist
militant. As overplayed by Richard Mulligan, he could be sec-
tioned, labeled Swift's Premium and sold in butcher shops.

Given such grossness, why should *Little Big Man* be counted as
a rambunctious triumph? Because in its 360° scope of slaughter
and laughter, the film has contrived to lampoon, revere or revile
the length and breadth of the entire frontier. On the trek, it dem-
onstrates inconsistencies and errata. For months audiences will be
talking about them. It also accomplishes that rarest achievement,
the breathing of life into an ossified art form. The seventies has its
first great epic. Blood brother to the 1903 one-reeler *The Great
Train Robbery*, *Little Big Man* is the new western to begin all
westerns.

Americana

DAVID DENBY

In *Little Big Man*, Arthur Penn uses the mode of comic
elegy in order to sustain a reverent feeling for the American past
without falling into sentimentality (his *Alice's Restaurant* was an
elegy for the present, or at least for certain ideals of the present
destroyed by madness and violence). Penn's version of the Old
West, adapted by Calder Willingham from Thomas Berger's 1964
novel, is bathed in legend, exaggeration, and nonsense; it is the past
transfigured in the telling, made accessible to the present through
comic stylization and an ambiguous, partly farcical treatment of
violence that is purely contemporary. If, at the same time, Penn
had been able to resist imposing certain ideologies of the present
onto the past, he might have made a great movie.

Little Big Man is probably as close as sophisticated men can
come to a genuine folk version of the Old West. Its central character, Jack Crabb (Dustin Hoffman), is not so much a hero as an
Everyman—an essentially passive recorder of vivid experience.
American history happens to him, runs over him, and fails to break

him. At the beginning and end of the movie we see him in some time vaguely the present, grotesquely alive at the age of 121. The movie consists of his reminiscing over his life as Indian fighter, general-store owner, con man, hermit, drunk, and occasional member of a Cheyenne tribe that raised him and that he comes to love. Forced to suffer through the slaughter and near-extermination of these Indians by the U. S. Cavalry, Crabb finally faces his enemy, General George Armstrong Custer, and tricks him into standing his last at the Battle of the Little Bighorn.

The movie tells wonderful lies, but it often has the *spirit* of actuality in a way that ordinary lying westerns do not. The obvious tall tales show up the less obvious absurdity of what we were once asked to believe in. Yet it's not a spoof; it's a movie that is reverent about certain human qualities—particularly those embodied in the slaughtered Cheyenne. Crabb himself is decent, competent, hopeful, and neither outstandingly courageous nor weak; life is sordid, absurd, and, as Crabb always survives, surprisingly persistent in its ability to make him suffer. Although Crabb as a character is not too highly individualized, one comes to respect his clear-sightedness, freedom from rancor, and acceptance of both pleasure and pain; he's a kind of higher spirit of common experience. Perhaps he's the perfect protagonist for a western that tries to do away with both the heroic style and the chamber-of-commerce morality that animate most examples of the form. The typical western hero, although he operates by himself or with only a sidekick, usually serves the interests of the great expansion, the great destiny; Crabb just wants to survive—until the great destiny kills everything he loves. How he finds the strength to survive afterward, we never know.

To make Crabb a credible folk representative, the plot involves him in many incidents and with many people. Most of this material parodies familiar movie conventions. With certain notable exceptions, Penn keeps the sense of reality in these adventures slightly deranged; this stylization tells us in each case how to respond to the material, and it doesn't always work.

It works best in the sequences dealing with Crabb's gun-fighting phase. First Carol Androsky, as Dustin Hoffman's sister, teaches him how to make "snake eyes" and "shoot before touching your gun." With this marvelous skill perfected to the extent that he can shoot three bottles thrown in the air at once, Hoffman strides into town, slipping and sliding on planks laid across the incessantly muddy streets, decked out in the fancy black clothes of the movies' born killers, his hair slicked up, his voice small and tight like Audie Murphy's. So far Penn has been gently mocking our belief in the power and glamour of movie gunslingers; but when Hoffman teams up in a bar with Jeff Corey (the character actor with Edward Teller eyebrows), who plays an extremely jittery Wild Bill Hickok, the tone moves further out into an eerie, nervous hilarity and finally explodes in our face with bloody violence. The absurd conventions we believed in always culminated in death, but when we actually see it with pools of blood, we want to turn away like the nearly fainting Crabb.

An example of stylization that fails is the recurring business with Faye Dunaway as the minister's wife who praises chastity and purity but can't keep her hands off men. Her exaggerated fluttering and posturing, which seem to parody the hypocrisy of the "good woman" in westerns, only lift the scene into the realm of different conventions—those of bad Victorian pornography, with its coy naughtiness. Nor does the repeated demonstration of Custer's prancing vanity work much better (although it *is* entertaining); as the villain of the movie, responsible for hundreds of deaths, he needs more depth, more development. Again we are moved from one unsatisfying convention to another—from noble heroism, the responsibility of leadership, and so on, to its nagging *Mad*-magazine parody, which can see only madness in heroism (for there's no doubt that the historical Custer was a hero, of a sort).

This playing with our memories and movie conventions reaches its height in the scenes set in the Cheyenne camp. Penn appears to have set himself two tasks with the Indians: first, to do away with the mumbo jumbo, the ignorant superstition, and the racist fears that have almost always characterized movie portraits of Indians; and second, to end the hypocrisy of those liberal westerns which have shown Indians being betrayed by treacherous whites, only to frighten the audience in the end with the Indians' aroused savagery —which justifies their slaughter.

These Indians speak in full sentences rather than grunts, they show a fairly wide range of personal characteristics, and although they are full of ritual and mystery, there's no spooky medicine man in sight, and they don't spend much time howling and dancing around the fire. It is not until late in the movie that we realize that we are being shown the gentleness, relaxed sexuality, and ignorance of technology that often characterize history's victimized civilizations. At the center of the community sits Old Lodge Skins (played by Chief Dan George), an elegant and kindly gentleman who is set up in the movie as an obvious contrast to Custer. He expounds the Indian view of life at considerable length, and just when we've had about enough and it's all getting a bit sanctimonious, Penn gently pulls the rug out from under him.

Nevertheless, Old Lodge Skins conveys the message of the movie: he explains the Indians' animistic philosophy to Crabb, claiming that they see life in everything—in earth, stone, and water; whereas for the white man, "everything is dead." We might accept these remarks if they weren't meant to carry so much weight: the whole latter half of the movie weaves Crabb's story into an account of Custer's genocidal compaigns against the Indians, and there's no interprctation other than Lodge Skins's for what happens. From the evidence of the movie, the whites didn't kill the Indians because they wanted the land, water, and skins, or because they were afraid of them, or even because they were racists. They killed them because it is the nature of white men to kill. And this sort of tautology is itself the essence of racism. Of course it's a new hip racism that will be very popular with certain sections of the young audience.

The two scenes of Indians being massacred are staged straight for terror and horror, rather than in the farcically scary style of the rest of the movie's violence (when the Indians themselves attack a stagecoach, for instance, it tips over going around a bend like an automobile in a Sennett two-reeler). The slaughter of the Cheyenne is particularly horrible, since we've come to know this community from the inside, but I don't suppose Penn trusted either himself or the audience sufficiently to do it any other way. I myself went dead on both these sequences, a victim of too many movie slaughters. My mind registered horror but I felt nothing. But there's no doubt that the scenes are intended to build up rage against whites, and they had that audible effect on other people in the theater. How can this rage be released? By another slaughter, of course, the slaughter of Custer and his men, which is the climax of the movie, and here again we are back to farce, with Custer ranting and staggering about until he falls flat on his face, seemingly knocked over by the two arrows that land in his back and that wind up pointing, like little flags, to the sky.

Leaving aside the question of Penn's altering the tone of the movie according to who is being slaughtered, I question the artistic and political ethics of building up the desire for revenge in the audience. Not only does it place the audience in a poor moral position, not only does it weaken the sense of outrage that the rest of the movie establishes, but it also contrasts badly with Crabb's narrative tone, which dwells on the sense of loss and is free of the ideology of hate. What starts as an elegy for lost values winds up as an exercise in white self-hatred, and although it may seem incongruous to say so, I can't help feeling that Penn's movie is another victim of the war in Vietnam.

HUSBANDS

Three Musketeers

PAUL D. ZIMMERMAN

Ten years ago, a young actor-director named John Cassavetes applied the techniques of improvisational theater to the making of a small, audacious film called *Shadows*. It reflected the strengths and limits of inventing a screenplay with the cameras rolling. Cassavetes failed to sustain any consistent quality or to control a coherent narrative line. But his spontaneous shooting caught gut feelings that programed screenplays rarely reach and created comic moments as fresh and fumbling as life itself.

One scene in particular rests in memory. It followed the romp of three pals careening about the Museum of Modern Art, full of mutual affection and brimming with energy. Cassavetes' latest and largely improvisational effort, *Husbands*, devotes itself entirely to such a trio of good friends—only now they are married, middle-aged, and menaced by the approach of death.

The film is a good deal more impressive technically than *Shadows* if only in the chiaroscuro surfaces of Victor Kemper's photography. And, like Cassavetes' second major film, *Faces*, its outlook is more serious and ambitious. But, in the end, *Husbands* benefits from the same spontaneity and suffers from the same inconsistency and self-indulgence that marked *Shadows*.

As the friends arrested in perpetual adolescence, Ben Gazzara, Peter Falk, and Cassavetes attend the funeral of a fourth musketeer and glimpse intimations of mortality that scare the hell out of them. They respond by running—to a health club to pit their aging bodies against time itself, to late-night bars to drown their desperation, to London for one last fling at a factitious freedom. There is a deliberate madness in Cassavetes' improvisational method. He is after a psychological naturalism in which his heroes unravel their intestines on the screen. He pushes his camera almost against their skin as they speak, willing to pick up the blemishes of their faces if he can't get at the sores on their souls.

But, more often than not, all he comes away with is the realism of ordinary speech uttered by characters under stress. And his insistence on close-ups adds shrillness to the constant ranting and haranguing. His improvisational mode works best in adversary situations where two actors can feed off one another. Gazzara's combat with his wife—physically bringing her to her knees in a forced confession of love, grabbing her mother's throat as a murderer grabs a hostage, beating both women in a futile assault on an unshakable maternal alliance—is one of the funniest and most frightening marital blitzkriegs ever filmed.

The fights between Cassavetes and the Olympian blonde he picks up in London also profit from improvisation. But the romance of Falk with a Chinese girl and Gazzara with a vacant tart fall apart. Falk, Gazzara, and Cassavetes are attractive and alive performers but they are not up to building characters of depth on their own. Instead, they fall back on attitudes, mannerisms, and reasonably consistent responses of fear, anger, and elation—all the standard tools of the nonimprovising actor.

This film is clearly a labor of love. The camaraderie that Cassavetes captures so well seems to reflect the private relations of the actors and the experience of making the film. But this special spirit that infuses the film with vitality also robs it of balance. The film runs two and a half hours, presumably because Cassavetes loves everything he has shot so much he cannot cut it. And it seems much longer. An early scene in which the boys get drunk and vomit endlessly is characteristically self-indulgent and so interminable that the film never fully recovers. In this sequence, the trio holds a singing contest among a bunch of broken old barflies, reveling in the quaintness of their battered companions. But, like most drunk parties, it is intoxicating for those intoxicated and boring to teetotalers. In the same way, Cassavetes and his companions get caught up so thoroughly in their own fun and pain and personalities that the audience is left outside, watching the making of a movie rather than the movie itself.

JACOB BRACKMAN

Now, with the audience fragmenting, budgets plummeting, and things generally going farther out, movies which issue from tight, insulated subcultures are finding mass distribution, and we are getting to see some dudes up there behaving in strange new ways. *Easy Rider* was the great groundbreaker. People who had never met anybody like that crew recognized their odd behavior as "real"; so did people who live among similar crews, yet never expected to view such antics on the silver screen. These were different kinds of recognition, to be sure. If you knew the scene, you found more to laugh with. You took it less seriously, perhaps, but dug it nonetheless. It was said in certain circles, and rightly, "Everybody got off on the picture at his own level."

For myself, I feel more intimate with the strange ways of East Village dopers, marginally making do (*Trash*), or even of hermitic pansexualists, brewing occult rituals (*Performance*), than I do with the ways of the tormented suburbanites who comprise John Cassavetes' special damned. I imagine I've learned a little about Cassavetes' people, indirectly, and I have no doubt that *Husbands*, his latest, fairly drips with realism. But still I may find it more disturbing than would a married man from Westchester. And he may find *Trash* more disturbing than I do.

When you live in the city, a certain powerful body of experience arises from standing witness, quite accidentally, to human interchanges so intense as to border often on the hysterical. I remember how unfailingly public "scenes" startled me when I was younger: a mother viciously berating an infant on the supermarket line; a couple at the next table ripping away at each other's weaknesses, no secret honored; inebriated, self-important men getting touchy with one another on a subway. I am used to such spectacles now, but that doesn't keep them from shaking up my day.

Perhaps I grew up at the tail end of an age which held firm against washing one's dirty linen in public. No sooner would ugly voices be raised than someone might be heard to stage-whisper, "Don't make a scene." It's been years since I heard that line, even though—as I live in the city—scarcely a day passes but somebody makes a scene in my vicinity. It seems no prudence can protect me from stumbling across them, charged mines laid out across my home terrain. They stand in a peculiar relation to the rest of my daily experience—a relation rather like that of Cassavetes' movies to everybody else's.

They have about them a kind of hyperreality—for pain and rage do seem more "real" than the neutral feelings with which I float through most encounters—and an awful unreality, as well: the emotion hurled across the curb, across the screen, seems invariably displaced. The concern at issue, the concern being screamed over, never in itself seems to justify the screaming. So one is left with the impression of people simply existing in a nightmare, out of touch even with the sources of their agony.

It's hard to come up with a handful of American films that equal *Faces* or *Husbands* in their capacity to influence how you feel for the remainder of an evening. Strangers color my mood more dramatically than friends do. On most days, nothing happening in my own life can begin to equal the force of what I overhear. One of the oddest features of a street episode or a Cassavetes film is my sense that I, a bystander, feel crisis more urgently than the protagonists themselves—as if the dynamics of crisis held them in such perpetual sway they could no more perceive its presence than a fish can perceive the presence of water.

Making a mess in public is evidently how the protagonists have learned to assert themselves in the world: their hunger for distinction so urgent and their claim to it so slight, they must become noteworthy if only by virtue of their obtrusiveness. They must emerge from the crowd or else they are nothing; emerge at whatever cost. They don't know how to have a good time, but their forced hilarity booms over every party—as if they knew how to show the rest of us what fun looks like. They swagger and bellow, grow sour, attack unpredictably, end up weeping for our forgiveness, whining inarticulate longings for some change in their lives. So they become special on the face of things! How otherwise might we suffer such behavior?

Characters in the city or in a Cassavetes film can act outrageously without any self-consciousness, without the slightest sense of irony about their gripe-of-the-moment. While one laughs at them, finds them ridiculous, one can never be quite certain how close to the edge they really are. In the back of one's mind lurks the possibility that the next outburst may terminate in the wail of an ambulance, white coats, a strait jacket.

Or so it looks from my shoes. I walk a high-rise corridor and hear wild giggling, yelling, weeping from behind the door of every other apartment. (Inside, do they break the china for drama? threaten one another with knives?) I recognize the characters in *Faces* or *Husbands* to be "real" from a distance. No doubt they seem real in quite another way—less portentously—to those who have better than a passing knowledge of life within the walls of these apartments, or wherever counts as home for men and women who can be driven to an emotional fever by a waiter or a doorman.

John Cassavetes and the actors with whom he works create a world of such people—failed at love, without insight, with the impacted cowardice that prevents one from ever confronting oneself squarely. In the weak, hung-over hours before sunrise, their bravado gives way not to any stark self-disgust, but to sentimental anguish, as murky (and, to the audience, uproarious) as the mania it supplants. The husbands—Cassavetes, Peter Falk, and Ben Gazzara—talk gloomily of a coming-of-age back around thirty, when they finally realized they would never be professional athletes, and to me it sounds as though each is mourning the death of every fine ambition he ever had.

But to me they are strangers, as I say; I suspect myself of finding too much of the tragic in their carryings-on, suspect that Cassavetes and Falk, at least, may be portraying men whom they see as quite like the run of men in their circle. Gazzara, however, by the end, even in his horsing around, seems something worse than infantile and truculent, seems to hate how his life has turned out with more than routine suburban passion. I believe he is meant to appear near bursting with poison, on the threshold of a breakdown. But maybe I'm wrong. Maybe Gazzara is intended satirically, and/or as somehow typical of a milieu I cannot hope to understand, of two cars, commutation tickets, air conditioning, pool membership, and a bitterness no mistress or pal can ever assuage.

I guess most of us now packed in closed space no longer expect each man to confine his extreme moments to the privacy of his studio apartment. The last half-dozen years have expanded the latitude for public behavior to embrace shows of craziness which the previous decades would have judged intolerable. Consider how far out the following struck us in 1963: sit-ins, men with long hair, marijuana, electric rock, dropping out, street theater, costumes— one could extend the list for paragraphs. Now even the armed services, faced with a drastically declining rate of re-enlistment, find themselves forced to suspend a host of "Mickey Mouse" regulations which sought to outlaw excess in personal demeanor.

A crucial distinction must be drawn here—though perhaps again it only looks crucial from where I stand. Can we compare the outlandish behavior of the past several years, of the new generation, with the outlandish behavior, newly exacerbated, of the middle-aged? To many, surely, they *do* look similar: both violate the circumscribed range of self-presentation which used to be permissible before strangers. Perhaps it makes little difference to the very young or the very old whether they run into, on a street corner, a marriage violently disintegrating, or a band of Hare Krishna chanters; a nasty boozer, spoiling for punishment, or a freaky panhandler, looking to scare up the price of a lid.

To me it makes an enormous difference. But I can appreciate that for many moviegoers, accustomed to adults in films conducting themselves within narrow confines, a movie like *Husbands* might seem close to *Trash*, even to *Performance*. They might seem alike in their strangeness. The less you know the respective scenes they depict, the more they are destined to sadden, frighten or discomfit you. Who in these movies strikes you as someone you'd hope to avoid? Whose narcissisms seem weirdest, most misplaced? Who's only "playing" when he makes a scene, and who's in scary earnest? Who seems a proper candidate for the asylum? These films establish a hyperbolic reality which the uninitiated can take for naturalism of the heaviest, ugliest variety—but which people who inhabit the milieu in question might be inclined to enjoy, to roar over, as superparody.

The husbands care desperately how they appear to others. Worrying over the impression they create makes them tense. They drink to unwind. But their looseness is affectation. They are at sea without their roles. Peter Falk has been sidling up to a shy Chinese girl with all the tenderness he can muster. When at last she turns passionate, aggressive, he backs off, shocked and suspicious. He can't get over her having ordered Coca-Cola, then slipping her tongue between his teeth. The husbands, especially Ben Gazzara, pride themselves on being *men*, some lusty middle-class version of what Hemingway stood for—Women's Lib's most loathed stereotype. They make jokes about queers. They feel it essential to come across masculine. They posture, swagger, and take offense in the service of that image.

No characters could be more alien from Joe Dallesandro in *Trash*. Or from Mick Jagger in *Performance*, playing upon a complex exaggeration of his satanic public image, and as himself in *Gimme Shelter*, the Maysles' harrowing record of The Stones' American tour, culminating in death at Altamont. Dallesandro and Jagger—either of whom could become a gigantic screen personality in the next few years or (just as possibly, I would guess) choose not to—are creatures of a shell-shocked age, droll and dreamy, without any grasp of how a man is supposed to act.

Androgynous, passive, ironical, languorously self-destructive— they pass easily between the sexes, between stoned and straight, downstream, past the most bizarre situations, not caring to control the responses of others nor to assert anything constant about themselves, disinterested in blame, looking only to drift on and, from time to time, get high. All these movies reverberate with bad vibes. But while the middle-aged heroes are crippled by frustration and inner conflict, the younger ones seem mysteriously accommodated to bad vibes, passing through every peril like insolent, invulnerable sleepwalkers.

2

AMERICANS AT WAR

PATTON

The Man Who Loved War

Pauline Kael

Patton runs almost three hours, and there is not a single lyrical moment. The figure of General George Patton, played by George C. Scott, is a Pop hero, but visually the movie is in a style that might be described as imperial. It does not really look quite like any other movie, and that in itself is an achievement (though not necessarily an esthetic one). The movie was shot in 70-millimeter and in "Dimension 150"; I don't know exactly what that means, but technically the movie is awesomely impressive. It was directed by Franklin J. Schaffner, and it looks a little like the early huge landscapes in his *Planet of the Apes*; the images, typically, are incredibly long, wide shots, taking in vast areas, with the human figures dwarfed by the terrain, and with more compositional use of sky than I've ever before seen in a movie. There's so much land and air—and it's so clear—that we seem to be looking at *Patton* from God's point of view. When Patton is in an interior, the interior is usually that of a castle, with doors opening into rooms beyond rooms in an apparent infinity, and one perceives the necessity for this—the need to keep the interiors consistent with the scale of the exteriors. The landscapes are full of men; the cast must surely run into the tens of thousands. But they're all extras—even the ones that *should* be important. There's really nobody in this movie except George C. Scott.

The Patton shown here appears to be deliberately planned as a

Rorschach test. He is what people who believe in military values can see as the true military hero—the red-blooded American who loves to fight and whose crude talk is straight talk. He is also what people who despise militarism can see as the worst kind of red-blooded American mystical maniac who *believes* in fighting; for them, Patton can be the symbolic proof of the madness of the whole military complex. And the picture plays him both ways—crazy and great—and more ways than that, because he's a comic-strip general and even those who are anti-war may love comic strips. I suspect that just for the reason that people can see in it what they already believe, a lot of them are going to think *Patton* is a great movie. I'm sure it will be said that the picture is "true" to Patton and to history, but I think it strings us along and holds out on us. If we don't just want to have our prejudices greased, we'll find it confusing and unsatisfying, because we aren't given enough information to evaluate Patton's actions. *Patton* avoids the clichés of famous men's personal lives by not presenting any personal life. Patton is treated as if he were the spirit of war, yet the movie begs the fundamental question about its hero: Is this the kind of man a country needs when it's at war? Every issue that is raised is left unresolved. Patton is a spit-and-polish disciplinarian and his men win battles. Do men fight better if their shoes are shined? (A boy near me whispered, "The Israelis keep winning victories.") Do men fight better, as Patton indicates, if they fear their leaders? Was Patton a great strategist or did he just follow classic theories? The movie shows us Patton's campaigns, which often seem to be undertaken for personal glory and with indifference to the possible losses, but then it balances this out with suggestions that his strategy was sound, and it doesn't give us enough data to evaluate one judgment or the other. Yet since the movie indicates that Patton can get his men to do more than the other generals can, it implicitly validates his ideas of discipline and of the value of instilling fear, even while showing him as an eyeball-rolling nut.

In approach, *Patton* is a synthesis of a satirical epic like Tony Richardson's *The Charge of the Light Brigade* and the square epic celebrations of the role of the Allies in the Second World War. It's a far-out movie passing as square, and finally passing over. I think the conception was to use Patton as if he'd been dreamed up by Terry Southern. (It's probably not altogether coincidental that

Scott played General Buck Turgidson in *Dr. Strangelove*.) But Patton is so much stronger than anyone else that he has glamour and appeal, even for liberals who will take him as the confirmation of their worst nightmares of the military. It could, of course, be a very smart liberal ploy to make Patton a monster-man among mice —to surround him with nonentities and thus present this monster as the true embodiment of military thinking rather than as its distortion—but it backfires by turning him into a hero.

Patton is enormous in scale; it cost more than $12 million. And, with the picture to himself, George C. Scott gives it all his intensity and his baleful magnetism. At the opening, standing in front of a giant American flag, he delivers a long, measured speech while holding the audience in a vise, and he continues to hold us whenever he's on the screen. He has practically all the good lines in the movie. Except for some briefly glimpsed Germans, who, naturally, have the most histrionic uniforms, and who are, by modern convention, elegant and epigrammatic, the movie is full of colorless, unattractive fourth-rate actors impersonating the English and American leaders. As Omar Bradley, Karl Malden is not as offensive as usual—he's merely negligible. If Bradley were presented as a contrasting kind of military leader—a brilliant but civilized officer —we might be able to get our bearings on what Patton is doing right and what he's doing wrong, but Karl Malden just stands around acting "restrained." Probably intentionally, the movie shows no *admirable* military leaders. The actors playing Montgomery and the others could be shoe clerks more easily than great generals. They have no class as actors, and their generals have no class; they're vain, small-minded competitors—mediocrities in drab uniforms. Scott's strength and scale as an actor make him the right hero for the imperial style of the picture, and since no one else has any star quality, the style itself validates him as a hero. It is an index to the oddness of this movie that Patton, the war lover, is so much more compelling than any other character that when Bradley is given the command Patton wants, it seems like injustice.

There are stylistic problems: the informal, dramatic conversations look a bit stiff and posed, as if Schaffner couldn't find a way to make the transitions from the implicit formality of the huge landscapes and horizons. (I point this out with full sympathy for what he was up against.) A larger problem is the continuity: the script doesn't follow through on the sequences presented. For example, the Germans guess Patton's strategy at one point, but we are never told whether they act on their guess or what the repercussions are. We are shown a great desert tank battle in which Patton's men are doing brilliantly until Nazi planes arrive, and then it is not made clear what the result is, or even whether Allied planes arrive, though Patton has been struggling with the British to get air cover for his men. And since we don't know how the scenes of war relate to the strategy of the campaigns, or even how this strategy works out, there is simply too much footage of exploding shells and burning tanks for its own beautiful sake.

The public-relations designation of this film is *Patton: A Salute to a Rebel*. Whom does Twentieth Century-Fox think it's kidding? What was Patton a rebel against except humanitarianism? The ads contain such lines as "*Patton* is a salute to a rebel *with* a cause," and "Patton was a rebel. Long before it became fashionable. He rebelled against the biggest. Eisenhower. Marshall. Montgomery. Against the establishment—and its ideas of warfare." One can scarcely blame the movie for the ads, but the movie is also busy trying to outsmart the public, presenting an arch-authoritarian as a rebel, the way one might present Spiro Agnew as a rebel against effete snobs. The pitch is, of course, that Patton is a straight-talking man opposing the stuffy bureaucrats, and that it's his uninhibited speech that scares them, because although they may agree with him they have to get along with the politicians. The movie is so manipulative that it flirts with the American jingo audience, which will probably agree with Patton even at his most rabid, when he wants to fight the Russians. (*That's* the kind of rebel he was.) And it flirts with the smart young audience, which may think the movie is really "tough" because it shows the military stripped of hypocrisy. The most treacherously clever bit in the movie comes when Patton is in disgrace for having slapped a soldier in a hospital. The Nazis (who throughout the film seem much smarter than the Allies) refuse to believe he isn't still in active command, because they can't imagine that the Americans would pull their best general out of the war for such a reason. It is an irony that will please every bully: See, the Nazis aren't weak and sentimental like us. We in the audience don't know any more about Patton when

Patton is over, but we've had quite an exhibition of winking at the liberals while selling your heart to the hawks.

M*A*S*H

Bloody Funny

Joseph Morgenstern

As you sit watching *M*A*S*H* you can only be swept along and occasionally under by its glorious madness. Later you wonder how the devil they did it.

It's characteristic of this cockeyed masterpiece, which ignores nonessentials with the most breath-taking courage, that it never bothers to explain its own slightly arch title, a military acronym for Mobile Army Surgical Hospital. The time is the Korean War. The place is three miles from the front lines or, according to an arrow nailed to a tree, 6,718.5 miles from New York Presbyterian Hospital. Surgical facilities in this sinkhole of the Eastern world consist of a jerry-built operating theater with plastic partitions, an erratic generator, a shortage of instruments, a surfeit of patients and a staff of young surgeons who are getting all the practice they could ever want in almost everything imaginable but preventive medicine. *M*A*S*H* is not black comedy; it's blood red. It sees war from the only true receiving end. Conventional war movies find the action in the shooting. *M*A*S*H* finds it in the bleeding.

Making a successful surgical comedy involves certain problems, especially when the bodies on the operating table are American soldiers. *M*A*S*H* has solved all the important ones by going all the way with the insanity—it's excruciatingly, barely bearably funny—and yet magically, even tenderly, retaining a sense of what is sane and precious in life: namely, life. You can't believe it until you see it, and you'll probably need to see it twice. Director Robert Altman, working from Ring Lardner Jr.'s adaptation of a Richard

Hooker novel, establishes his style in the first few seconds of film and rarely departs from it. Everyone jabbers at once, in the most adroit use of dialogue overlaps since Orson Welles. Helicopters deliver hideously wounded men to a cheerful nut house where the commanding officer devotes much of his time to fishing, the blood refrigerators are chock-full of Budweiser, the nurses chatter about their complexion problems, and Radio Tokyo dispenses "The Darktown Strutters' Ball" at full blast in Japanese over the public-address system. *M*A*S*H* has a sublime contempt for any and all things military.

As a counterpoise to all this deadly idiocy, the movie gives us three freewheeling young surgeons, played faultlessly by Donald Sutherland, Elliott Gould, and Tom Skerritt. They're the villains of the piece, in military terms, and the heroes, of course, in human terms. They're medical men who refuse to be military men, who refuse to give a damn for discipline of any sort but surgical. They were drafted, after all. Even in the operating theater they carry on as happy-go-lucky hedonist-nihilists, except that they do have the skill and do not have the facilities, and keeping a certain emotional distance from a boy whose skull is beneath your surgical hammer and chisel is the only way to keep your own sanity and your own limited power to heal.

The surgical scenes are the crucial ones on which reactions or stomachs will turn. No shot is ever fired in the film, except by a referee on a football field toward the end, but the war becomes an offstage mulching machine that breaks bodies and spews bleeding chunks and pieces of them into the operating theater. The original novel was written pseudonymously by a surgeon, and someone who saw such mobile hospitals during the Korean War tells me these scenes are not exaggerated. My own feeling, having seen nothing but the movie, is that they're almost completely successful. They're ghastly, but at the same time, in a weird way, they're abstracted and hilarious. The director knows that we know it's not real blood and gore. We're not the same audiences that recoiled in horror at the amputation scene in *Gone With the Wind*. But we are, hopefully, an audience that can spot genuine lunacy when we see it, and the lunacy here is war.

M*A*S*H is much more than a one-joke comedy, even if its best joke is up there in the same league with Swift's baby-munching in "A Modest Proposal." Sutherland and Gould play brilliantly together in a sly, easy camaraderie of men who love life too much to live it by infantile rules. Equally brilliant is a complementary duet for fanatics played by Robert Duvall and Sally Kellerman. He's a surgeon and religious nut, she's a chief nurse and Army nut, and their seduction scene is as funny a bit of business as anything in the movie. But you can go on indefinitely about funny business in the movie: a dentist's suicide (funny and strangely touching too), Miss Kellerman's rage about having her true colors revealed, and a wildly funny football game that's only slightly less lethal than war, as body contact sports go.

A few of the film's minor ironies are pretty heavy-handed, and the script goes noticeably soft in a sequence in Tokyo. For the most part, though, M*A*S*H is a remarkable achievement, and I confess complete bafflement as to how the people who made it ever achieved what they did, a hyperacute wiretap on mankind's death wish. It's ensemble work of the highest order, and credit should go not only to Altman, Lardner, and the cast but to the director of photography, Harold E. Stine, the editor, Danford B. Greene, and also the songwriters, Mike Altman and Johnny Mandel, for the major irony of their "Suicide Is Painless" ("It brings on many changes . . ."). Brave men and women all!

Breakthrough

David Denby

M*A*S*H, the celebrated American comedy about three Army surgeons in the Korean War, is not a great work, but it is joyous and liberating in the way that European movies which are great works almost never manage to be. And it's the kind of movie we need in the present moment—M*A*S*H (an acronym for Mobile Army Surgical Hospital) may be set in Korea, but who in the audience can help thinking "Vietnam"? Sardonic antimilitary comedy suits our mood; this one may rescue us for a while from the hopelessness we feel. The film makers take for granted a certain alienation and disgust, but they don't rely on it completely for their effects, as Antonioni has in *Zabriskie Point*, his shockingly lazy vision of America as a corrupt society. Director Robert Altman and his company work with a happy, bright energy that makes you want to go along with the movie, even with the scenes that don't quite come off. They create their own world and earn the right to their attitudes. After a cautious beginning in New York and Los Angeles, Fox has now opened the movie all over the country. The Army, however, announced in late March that M*A*S*H would be banned on all its bases.*

M*A*S*H is the breakthrough in the realm of popular culture that The Graduate was supposed to be and really wasn't; its great achievement is to establish an acceptable heroism. Neither solemnly forbearing in the Gregory Peck tradition, nor beautiful and ineffably sweet, as in the canting youth movies (The Graduate), its heroes are really something to admire. Carnal and witty, chivalrous but not soft, these men do something in the world with pride and success and have graciously retained the wildness of adolescence. Only the most unimaginative standards would find them disapointing; doubtless they aren't "mature"—that insulting, coercive notion which requires us to give up so much to succeed.

The mood of the picture is sustained by a tremendous secret excitement that passes among the three men (played by Elliott Gould, Donald Sutherland, and Tom Skerritt) and radiates from them to the audience, a tense unspoken understanding of the reality of the situation: that the war is absurd, an offense against rationality too deep for words; that the field hospital is inadequate to handle the flow of mangled bodies that pass across its operating tables; that the doctors must work with intensity, skill, and improvisatory daring to have any effect at all; and that away from their wives and civilian careers, they have been offered a second chance at recklessness and boyhood, a chance they joyously accept because it is the only way to remain sane and keep working. These doctors really know about health; they know what supports life and what kills it. The elaborate bad taste, the detailed attention to games and trivia, the constant intrigues of everyone sleeping with everyone else—all this enforced atmosphere of a disorderly summer camp or coed frat house is a kind of therapy. Several reviewers have complained that the surgeons are excessively brutal to people they don't like, but it seems natural to me that personal relations in a

* The ban was subsequently lifted.

military emergency hospital would become exacerbated to the point where every quirk would become unbearable. The tensions are relieved either with obscenity and kidding ("If you didn't have such a good body, nurse, we'd get rid of you") or, in extreme cases, with personal vendettas.

Their wildness would be stupid and merely cruel if they weren't such good, competent surgeons. The scenes in the operating room, with blood spurting from open wounds and doctors running from body to body, are both harrowing and funny—this butcher-shop mess is war's final truth. The humor is bitter but not sick—not black comedy, but something warmer, with the outrage closer to the surface. Richard Lester tried to bring down the curtain on the traditional hypocrisy of war movies in *How I Won the War*, but his style—absurdist farce—backfired on him; his vision of war wasn't shocking and grotesque, it was just silly. Audiences were justifiably bewildered, and their resentment shifted to the movie itself. Altman sticks close to the realistic level, and his esthetic conservatism works for us: the mess in the operating room creates in us the same explosive tension and near-hopelessness that the doctors feel, and we experience the relief that they do when they get the chance to go wild.

Many elements in this production, from the acting style to the sound quality, are innovative in ways that could be important for the big studios, which must learn to work cheaper and bring in fresh talent if they are to survive. First, who is Robert Altman? When I talked with him in Hollywood recently, he told me that the New York journalists who interviewed him after *M*A*S*H* opened couldn't understand why they hadn't heard of him before; surely he was a Canadian or had spent ten years in jail as a political prisoner? Actually, Altman, at forty-five, has been kicking around the film business for years. He has done shorts and documentaries in Kansas City, lots of television in Hollywood, and three features that went largely unnoticed, including *That Cold Day in the Park*, a Sandy Dennis vehicle that was both sordid and dull. Altman got to see Ring Lardner, Jr.'s script for *M*A*S*H* after other directors had turned it down. He accepted the project and independent producer Ingo Preminger came up with $3.5 million from Twentieth Century-Fox, which by the crazy policy of that company was actually a modest budget.

Left on his own by a studio worried about leviathans like *Hello, Dolly!* (over $20 million) and *Patton* ($12 million), Altman was free to experiment. A run-down, garbage-laden field hospital was built on the mud flats at the studio ranch in Malibu Canyon. With the veteran Harold E. Stine as his cinematographer, Altman went after a drab, drizzly look by using a zoom lens with a fog filter. *M*A*S*H* seems entirely composed in greens and browns, except for the operating sequences, where the blood becomes even more shocking by being the only color in the movie. Rather than scheduling his cast members to fly in for three days here, four days there, as is usually done, Altman gathered an ensemble company, mostly at low pay, and held it together for the entire six weeks of shooting. Many of these actors were hired from the American Conservatory Theater and the satirical revue *The Committee,* two San Francisco institutions whose members specialized in ensemble playing and improvisation. Eight of them had no parts in the script when hired, but Altman put them in costume and let them join the group on the set. As tensions and friendships developed, roles emerged for these actors and lines and routines for the company at large—just as they might at a close, working community like an Army base. Some of the actors developed such a strong sense of the community that they voluntarily removed themselves from scenes where they felt their characters didn't belong. Anyone who knows actors may have trouble believing it.

In a movie devoted to the destruction of pretense, overelaborate or florid readings, however skillful, would be all wrong; Altman allowed his performers to improvise frequently, and they seem to be relaxed and enjoying themselves. Here, as in *Bob & Carol & Ted & Alice,* Elliott Gould is extraordinarily evocative of someone we may vaguely remember from summer camp or school; he has that air of a self-absorbed adolescent, acting out his private sense of amusement. As for Donald Sutherland, he appears to be stoned most of the time, which gives his favorite ploy of mock formality a rather muzzy and decrepit tone. These self-loving performances, probably indistinguishable from the actors' personalities, work perfectly—in the Army a man must become a "character" or he loses all individuality—whereas Tom Skerritt, who does some straight acting as a Southerner, is merely effective and likable. Almost everyone in the large cast has his own lovely moment of eccentricity or wit, and we don't see the mugging typical of supporting actors desperate to make an impression.

Since mood was more important than the details of a loosely episodic plot in which no given scene was abolutely essential, Altman could take big chances while shooting and hope for the craziness and pacing that more anxious preparation often kills; naturally, he had to throw a lot away. It would probably be impossible to do improvisation without using the sloppy sound recorded on the set; post-dubbing, the usual procedure, could never reproduce that excited intensity of actors building a scene without knowing exactly where they are going. By committing himself this way, Altman may have lost a few big laughs when dialogue overlaps (sometimes the overlap is itself funny), and there are occasional lines we simply can't hear, but he came up with the liveliest sound track on an American film in years. Many scenes begin in mid-conversation, but we catch just enough to feel the texture of relationships, the amount of living, that might be going on. It's not only the dialogue that works well. The hospital camp's loudspeaker system, for instance, becomes a major character in the movie, establishing the weirdly banal official atmosphere in which everyone must work. "The American Medical Association announced this morning that marijuana is a dangerous drug," it says, during one of the ghastly operating scenes.

Almost every minute of M*A*S*H is filled with detailed invention; the movie has a prodigal, throwaway quality that may remind some viewers of a vintage thirties comedy like Howard Hawks's *Bringing Up Baby*. I wouldn't be surprised if it became a college-film-society classic and was loved by generations of students.

Brad Darrach

If you believe in God, America, Virginity, Temperance, Not Swearing, Military Discipline, and The Sacred Relationship Between Doctor and Patient, pass on to the next review, please. No? Well, you've been warned. M*A*S*H is the deftest, leftest, assiest, grassiest, side-splittingest, throat-slittingest little medicomedy that ever told the Five Deadly Virtues to go stuff it.

The story starts out like a regulation dogface farce, the kind you used to see Tom Ewell and David Wayne in. But then. Then all at once you find yourself in a bloodbucket called a Mobile Army Surgical Hospital set up in a gully about three miles behind the front lines in Korea. On the operating tables, mutilated bodies gurgle gore while casual young surgeons hack them up, kick pieces of human flesh around the floor and fling gems of med-school humor at each other. First surgeon: "Is this an officer or an enlisted man?" Second surgeon: "Enlisted man." First surgeon: "Make the stitches big." Off duty the medics while away the rustic tedium like pashas—sipping cold martinis, nibbling warm nurses. When they get bored, they steal a jeep or maybe bootleg a little amphetamine to the natives.

What they dig the most, though, is to chump the chaplain or some other godly bod ("Say, were you religious back home or did you crack up over here?"). The shafting of Captain Burns, whose priggery is exceeded only by his incompetence, is their masterpiece. It begins when they bug and broadcast the Captain's first attempt at fiddle-dee-dee, and concludes the following morning, when a surgeon chummily inquires if the Captain found Hot Lips Houlihan "any better than self-abuse."

You get the idea: use the formula but freak out on it, speak up through it. Speak up but stay cool. If you can't see why they go amiably ape, those two swinging surgeons (Elliott Gould and Donald Sutherland) are in no sweat to tell you, and neither is Director Robert Altman. You get an eerie feeling from time to time that while you're laughing at them, they're laughing at you.

CATCH-22

ARTHUR SCHLESINGER, JR.

What went wrong? Here was Joseph Heller's hallucinatory satire, the wildest and most murderous of contemporary visions of war; here was Mike Nichols, the director whose intelligence, wit, and sardonic imagination qualified him perfectly to convert the novel into a film; here was Alan Arkin, who must have been the man Heller had in mind when he conceived Captain Yossarian. Yet the result, despite flashes of excitement and originality, is in the main laborious and leaden.

One thing that went wrong, I think, is that Nichols got his wars mixed up. As a novel, Catch-22 was about World War II. Its point, I take it, was that the inherent momentum and madness of the military machine generated monstrosities even when the war was good and necessary. As a film, Catch-22, while still set in World War II, is really not about that war at all. It is about the war in Vietnam—a war in which monstrosities occur not in spite of but because of the nature of the war. Instead of an attack on the military machine, it becomes an attack on war in general. But has the Vietnam war really reduced all wars to its own level?

The film constantly intimates Vietnam parallels. In the novel Colonel Cathcart, the commanding officer, is thirty-six years old. Played by Martin Balsam in the film, he is a grizzled maniac in his fifties, bearing a considerable resemblance to Lyndon B. Johnson. To remove any doubt in the matter, Colonel Cathcart is given a scene, not to be found in the book, where he receives a subordinate while sitting on a toilet—an unmistakable allusion to what is said to have been one of the less beguiling administrative habits of the former President. Thus Cathcart's escalation of his war seems to spring from the basic policy madness of Vietnam, not from the more complicated problem of military madness within a rational policy as in World War II.

Joseph Heller achieved an extraordinary tension between horror and farce. The film is too often heavy-handed. Take the elaborate overemphasis in the chaplain's reaction to Colonel Cathcart on the toilet, for example; or the ponderous irony of a scene where two characters, walking a landing strip and discussing a business deal, remain oblivious to the plane skidding by them and exploding into flames. The movie Catch-22 lacks the poise and control necessary to walk its high wire.

This may derive in part from the difficulty of compressing a long, perhaps overlong, novel, with a complex structure and a mob of characters, into a two-hour movie. The screenplay skims so many episodes so quickly that the dramatis personae are, in many cases, inadequately established and the pattern of the film is hard to follow. Among the actors, Alan Arkin seems an unduly passive and even somnambulistic Yossarian. Perhaps Anthony Perkins as the chaplain and Orson Welles as General Dreedle come off best; but the kaleidoscopic style of the film makes it hard to judge performance.

Can one's disappointment come from having expected too much? Certainly the film has its lovely moments, both visually (a squadron of planes taking off in a shimmering dawn) and dramatically (Yossarian in the hospital). But I cannot resist the feeling that a much less pretentious, polished, and worked-up film—I mean, of course, M*A*S*H—comes closer to catching the gay and savage anarchy of Joseph Heller's novel.

Some Are More Yossarian Than Others

STEFAN KANFER

McWATT'S VOICE (filtered, yelling):
  Help him! Help him!
YOSSARIAN (into mike, yelling):
  Help who?
McWATT'S VOICE (filtered, yelling):
  Help the bombardier!
YOSSARIAN (into mike, yelling):
  I'm the bombardier. I'm all right.
McWATT'S VOICE (filtered, yelling):
  Then help him. Help him!

The chronicle of war is the Bible of irony. The original victim of that mistaken-identity crisis was a B-25 bombardier named Joseph Heller during a World War II raid over Avignon. He was a dozen feet from the pilot; yet they were separated by layers of chaos and terror. It was not Heller who was hurt—it was his gunner who was bleeding copiously into his flight suit. It was Heller's thirty-seventh mission. From that instant of agony he grew petrified of flight. When his war ended, he took a ship home; it was some fifteen years later before the flier entered another plane.

The experience was too extravagant to be fiction and too real to be borne. Heller furnished the corpse with a vaudeville wardrobe, mixed in fifties America, and called his novel *Catch-22*. Black, mad, and surreal, it told of a bombardier named Yossarian impaled on the insanity of war and struggling to escape. Undergraduates still see Yossarian as a lionly coward, the first of the hell-no-we-won't-go rebels who had to go anyway. To them, the book's final sentence limns the human condition as well as the hero's: "The knife came down, missing him by inches, and he took off."

Catch-22 smacked of Restoration comedy. The characters trapped with Yossarian in the 256th Squadron had arch names: Major Major, General Dreedle, Colonel Korn, Milo Minderbinder. The contents seemed to be a series of hyperbolic World War II anecdotes, but its author confesses: "I wrote it during the Korean War and aimed it for the one after that." The book was criticized as flatulent, self-indulgent, and anachronistic—"Engine Charlie" Wilson's General Motors, thinly disguised, was one of its archvillains. Moreover it followed Hilaire Belloc's irritating dictum: "First I tell them what I am going to tell them; then I tell them; and then I tell them what I told them."

Nearly five million readers nevertheless found it one of the most original comic novels of their time. They found it so funny, in fact, that surely half of them ignored Heller's own warnings: that *Catch-22* is no more about the Army Air Corps than Kafka's *The Trial* was about Prague; that "the cold war is what I was truly talking about, not the World War"; and that the second biggest character in the novel is death.

The biggest, of course, is Yossarian. Like most larger-than-death heroes, he is Everyman. Still, some men are more Yossarian than others. Mike Nichols knows. And Alan Arkin knows. And Mike Nichols knows that Alan Arkin knows. "It was the only part I've ever worked on which didn't demand a conception," says Arkin, "because there isn't much difference between me and Yossarian." Viewing Arkin in the film of *Catch-22* is like watching Lew Alcindor sink baskets or Bobby Fischer play chess. The man seems made for the role. Fear rides on his back like a schizoid chimp. His voice climbs from neurosis to hysteria—and winds back down again, without missing a moan. On Yossarian's tortured face is a look of applied sanity that befits only saints and madmen. He walks through a closed system to which everyone but the dreamer has a key.

Arkin's complex, triumphant performance is due in part to good genes—he looks more like Yossarian than he does like Arkin. In part it is due to a virtuoso player entering his richest period. But in the main it is due to the quirky talent of director Mike Nichols, whose previous successes have been wrung largely from the bland and facile. It is as if Neil Simon were to turn out *Endgame* or Peter Sellers to turn into Falstaff.

The film is far from whole. Occasionally, it moves too slowly. Despite its determined timelessness, it suffers from inescapable time lag. The feudal state of the Army has the aspect of ancient history; bombing in World War II was like bombing in no other war before or since. When the novel was published in 1961, its nonviolent stance was courageous and almost lonely. But antiwar films have become faddish lately, and *Catch-22* runs the risk, philosophically, of falling into line behind *M*A*S*H* and *How I Won the War*.

Comedy, of all things, is the film's weakest component. As an adapter, Buck Henry has supplied a terse, sufficient script; it is as a comic actor that he is wanting. In the part of Colonel Korn, he violates the first rule of humor: if what you're doing is funny, you don't have to be funny doing it. Playing outpatients of *Dr. Strangelove*, he and his Tweedledummy Colonel Cathcart (Martin Balsam) italicize every punch line. Even their faces are overstatements. As General Dreedle, Orson Welles sweeps past like Macy's Thanksgiving Day Parade, all plastic and gas. Dreedle need only have GREED lettered across his middle to complete the cartoon.

But Nichols was not making *Super-M*A*S*H*. From the beginning, he was aware that laughter in *Catch-22* was, in the Freudian sense, a cry for help. It is the book's cold rage that he has nurtured. In the jokes that matter, the film is as hard as a diamond, cold to the touch and brilliant to the eye. To Nichols, *Catch-22* is "about dying"; to Arkin, it is "about selfishness"; to audiences, it will be a memorable horror comedy of war, with the accent on horror.

With psychiatric insight, Nichols has constructed *Catch-22* like a spiral staircase set with mirrors. Yossarian ascends by dols, units of pain, glimpsing pieces of himself until he comes to a landing of understanding. It is 1944, Mussolini has collapsed, and Allied victory is inevitable. But for the bombardment group, there is no surcease. Colonel Cathcart compulsively keeps raising the number of missions required before an airman can be rotated Stateside.

Like a carnivore among vegetarians, Cathcart careers through the defenseless. The chaplain (Anthony Perkins) is chewed out for not writing inspirational sermons that will gain the unit a spread in *The Saturday Evening Post*. The fliers are ordered to raid civilian towns so that they can concentrate on producing nice tight bomb patterns in the aerial photographs. Most horrible of all, Lieutenant Milo Minderbinder (Jon Voight) is encouraged in his murderous wartime profiteering.

Yossarian moves numbly through it all, reminiscent of the Steinberg drawing in which a rabbit peers out of a human face. He begs Doc Daneeka (Jack Gilford) to ground him as being insane with fear. But the flight surgeon dutifully recites the Air Force manual's imaginary Catch No. 22: Naturally, anyone who wants to get out of combat isn't really crazy. So supernaturally, anyone who says he is too crazy to keep flying is too sane to stop. On such circular reasoning rests the plot, the dialogue, and indeed the film's essence.

The dominant image is the circle. *Catch-22* is as cyclic as the Soldier in White, a mummylike form completely encased in bandages. At one end, a bottle feeds fluid into the region of some upper vein. At the other, a pipe conducts the fluid out of the kidney region and into another bottle. At a given signal, preoccupied nurses exchange the bottles, and the cycle begins anew.

Fully loaded, the bombers take flight, make their lethal gyres and return empty. Under Nichols' direction, the camera makes air as palpable as blood. In one long-lensed indelible shot, the sluggish bodies of the B-25's rise impossibly close to one another, great vulnerable chunks of aluminum "shaking" as they fight for altitude. Could the war truly have been fought in those preposterous crates? It could; it was. And the unused faces of the fliers, Orr, Nately, Aardvark, could they ever have been so young? They were; they are. *Catch-22*'s insights penetrate the elliptical dialogue to show that wars are too often a children's crusade, fought by boys not old enough to vote or, sometimes, to think.

Yossarian's mind circles five times to that instant in which McWatt calls out "Help him!" Each time Yossarian's arc of memory lengthens as he bends to aid the mortally wounded Snowden—until at last he sees the man's flesh torn away and his insides pour out. It is at once the film's most repulsive and instructive moment. From that time Yossarian cannot accept the escape bargain his superiors finally offer him: "All you have to do is like us." He cannot betray his fellow victims of what Norman Mailer called "exquisite totalitarianism." It is then that the rabbit must run or perish.

Most of the film has the quality of dislocation. It is lit like a Wyeth painting and informed with the lunatic logic of Magritte. Only twice does it grow didactic. In an Italian whorehouse, nineteen-year-old Nately (Art Garfunkel) confronts a 107-year-old pimp. The scene is photographed narrative, almost word-for-word from the book's symbolic and simplistic confrontation: weary but supposedly immortal Italy versus vigorous but naive and supposedly doomed America. When the boy accuses the ancient of shameless opportunism, the centenarian defends himself with the ultimate weapon: age. "I'll be twenty in January," answers Nately. There is no answer to the old man's Parthian shot: "If you live."

As the film progresses, Lieutenant Minderbinder descends from mess-hall hustler to full-time racketeer. In a crude and overdrawn caricature, the loutish blond fly-boy suddenly becomes a Hitlerian symbol who bombs American bases in a deal with the Germans and sells stocks in the war because it is good business. Here Nichols —like Heller—cannot let hell enough alone, and Engine Charlie's oft-quoted G.M. dictum is paraphrased: "What's good enough for M-M Enterprises is good for the country." But not for the movie.

The Catch

HOLLIS ALPERT

Although made with evident skill, conscientiousness, and even rigorous dedication by the gifted Mike Nichols and his many gifted associates, *Catch-22* simply does not come across well as a film, and it is not merely a matter of flaws, of humor failing to be funny, of performances misfiring, but the management of the material itself. Joseph Heller's novel, while often belaboring its assumption (with which I am inclined to agree) that military bureaucracy is by its very nature insane, was a wild, exuberant mixture of gruesome realism and outrageous comedy. Somehow it worked, held together by its style. That style hasn't been totally transferred to film. What we have instead is an uneasy blending of two mediums, the novelistic and the cinematic.

By way of illustration, there is a quite haunting scene in the film: A plane, piloted by a member of a World War II squadron, buzzes a recreation beach and an offshore raft. On the raft is a cheerfully waving airman. As the bathers on the beach watch, the plane heads toward the man and cuts him in half. The lower half of the body slowly falls, and the pilot goes on to crash into a hillside. A similar moment occurs in the book, but with a vast difference: We know the pilot, the man on the raft, and those on the beach. Heller goes on to relate the consequences of the eerie, horrible happening. But in the movie, it comes out of left field, so to speak.

And I think this may pinpoint the major problem of the film. Heller's people were improbable at times, but they were always people. We got to know them. In the film, they are seldom more than faces. They pass by like figures in a nightmare landscape. Who piloted that plane? McMann, of course. But, let's see, just who was McMann? And that man on the raft? Perhaps it was the need to compress so much into a limited time span that caused Nichols to slough off his people, that caused him to choose a form of nightmare—Yossarian's nightmare—in which other nightmares cyclically occur.

Yossarian wants to escape from insanity by feigning insanity. But that's the catch. It's normal to want to escape, and therefore he is sane. Yossarian, as played by Alan Arkin, is the heart and center of the film, and yet we don't know him well either. The film begins with his dream of his end. Or does it? Nichols doesn't anchor us solidly to this form. It literally requires a knowledge of the novel to know who is who and what is happening. That GI in fatigues who knifes Yossarian. If we know the novel, we know it is an Italian whore. If we don't know the novel, we just don't know. Finally, near the end, we are *told*.

Among those who pass by and through and who are limned with relative clarity are Colonel Cathcart (Martin Balsam), Dr. Daneeka (Jack Gilford), Chaplain Tappman (Anthony Perkins), and General Dreedle (Orson Welles)—but, to freeze them, Nichols often resorts to caricature. They are a little overdone and seldom funny. However, does Nichols (and Buck Henry, the screenwriter) want them to be funny? I doubt it. Their justified outrage makes them cold and grim, and the film is overcome by the awfulness of what they are showing. Thus, there is little or no humanness in the film, no real heart that bleeds. And yet there are moments of icy brilliance. I rather think that Mr. Nichols was never quite able to resolve the conceptual tensions between his vision and that of Mr. Heller.

JACOB BRACKMAN

Whatever else you care to say about war, it's ideal for the movies. Our recent experiences with real war, however, have rendered the old chauvinisms which informed movie war cruelly ridiculous. The problem of modern war movies, therefore, is to retain the emotional power (men going their limits of endurance and pluck) and the kinetic power (planes, tanks, explosions, bodily injury) within an over-all vision of war as senseless and bestial.

Once our war movies seemed manufactured as U.S. troop entertainments. (Think of the guts-and-glory previews forever blaring from the M*A*S*H camp P.A. system.) But a modern base would be masochistic to play M*A*S*H, or Too Late the Hero, or any recent war film. Even Patton, a celebration for hard hats, is suffused with disturbing pathology and shameful motives. Medals, all displays of military pride, have become a joke. If a movie soldier now launched into a patriotic speech, we'd take it as a sign that combat had driven him insane.

At one or another level of sophistication, the argument proceeds rather like this: "I'm trapped in a huge chaotic war. I don't understand it. I am helpless to alter its course. I'll soon be back at the front where I can die at any instant. So why not take the same risks on my own behalf?"

Over the decades, American war movies have familiarized us with all subversive lines of argument—but only, until most recently, as a first step toward undermining them, denying their sense. There was never much hope of denying the existence of the "selfish" way of looking at war and the outrageous claims war makes upon one. A next-best solution was to embody such wrong-headed perceptions in characters who could be easily written off.

Sometimes, simply, unpatriotic ideas would be voiced by reprehensible men—closet fascists, bigots, cowards who could betray not only their country but comrades in adjoining foxholes. (Only an unshakably un-American viewer might identify with their analyses of war.) Sometimes they would be voiced by a protagonist wearing a *mask* of cynicism, one who ultimately exhibited the very self-sacrifice he'd scoffed at. (Bogart often played a variation of this character.)

But whatever attempts were made to negate it, this resentful underside of jingoism has been there all along. Someone was nearly always saying: "You lost your legs for nothing." "You lost your son for Wall Street." "You lost your sight, your sanity, your sweetheart, for a stubborn misunderstanding."

This underside of cynicism has now crept around and spread over everything. Even though the old sorts of ingenuity and valor still get called into play in movies like *Too Late the Hero*, no soldier cares for anything beyond saving his own skin. The war makes no sense to anyone. Not even World War II makes sense anymore.

Our war movies have always been built around sides: ours, theirs; good, bad. The special loyalties which *our* side called into play—from the thirty-foot GI, and from us chewing the popcorn—depended upon that vast and now defunct reticula of understandings about what the United States stood for and how our nationalism might reasonably be appreciated as a species of universal idealism. In retrospect, we recognize that idealism to have been righteous smugness, pathological arrogance, and the war movies we shall be seeing for a while will reflect reaction against patriotic falsehoods.

There's always a catch. If you're crazy, they have to take you out of combat, but the catch is you have to *ask* them, and if you're trying to get out of combat then you can't be crazy. That's Catch-22. If you think about it hard, it can drive you crazy. Then maybe they'll let you out. No, because you'd have to ask them first, remember? That same catch, number 22, may also be a law according to which certain women can be summarily seized to become servicemen's whores, all profits to a syndicate so gigantic it makes deals with major powers, a syndicate controlled by a bland, personable Acting Mess Officer. But obviously that's nonsensical. Selling shares in devastation! Does war make men crazy? Do men make war because they are crazy to begin with? If you think about it hard, you can tumble into an unbalancing circularity. That's not exactly being crazy, but sometimes it's hard to know just where to draw the line. Like when there's war and you find yourself in the middle of it, even though the war is over. Like when what you destroy doesn't matter so long as you produce tight bombing patterns for the aerial photos. Why not ask your friends? The zombies, murderers, and corpses. But if *Catch-22* had been directed by Brian Hutton or almost anybody out there, it would have wound up indistinguishable from *Kelly's Heroes*. (Material about *Kelly's Heroes* has been edited out of this review.) Under Mike Nichols, this is true only about forty percent of the time.

The unsavory part of me that sat looking over *Catch-22* with an appraiser's eye kept commuting, it seemed, between two movies that had been intercut by some moon-struck studio editor. The one a dark, hysterical masterpiece, a *Moby Dick* of movies. The other a dumb, undergraduatey jackoff, a $15 million Hasty Pudding Show. The one as if Lewis Carroll had redone *The Inferno*—to make you laugh and steal the sound of your laughter. I respected it; even, a few times, stood in awe of it. For minutes at a stretch, I'd feel I was undergoing something like a new *kind* of movie, and therefore one of historical eminence.

From the movie I admire, a few sequences: the refrain around which Yossarian's epic undulates: Y alone in a bleached-out frame, receiving radio instructions over earphones. Then ineptly reassuring Snowden, the wounded gunner: "You're going to be okay." Five times the scene returns, each time elaborated, like a repressed trauma floating back piecemeal from the edge of childhood memory. Next time, a spurting leg wound revealed. "Listen, kid, it's not bad. I'm gonna put a tourniquet on it." Later, when Snowden complains of the cold, Y sees the red blotch of his body wound. Finally he conjures, in a millisecond's image, the body ripped wide, spilling its innards. The plane careens. Snowden shivers. Arkin careens, a silly smile plastered across his face. "There, there," he keeps repeating.

A vision from his delirium: Y swimming toward Nurse Duckett on a raft. She strips and beckons playfully, her breasts slow-motion jouncing. Amazed, frantic with longing, he seems almost to rise like a porpoise from the water. He quickens his stroke. Exhausted, he begins to sink. Through the foregoing, the sound of wind and distant guns.

The airstrip brilliantly lit by searchlights, installations exploding along its perimeters. Minderbinder (lit, as usual, from down low) directing the air raid over loudspeakers, from the control tower. The strafing begins. Y running, his pistol absurdly at the ready, reversing his direction, yelling for Nately, panic and incredulity doing battle in his eyes.

But spritzled all through this order of stuff is a bomberload of fairly contemptible burlesque. The General's WAC (an early-forties Betty Grable type) licks her lip and twenty-seven fly-boys fall all over each other offering her twenty-seven folding chairs. The General warns against further moaning; the Major moans (not over the WAC) and the General orders that he be taken out and shot. The Lieutenant Colonel screams, like a quarter-pint Bilko, at the frightened chaplain.

The *Catch*-22 I hold cheap features Martin Balsam as Colonel Cathcart, Buck Henry as Lieutenant Colonel Korn, Bob Newhart as Major Major, Orson Welles as General Dreedle, Austin Pendleton as Colonel Moodus, and sometimes Jon Voight as Lieutenant Milo Minderbinder. (Minderbinder, a borderline case, seems to play a role in both movies.) Not that these performances are poor —just apparently conceived to suit a broad, inconsequential entertainment, like *Kelly's Heroes*. With Arkin trying to make the devil roar, these fellows second banana as if to a Westbury matinee.

Self-conscious, lap-over transitions zap us from one sequence into the next. For instance, the Colonels Balsam and Henry put their heads together, chortling over how General Dreedle would handle Y's malingering. One pipes up, "Kick 'im in the balls." Bam! cut to Nurse Duckett kicking Y in the balls as he fumbles for her buttons. Most of the transitions operate in just this dimension of cleverness. Yet often as not they're connecting moments of substance that elicit dense emotional responses; moments which can be laughed at, but don't *demand* to be laughed at. The cutesy cuts turn out to be most destructive in their trivializing, because the film's structure—a new . . . disjointed time-jumping spiraling swirlback—turns out to be the most harrowing thing about it. Second most harrowing: how, in the fearful dissociations of war, friendship is impossible. Friendship was the last redeeming myth.

Some of *Catch-22* is so impressive—startling, really—that I like to think Mike Nichols is finding his grown-up stride at last. I begin here to sense the man's complexity, to hear something of the cry beneath his facile send-ups, to anticipate large work from him. However, to account for all the choices which only serve to reintegrate his schizzy *Catch-22* back within the safe conventions of Service Comedy, I must imagine he still labors under the residual bad advice of old, flyweight buddies. Weight classification, a Norman Mailer metaphor, of course, reminds me that Mailer once (in a stroke of that colossal, brutish blindness we allow him, not always cheerfully) miscalled Salinger "the greatest mind ever to stay in prep school"—a title which, a number of us are coming to suspect, properly belongs to the lively Mr. Buck Henry, author.

Can I quit without avowing that *Catch-22* just shines on when Arkin's in the frame? His Yossarian is one of the all-time *full* movie characterizations. This Arkin is inexhaustibly original (he never reads a line the way anyone else might read it) and totally human (you always know him from somewhere). There's also a wonderful performance by the young actor who, in *Midnight Cowboy*, picked up Jon Voight on Forty-second Street and did the virtuoso four-minute turn through lust, nauseated guilt, and, as he finally reneged on the promised payment, terror. Here Bob Balaban plays a wry, mysterious pilot of sudden smiles—a child, like most of our fighting men—whose propensity for crashing into oceans may just be in dress rehearsal for a master escape.

He symbolizes for Yossarian the most urgent personal question about war, a question that stands at the precise center of *Catch-22* and, now, of several million young lives: How can it be escaped from?

SOLDIER BLUE

The Red and The Blue

HOLLIS ALPERT

A bullet drilled the blue uniform of the cavalry officer, and a small fountain of blood spurted from his heart—and it was at this point during the screening of *Soldier Blue,* a film directed by Ralph Nelson, that an esteemed lady reviewer for an esteemed publication got up from her seat and left the screening room, never to return. The picture had been under way no more than ten minutes, and since I stayed to the gory end, I can vouch for the fact that worse, or more, violence was yet to come.

A solemn foreword to the movie did attempt to prepare us for some of its horrors. The massacre of several hundred Cheyenne Indians, portrayed toward the close of the film, was to be regarded as true. There had been such a shameful event in American history. As was further made clear by some material supplied by the releasing organization, Avco Embassy Pictures Corporation, there had been two such events. One was the Sand Creek massacre, which took place in 1864; the other was the Wounded Knee battle of 1889. Research on both was used as the basis for the reconstructed version in *Soldier Blue.* Thus, for Mr. Nelson, presumably, there was sufficient justification for telling it—or, rather, showing it—like it was.

But was there such justification? On Mr. Nelson's side, the recent *alleged* (italics mine) massacre at Mylai can be cited as a parallel, and with it the plain insinuation that the American character, so called, has always been tainted with blood lust. Surely, then, anyone with the facts would be rendering a human service by bringing them to light. On the other hand, Mr. Nelson doesn't give us only a massacre of Indians, he opens the film with a massacre of U.S. Army soldiers by the Cheyenne, violent enough to make the aforementioned reviewer walk out. And he fails to tell us whether or not *that* massacre was based on an actual event.

Mr. Nelson, then, is giving us fiction, and between those two prolonged acts of violence he places what he has termed "an intimate story," and one based on no fact whatsoever. It is so preposterous a story that it gives rise to unwitting laughter, caused partly by Candice Bergen as a girl captured by Cheyenne warriors and turned into a chief's squaw for two years before being released, apparently for incompatibility. Fiction, of course, whether written, spoken, or shown, is not required to follow factual truth, but rather seeks relevance, meanings, emotional and esthetic responses, and there is no more cliché cop out for failure than for its author to say: "But it's all true! It all happened!"

Ever since American movies began losing their inhibitions, once the Production Code was all but laid to rest, film makers have been in a kind of competition to see who can shock the most. A whole new set of clichés has sprung up. The standard reactive line of dialogue for a pretty girl to speak is now "bullshit!" Miss Bergen, playing a girl of a century or more ago, not only says "bullshit" to her lover, but, on another occasion, "balls." Even historical films, it seems, must be "now" movies, especially in their speech patterns. Mr. Nelson, again, has admitted candidly that his aim was to tell a story of then in terms of now. But where he and others who present nauseating violence (not to mention whole catalogues of sexual aberrations) err is in assuming they have artistic license to do so.

Never, for one moment, do such film makers as Nelson (previously responsible for such sentimental efforts as *Charly* and *Lilies of the Field*) and Sam Peckinpah (*The Wild Bunch*) mention that a plethora of blood on the screen is commercially exploitable. Heavens no! They spend their $3, $4, and $5 million budgets showing us truth and assisting us in changing our errant ways. The advertising arm of the industry is not so easily taken in by this kind of b-----t, however. One big ad for *Soldier Blue* is headlined: THE MOST SAVAGE FILM IN HISTORY. Another film, too nicely titled *Too Late the Hero*, evidently hasn't been attracting enough customers; so it has been retitled *The Violent Bunch*. Suitable for kids, too, since it has been given a GP rating.

All in all, it has been a depressing summer. With our film makers freer than ever to create their visions, they have been foisting on us one benighted effort after another. It is not that our sometimes shameful history needs hiding; it is not that facts of life need covering. It is the pandering to some benighted film audience out there somewhere, supposedly, that sickens the heart and the conscience. The massacre in *Soldier Blue* is not only of the Indians.

3

IMAGES OF REVOLT

THE MOLLY MAGUIRES

Arthur Schlesinger, Jr.

The Molly Maguires is a movie about violence in America. Its subject is a secret society of Irish miners in the coal fields of Pennsylvania in the 1870's driven to terrorism by the harshness and brutality of the mineowners. The film, directed by Martin Ritt and written by Walter Bernstein, tells the story of James McParlan, the Pinkerton operative who penetrated the Mollies and reported on them to the law.

Opinion has vacillated as to whether the Mollies were hateful terrorists or early martyrs of the labor movement. Sir Arthur Conan Doyle, who used them for a late Sherlock Holmes novel, *The Valley of Fear*, transforming James McParlan into a character named Jack McMurdo, embraced the terrorist theory. In the best book on the subject, *The Molly Maguires*, published in 1964 (this is *not* the paperback novelization of the film now available under the same title in the drugstores), Wayne G. Broehl, Jr., suggested that their grievances were genuine. In any case, leading Mollies were eventually brought to trial, with the Pinkerton man as chief witness. Twenty were hanged, ten in a single day.

This wild and savage tale has been considerably trivialized in the film. Ritt and Bernstein, those two old Hibernians, see their Irish characters as stereotypes, given to much lusty drinking, cursing, and brawling. There are meaningless alterations of fact: The events are placed in 1876 when they actually occurred in 1873–1875; three

96

Mollies are hanged rather than twenty; John Kehoe, a Molly leader, is a miner rather than a saloonkeeper; and so on.

Facts are not sacred, except to the historian; and the novelist or film maker may use them as he wishes so long as the imaginative reconstruction is persuasive. What matters, as Georg Lukács has written, "is not the retelling of great historical events, but the poetic awakening of the people who figured in those events. What matters is that we should re-experience the social and human motives which led men to think, feel, and act just as they did in historical reality." This is what William Styron accomplished with such success in his book *The Confessions of Nat Turner.*

But the makers of the film *The Molly Maguires* have brought no particular insight or flair to their subject. They have, for example, no very vivid period sense. In 1876, their chosen year, America was in a depression, but there is no sign of this in the film. Nor do they illuminate the motives of the Mollies, their opponents, or the Pinkerton man. They put out chic, contemporary signals about violence and law and order, but this is not done with sufficient depth to make *The Molly Maguires* a parable, say, of the Black Panthers. Nor can they seem to decide whether McParlan was a hero, a scoundrel, or just a man doing a job.

For a passionate story, this comes out as a cold, dry, and rather perfunctory film. It does not appear to have engaged Martin Ritt as *Hud,* for example, so powerfully engaged him, and the actors— Richard Harris as the Pinkerton man, Sean Connery as John Kehoe, Samantha Eggar as a miner's daughter—perform their roles without amplifying them. What could have been a searing exploration of our national propensity toward violence ends as a pointless anecdote.

GETTING STRAIGHT

JACOB BRACKMAN

As a moviegoer of shrewd discrimination, doubtless you go suspiciously anyway to a movie that promises you onturnage, incoppage, outfreakage, blacks, the draft, the pill, campus revolt, LSD, SDcetera. But if you nonetheless can't quite put your finger on where *Getting Straight* is at, well, scrutinize those placards in the big confrontation scenes. Imagine. Hiring hundreds of actors and crew, spending all that time, energy, and dough to make everything look right, then issuing protest signs with all the specificity of "Down with the Establishment." Some of the signs complain that narcotics spies have been planted on campus. Some bear the nuclear-disarmament symbol. PEACE BROTHER. Mostly, like LET THE PEOPLE DECIDE, the particularity's been squeezed out of their grievances altogether. We've grown accustomed to the mechanics of overscrupulous inoffensiveness, mainly from TV, where networks and sponsors are said to blanch even at political euphemisms —but a more cynical, more gratuitous principle is operating here. These placards, in a film that seeks so zealously to cash in on these components of our national agony, border on outright contempt. It would be nicer even to suppose that they'd been drawn up and substituted at the last minute, by executive fiat, right there with everyone waiting around on the set, because some young propman had brought in signs that cursed, named names, were just too hot. It didn't happen that way of course. Is it just niggling to complain of placards which extras carry—if they become a sudden emblem for a hundred other invidious falsehoods? The students' signs and their contentless chant—ACTION Now!—prepare us for the subsequent battle sequences down in that apocalyptic subbasement where the most tortuous politics of human history are reduced to kinetics.

Elliott Gould plays an overage, oversexed graduate student, who several years back was a celebrated campus longhair and rabble-rouser. He's dropped in again after six years because, however saltily, however acri*moni*ously for chrissake, he comes on about the crises of the day, he's dewy-eyed at the prospect of awakening youthful minds. He wants to teach high-school English, coach a tennis team, win the day at Hi-Y dances. A practice instructor of Dumbbell English, he catches one of his students, a Mexican-American (or a Puerto Rican) named Garcia, with a Batman comic. Expecting a scolding, Garcia winces in advance. Instead, Gould leafs through the comic and brays enthusiastically, "You know, there's a great similarity between Batman, Captain Marvel, Red Ryder and . . . Don Quixote! It's that nineteenth-century Romanticism that twentieth-century heroes are made of." (Cervantes was writing before Shakespeare. Gould is a literature major.) Later, he hands his girl friend Garcia's final blue book, from which she reads aloud, her tears flowing freely. It seems Garcia's been inspired all the way to the library, where he's checked out, figuratively, Don Quixote: "He *better* than Batman. He braver." The girl friend sobs, "Oh, Harry, that's beautiful." Gould's name is Harry.

At one point, he's trying to study for his master's orals in a room full of undergraduates who are debating strike strategy. Listen to their discussion. They take stands on issues from coed dorms and drug legislation to R.O.T.C. and Black Studies; propose tactics from asking for permission to circulate a petition to Up Against the Wall. They appeal to Gould as to an elder statesman. Barely glancing up from his books, he grunts his approval to anyone who asks for it. An angry black student attacks his indifference. Impatiently, Gould lets on he'd be more impressed if they were protesting in the outside world, where they'd risk bigger bruises—like in Selma. The black is infuriated. "What right have you got to bring up *Selma*, man, as if you'd been there?"

Gould replies quietly, evenly, "I *was* there, man."

Pan to a cluster of openmouthed students. It's a heavy moment. (If you think about it for a minute or two, however, it collapses under the weight of its own referents, and starts stinking.) One earnest, wholesome-looking boy—whose father is president of the alumni association, and who is certain no C.I.A. agents have infiltrated the campus—asks Gould querulously, "Then, you mean, you think what we're doing . . . isn't important?" Gathering his books under his arm, making for the door, Gould can afford to be conciliatory: "Of course it's important. I've just done it already."

Some minutes later in the film, Gould has become a reluctant intermediary between the administration and the kids. He's inside a paneled office, arguing with the university president. "I'm not as square as some of you might think," the president says. He's one of those benign, twinkly-eyed, totally-out-of-touch administrators who—with the Turks already howling at the gates—is prepared to offer a few extra hours of coed visiting in the dorms. Meanwhile, the wholesome alumni son has become a flaming Cohen-Bendit; he can be seen outside the window charging around like a crazed animal, shrieking, "Pigs go home!"

"A week ago, that kid just wanted to get laid," Gould tells the president. "Today, he wants to kill somebody. You should have let him get laid."

All these greedy little inauthenticities don't add up to a moral affront until the police remove their badges and turn on the fire hoses. Then the students, with their divers silly goals, can all be choreographed into the violent Weatherman ballet, and Gould can make goo-goo eyes at Candy Bergen across a sea of carnage. Finally, for his own very particular reasons—his teaching dreams were shattered after he was caught pulling a Ted Kennedy on his Visual Arts exam—he gets to fling his own sexy rock through a plate-glass window. And won't the kids cheer their little lungs out for *that?* Columbia could scarcely have expected *Getting Straight* to bow so opportunely. For the first time, only days before its premiere, students were shot to death on American campuses.

THE STRAWBERRY STATEMENT
and
GETTING STRAIGHT

Commercials for Revolution

DAVID DENBY

When people of my generation—the under 30's—look at the socially conscious movies of the thirties and forties, we can usually sense the evasions and distortions, even if we are too young to know what those periods were actually like. Anyway, we may enjoy the "phony" things in an old movie the most; the attitudes that are revealed toward what was then the present are as interesting as a historically "straight" version might be, and perhaps as important. Movies that are made now about the past also tend to go in for a lot of heavy attitudinizing. Since the natural inclination of the mass media is to sell the current moment as the most important and interesting in history, the past is often shown as quaint or slightly contemptible, or as a curiously underdeveloped but definitely recognizable version of the present. We may not be aware of this stylization when we see it; and if we are, we may not care—at the moment contempt for the past is also very strong among young people. But we do get angry about lying movies set in the present, particularly if we have lived through an experience someone is trying to put on the screen.

Matching movies against "the truth" may be a limited and rather philistine approach to criticism, but I don't see how it can be avoided now that the studios think they can make money by releasing movies on public issues that heavily involve us in our lives outside the theaters. The audience has powerful, unresolved feelings about a subject like student protest, and as a result, *The Strawberry Statement* and *Getting Straight* were awaited with grander and more naive expectations than usual. Older members of the audience may have been seeking explanations for things they didn't understand; perhaps the younger ones wanted justification, or at least an image of their experience that they could share. When the movies turned out to be rotten, the reviews and personal comments were filled with charges of betrayal.

The men who made these movies didn't take the trouble to get inside the material; instead, they relied on slogans and symbols that have always been the clichés of mass-media coverage of the student movement. Did they think the movie audience would be offended by seeing or hearing something that wasn't familiar from television news? They also fell back on the conventions of youth movies, a period style as deadly as any in movie history. Visually, the principal elements of this style are an indiscriminate and empty lyricism, relying heavily on zoom lenses and change-focus shots, and rapid "shock" cutting from extreme close-up to extreme close-up. It doesn't seem to have occurred to the moviemakers that these used-up visual mannerisms would be inappropriate for a "serious" movie. I'm sorry to say that the young audience doesn't throw anything at the screen during these sequences. College students going to film revivals often ridicule such conventions of the forties as elaborate flashbacks, throbbing violin passages, and sentimentality about family and courtship, but give them the tenth current example of young "spontaneous" people running through Central Park with a red balloon while Simon and Garfunkel sing of peace and love, and they will sit as quietly as lambs. They don't jeer at the celebrations of freedom that look like extended toilet paper commercials, and they aren't restive during the scenes of violence or rapid movement that are so brutally cut that it's impossible to see what is supposed to be happening or even where the participants are in relation to one another.

Fully a third of *The Strawberry Statement* has been given over to that awful romping and larking about, and the locale has been shifted from the grimy Columbia of the book to San Francisco, where the sun shining through the unpolluted air can flash in the lens as the cameraman staggers, circles, and finally tilts to the sky to get that unfettered, full-of-joy look. After a few minutes of the movie, it becomes clear that the hero (Bruce Davison), an undergraduate at a fictional university, is a nice kid with many good, clean impulses. But as he gets seriously involved in a campus sit-in, we're eager to know *more* about him: if he wasn't interesting to begin with, then maybe the experience is doing something to him. Instead, when Davison is away from the strike, director Stuart Hagmann wastes valuable minutes chasing him over every hill and up every tower in town, until finally the movie ends with his darling head being busted by the police. Is it necessary to assert at this date that although the radical students may be many admirable things—tough, courageous, morally earnest—they aren't totally innocent? It's as if Hagmann and screenwriter Israel Horovitz were afraid that we'd lose sympathy if the hero were shown to have any ideas or aggressiveness, guile or significant confusions. The most insufferable part of youth movies is the conception of young people as a morally and existentially distinct species of humanity—noble, loving, bountifully but innocently sexual, and most of all, free.

Putting a cipher, however free-spirited, at the center of the movie was bad enough, but Horovitz compounds the error by having Davison fall in love with another cipher (Kim Darby) in the middle of the strike. It's an example of real condescension to the audience: why should we have to watch these astonishingly conventional boy-meets-girl, boy-loses-girl, boy-gets-girl routines? The teen romance seems like a hangover from a surfing-party movie, and adults who might be turned off by the politics can say, "See, they're just ordinary good kids who got mixed up in protest by mistake." Surely a couple so awkwardly and beautifully in love couldn't be serious about all those unpleasant criticisms of the university.

The Strawberry Statement isn't distorted from the left or right; it's simply empty. Occasionally some of the student idiom comes through, and Hagmann has staged a witty sequence in a police wagon in which a strike leader does an easy soft-shoe on the way to jail while the others sing "God Bless America," but these bits are all too short, and the important scenes in the president's occupied office are wisps and fragments of good lines that don't build to anything.

To gain an idea of one kind of complexity that's been left out, consider James Simon Kunen, whose diaries of the Columbia strike in 1968 provide the title, the hero, and some of the situations and dialogue. Kunen strikes one as a pleasant, bright kid with a wry sense of humor, but his literary style, so carefully modest and winning, is probably the result of shrewd calculation. Kunen began publishing his diaries in mid-strike in *New York* magazine; subsequently he became a minor celebrity and youth "spokesman," was attacked by the left for making money off the strike, donated some of his earnings to the Black Panthers, and so forth. He appears briefly in the movie as a strike leader, and is overheard explaining to someone that the media are biased against the strike because the same people profiting from the war and serving as trustees of the university are also running the press, television, and *the movies*. This last reference, coming as it does in a movie from which Kunen is making a small fortune, reveals confusions of cynicism and honesty that take the breath away; yet with such a walking bag of contradictions—an Abbie Hoffman in the making—standing right in front of them, the film makers didn't learn very much about their subject.

Since the strike begins in time before the movie opens, and the hero joins it in full swing, there's no sense of how a movement grows—how, for instance, an originally small group raises the level of provocation and induces the administration to reveal its contemptuous attitudes toward students, thereby creating a mass movement, and how the recklessness of that group is at the same time a form of responsibility to the movement; nor is there any feeling for the volatile and intimate relationship, alternating between trust and angry suspiciousness, that exists between the leaders and the rest; nor any indication of the way students hitherto lost in the university find an identity for themselves and an idea of what a university could be in the example of the strike community itself; nor a hint of the extraordinary amount of intellectual activity that goes on in that community, the wicked excitement of turning the moral passions learned in the classroom against the teachers and the university; and so on.

The issues that inspired the strike are spelled out clearly enough —far too clearly, in fact. The university is going to put up an R.O.T.C. building on some of its land being used by neighborhood black children as a playground; later the students find out that the land is being held tax-free in a tricky deal with a water-and-power company whose president is also a trustee. By first simplifying and then combining elements from the Columbia strike and the People's Park furor at Berkeley, Horovitz has concocted an outrage so blatant, morally so open-and-shut, that even Governor Reagan might support a strike against this university. Why didn't he accuse them of polluting the river with used IBM cards or doubling the library fines for black students while he was at it? It's a classic case. Here is Hollywood making accusations against the universities that would make a Weatherman blush, and it's all being done to make the audience sympathize and identify with two kids who don't look or sound like radicals for a minute.

The bust at the end of the movie, with police gassing, kicking, and clubbing students until we can't stand it anymore, is finally an effective piece of film making. But what could be more pathetic than Hagmann & Co. getting the violence right after fudging everything else in the movie? Conceptually, violence presents no problem for them, and we in the audience can sit there with scalding tears and voluptuous feelings of indignation. As a solution to the incompetence of the movie, it's as hopeless as university administrators calling in the cops when *they* can't figure out what to do.

Some of the male students in *The Strawberry Statement* join the strike to meet girls; the men who made *Getting Straight* would have us believe that sex is what the whole movement is about. When graduate students Candice Bergen and Elliott Gould make love after a heavy police bust and Gould says that riots are good because they make everyone feel sexy, we think he's teasing her radical "commitment"; but there they are at the end of the movie, tearing off their clothes while heads are being cracked all around them in another riot. As a freak-out ending it beats the current competition, but what could it mean—that making love is a revolutionary act? When the Living Theater troupe took off their clothes in Berkeley last year and proclaimed "Revolution," the student audience jeered, but this "radical" nonsense may be a plausible money-making idea for film makers (Antonioni tried it in *Zabriskie Point*), even if the radicals themselves will have none of it. In a scene of paralyzing stupidity (written by Robert Kaufman) Gould confronts the president of the university and demands liberation: "Haven't you heard? Repression breeds revolution. See that kid? A week ago all he wanted to do was get laid, and now he's ready to tear the place apart. You should have let him get laid!" As political analysis it's fairly insulting (they'll be lucky if the students don't tear the theaters apart), and of course the student could have done what Gould suggests without help from the administration. What makes these film makers think that college kids in California are having trouble getting into bed with one another?

Gould plays a volatile intellectual in his late twenties who has been around and done everything and now wants to settle down and get a teaching credential—only he can't do it, he's too active mentally to accept anything. He might not be a bad character, but Kaufman has used him to deliver all those fine bold speeches we all rehearse in our heads about Vietnam, education, suburbia, etc., and we're supposed to think that Gould is saved because he can't resist telling people off. We're also supposed to see that his vivid temperament exposes the inhumanity of official pedagogical theory at the School of Education, but from the beginning all we can think is that a man this mercurial and unstable isn't going to be happy teaching in *any* kind of high school; it's sentimental to assume that the system is a failure because it can't accommodate him. But this is what the movie insists we do: after Gould purposely fails an oral examination conducted by corrupt and physically loathsome academics, he joins the students rioting outside and throws a brick through the window—a sign that he has achieved sanity at last and really gotten "straight."

Since the adult authorities are all either stupid, power-mad, or ineffectual, the system isn't exactly presented at its best or its typically suave, appearances-minded worst. Shifting the disgust this way to adults who are sexually out of it or morally grotesque is a displacement in meaning typical of youth movies, which make their appeal directly to the narcissism and sexual snobbery of the young. These feelings may be severe to begin with, and in the advanced industrial countries they are savagely enlarged and exploited by the ubiquitous advertising culture. Neither of these movies transcends that culture for a second.

Isn't there an American Godard lurking somewhere among those thousands of film students who could make a movie equal to the passion of the radical young and show the Establishment that it won't always be making money from the rebellion against it?

THE REVOLUTIONARY

Compulsive Revolutionary

JAY COCKS

He is the one who sits quietly at the back of the class, always attentive, always taking meticulous notes. He stares myopically through steel-rimmed glasses and speaks with a halting, stumbling shyness. He has been at the university for years now, studying long nights in his shabby apartment, breaking away only for leafleting or demonstrating. He has become politicized as much by his own loneliness as by history, and any kind of action he may take contains equal parts of activism and self-affirmation. As his sense of isolation increases, so does his political commitment. A subtle, intelligent new movie called *The Revolutionary* charts the course of his radicalization with cool precision, showing that this student mixes in revolution because he must.

The student, called A (Jon Voight), attends a large university "somewhere in the free world" and faithfully goes to meetings of the Campus Radical Committee, a group whose militancy is pretty well confined to *in camera* debates. A gets busted for disrupting a political rally, and eagerly lies on the stone floor of his cell, scribbling a ringing "statement to the court" on a length of toilet paper. He is freed the next morning without a chance to read it.

In a fit of pique, he quits the committee and goes to work for an Old Left group of factory workers. He is expelled from the university for unspecified reasons, then allows himself to be drafted into the Army. He discovers that his unit is going to be sent in to quell a riot in a neighboring town, and so he deserts. Back in the university town, he falls in with a kind of surrogate Weatherman type who keeps taunting him by saying, "You got to have action, right? A little action, huh?" With him, in the film's galvanic last scene, he is about to bomb an unfriendly magistrate.

A's progress from liberalism to violence may be intended as a paradigm of contemporary student politics, but director Paul Williams is equally interested in the human impulses that shape history. A is certainly no hero, and as a political figure he possesses about as much charisma as the neighborhood poll watcher. His gimpy right leg cripples him physically, and his academic training —plus a lower-middle-class upbringing—tends to paralyze him politically. Unfortunately, *The Revolutionary* sometimes suffers from the same lingering paralysis. The crucial climactic scene ends with a frame-freeze as A confronts the judge: Will he throw the bomb or not? "The question isn't resolved," says director Williams, "because I wanted to throw the choice back to the audience." Well and good, but the ending crests without climaxing, reducing the whole scene to "Lady or the Tiger" trickery. Williams also errs occasionally in reproducing the monotony of A's life; the boredom is sometimes not intense enough to be more than just boring.

As A, Jon Voight gives an extraordinarily fine performance—his best to date. He can be comic, confused or concerned with equal finesse. The force of his personality gives the role depth, but never overwhelms and smothers it. Collin Wilcox-Horne, as Voight's sometime mistress, has maddening mannerisms that transform her every scene into something akin to an Actors Studio exercise. Jennifer Salt (as a rich girl who becomes interested first in Voight and then in the Movement) and Robert Duvall (as the radical factory worker) help keep the proceedings in a more realistic perspective. Seymour Cassel gives the agitator an interesting twist of paranoia as well as the requisite shot of adrenalin.

There is a good deal of talk these days about bright young film makers, guys in tinted shades who spin their cameras around like tops, talk "commitment," and produce exploitative films like *The Strawberry Statement* and *The Magic Garden of Stanley Sweetheart*. But they are merely today's equivalent of the old studio hacks; it is with film makers like Paul Williams that the future of the industry lies. Williams has talent and insight far beyond his twenty-six years. He has enough respect for his script—and for his actors—to let the camera record the scene instead of orchestrating it. *The Revolutionary* is not a totally successful film, but it is an extraordinarily good one—honest, compassionate, meticulously executed. It marks Williams as a film maker not only worth watching but also worth waiting for.

BRUCE WILLIAMSON

Jon Voight, totally in command of an oddly pitched voice and an awkward, ambling gait for his role as *The Revolutionary*, should hearten those fans who consider him the best movie actor since Brando. While it's true that Voight goes a long way with whatever the moguls give him to do, they don't give him nearly enough in this adaptation of a novel by Hans Koningsberger. Edward Pressman and Paul Williams, the young producer-director team responsible for Voight's very first picture, *Out of It*, seem beyond their depth in Koningsberger's study of a student activist named A (we're in Kafka country, you understand—a nameless place in the so-called free world at an unspecified time in history) who leaves school to join a more radical workers' movement and ultimately comes to his moment of truth when he is asked to back up his revolutionary zeal with an act of violence. Though the hero quotes Robespierre and everyone talks about oppression, the movie gets into trouble because the particular revolution at hand appears to be taking place in a social vacuum. The decadent society A seeks to overthrow remains an abstraction. Filming in England, Pressman and Williams create a dreary gray world of slums and slag heaps, but the character Voight plays so well is simply a cliché dressed up in the fashionable jargon of dissent. *The Revolutionary* is aggressively boring from first to last, despite some nice naturalistic touches in the love scenes between Voight and Collin Wilcox-Horne, as a comrade-in-arms, and comely Jennifer Salt, as the rich upper-crust girl who symbolizes—you can be damned sure—the hero's sentimental attachment to his bourgeois past.

ICE

Kamikazes

PAULINE KAEL

Ice is a surprisingly honest, comprehensive view of the life-style of young American revolutionary terrorists; though nominally set in the indefinite near future, when the Vietnam war has been superseded by a war in Mexico, it is simply an extension of current urban-guerrilla attitudes and activities. However, the film generates far more interest when you talk about it afterward than while you're seeing it. As a piece of moviemaking, it is gray and grainy and painfully stagnant, and when you strain to make out the over-lapping mumbled conversations you discover that nothing in particular is being communicated. Though it's an acted film, it has a hazy semi-documentary style, as if a stoned anthropologist were examining his own tribe and were so indifferent to the film-making process that he hadn't learned how to read a light meter or bothered to work out a continuity. It's a film about political commitment that is made not only without commitment to film as an art form but without any enthusiasm for its own political commitment.

The director, Robert Kramer, has perhaps the least ingratiating style imaginable. In *Ice*, as in his 1968 film *The Edge*, the viewer is likely to get the characters confused, because they're not introduced to us or individualized; we are left to sort them out for ourselves, if we care about the particulars. Obviously, Kramer doesn't, because he doesn't follow such elementary theatrical principles as not casting look-alikes, or costuming people so that they can be readily distinguished. The only care in *Ice* seems to have gone into the violent scenes, and then only into their staging, not into their dramatic function. The film offers a cross section of guerrilla activities, without explanations. We are plunked into the middle—into receiving guns and hiding them, into meetings, killings, sabotage—without being informed why someone is being killed, or who he is, or why someone else is being tortured. When things go wrong, we don't know why, or even which side they're going wrong for; we're not sure who the opposition are—whether they're police or right-wing groups or left-wingers with a different ideology. And since the scenes don't build out of each other, you get the feeling that the significant parts must be missing, and you become impatient—you feel you're getting the fringe details and mumbo jumbo of conspiratorial organization rather than the heart of revolutionary activity. It all seems pointless and utterly unreal as you watch kids playing at being guerrillas in their parents' tasteful apartments in the Belnord and other upper-West Side bastions of the middle-class left. When they go out to liberate a luxury high-rise, the nuttiness of it all may make you groan.

But these weaknesses in the movie as plausible dramatic entertainment are just what make it such a revealing account of the anomalies in this movement that *is* concerned with immediate destructive actions rather than a vision or a long-range plan, this movement whose participants do indeed look alike, and talk tonelessly, as if anesthetized, and who are indeed likely to be upper-middle-class kids whose parents support them and, in varying degrees, agree with them and cooperate. It's obvious that some parents made their homes available to Kramer, and some appear in the film. *Ice*, though it cost only twelve thousand dollars (from the American Film Institute), has a cast of two hundred and fifty. Kramer gives a remarkably accurate picture of the world he is part of, and, in a very peculiar way, which I think rarely occurs, his style as a moviemaker—which is to say his *weaknesses* as a moviemaker—is part of the style of life he chronicles. This long, ambitious picture is passive and demoralized and mechanical; it's as alienated as its characters. I don't think Kramer has merely projected his own alienation onto them; I think he shares in their absence of goals, and that's why his movie is so paralyzingly boring.

Ice is the cold, dank side of the youth consciousness; it is concerned primarily with life-taking and with routinized self-sacrifice. *The Edge* was a chronicle of the disillusion of a group of once active civil-rights workers living together in a community; one of them made plans to assassinate President Johnson, failed, and committed suicide. In *Ice*, the actions planned seem just as senseless and suicidal, and are presented that way. The movie is a kind of aging New Left self-examination, a where-we-are-now—a record of random violence and grubby, inane discussions. The movie appears to be coldly objective, and one may think that it is almost obsessively introspective and self-critical until one recognizes that the objectivity is a matter of tone, not of method. Television has accustomed us to thinking that objectivity lies in not evaluating the facts, and this movie, which does not interpret what it shows, and which is so diffuse that the shots don't even appear to be framed, carries "objectivity" so far that the picture seems to be visually decomposing while you're watching it. But though it is not a propaganda film in any obvious sense, there can be no doubt that the presentation is made from inside. *Ice* takes a despondent view, but it believes in the revolutionary actions it shows. It doesn't believe in them *much*, but it believes in them more than it believes in anything else. The commitment is implicit not only in the fact that the movie finds nothing strange about this way of life but in what it takes for granted by starting at the point where all other possibilities have been excluded—which is why it seems totally nondramatic. The characters have already resigned themselves to becoming bodies to be put not just on the line but over it. Kramer doesn't sentimentalize details, any more than he dramatizes situations, but he does sentimentalize at the most basic level in presenting this communal-guerrilla mode of living, on behalf of the poor and victimized (whether they want it or not), as a necessity. And the slight pretense that we're in a future police state makes the underground guerrilla network seem inevitable. However, there's little doubt that some, perhaps many, believe it's inevitable now, and the participation in terrorism by young, privileged, well-educated people is not likely to disturb the younger movie audience, who may accept *Ice* as where things are—and conceivably even as an affirmation.

The extremists are not colorful, emotional, wild-eyed revolutionaries. They go about their plotting and bombing as if revolution were an unpleasant business they were engaged in—a dangerous business that was going to turn out badly for them but that they must go on with. Though the characters are not stereotypes in the Hollywood sense, they nevertheless seem stereotypes rather than people, and this is, I think, part of the revelation of the film—the revolutionaries' interchangeability. They have accepted their roles as cogs in the revolution, and, being devoid of strong personality or flamboyant passions, they *are* alike. They seem to believe they are rational political beings because they are not romantic in style; they have managed to make nihilism banal. They are like the mild, affectless terrorists making bombs in their parents' Village town house; their voices are as low-keyed and lacking in ardor as the Bernardine Dohrn tape. They don't really choose violence; they acquiesce in it. In the movie, they're trying to bring about an apocalyptic change that they don't expect to survive, but they go about their tasks methodically. They have rationalized their irrationality, and they have domesticated their alienation in communal living. (They do not lose their alienation in communal living; instead, they reinforce it, because their alienation becomes the life-style that links them.) One could almost say they carry out their tasks like the anonymous workers on a cathedral—for the greater glory of the poor.

They seem to be wiped out as people, but though their dreariness and their acceptance of the self-obliterating life go together, we can't tell which came first. The movie isn't illuminating on this point, yet from the evidence in the film (and elsewhere) I infer that this depersonalization is not distressing to the depersonalized. Maybe their acceptance of conspiratorial action gives them a mission that justifies the depressed state they were in anyway—gives them a definition as people that they hadn't had before, a *reason* for losing the lives that they'd never fully found. They may *feel* less depersonalized in the movement because they no longer feel the need to express themselves individually. The fact is that within the last couple of years well-educated students have accommodated themselves to terrorism with startling ease. *Ice* shows them to be as blandly programmed as they do indeed seem to be in newspaper accounts. One begins to see the movie as part of a phenomenon, and to look into it for clues to how it is that some of the most freely brought-up children in our society—the children of poets and professors and analysts and successful businessmen—are so personally depressed about "Amerika" and so affectless about violence that they have turned into Kamikazes. In the movie, the guerrillas talk about their regional offensive as part of a spontaneous revolution that, by the meshing of many groups like theirs, will overthrow the warmaking Establishment, and yet nihilism is their normal, everyday outlook. They have commitment but not conviction.

They are conspirators in violence, but they aren't like revolutionaries as we've traditionally thought of revolutionaries, because they don't seem to be carriers of revolution—they don't have any revolutionary *spirit*. The film itself raises this question, as it raises so many others, only to drop it in, like the TV producers who think that when they mention something they have covered it, though they have only covered themselves against the charge of having omitted it. The characters in *Ice* relax with drugs or sex, and there is never a hint of intellectual excitement or of any pleasure in thought. They are a joyless, unhappy group, and one gets no sense of how they want society to be, of what their dream of the good life is. Even their despair is neutral. One looks at them and thinks, What kind of revolution could they conceivably make? What kind of life do they visualize? From the evidence, they have no sustaining vision beyond smashing the state. They speak of better conditions for the poor, but they speak of nothing for themselves—not even survival.

Self-abnegation pervades the movie. One can only surmise that these people don't really believe in a liberating revolution—that they believe only in the repression they constantly expect. With the specifically modern look of being faintly blocked emotionally that is as common in the faces in suburban supermarkets as it is in the faces of the girl defendants in the Tate case and the girls sought for bombings, they accept a conspiratorial role, as if everything political had been settled except the details. They carry out their actions like the girl in *La Chinoise* who, having got the hotel-room numbers mixed, assassinates the wrong man, curses herself for her mistake, and goes back into the hotel and shoots the right man—a bureaucrat whose crime is that he carries out orders mechanically. The depressed state of the conspirators suggests that mechanized equality is their goal. One gets the strong impression that it is not politically but psychologically that the terrorists have lost interest in nonviolent alternatives, and that they *prefer* this conspiratorial, terrorist nonpolitics, in which they don't have to believe in anything or try to make actual contact with blacks or the poor, who might rebuff them. They don't have to leave their own middle-class group. The mechanical solutions of terrorism—the simple acts of destruction—can satisfy their desire for accomplishment. When they blow something up, they have tangible results—not the frustrations they heard about from those who worked in the South or in the ghettos or in the McCarthy campaign. Terrorism is the ultimate materialism. Functioning this way, they don't develop as people; they become like guns.

The atrophy shows in the film-making process: Kramer throws in flaccid derivations from Godard—agitprop statements, some revolutionary "theater," some war toys, a documentary montage. The political slogans that are recited might be a comment on left-wing sterility, but who can say? In this spongy atmosphere, sterility and comment on sterility are not distinguishable. Kramer's work has an ill-defined self-consciousness; almost anything one can perceive in the film might have been put there deliberately or might have found its way in and been accepted as belonging there. The title itself may refer to the frozen rigidity of the movement as it waits for mass support, and it may indicate a recognition that to live just to "smash the state" is not enough. The director, disengaged from film making while engaged in it, is also disengaged from the results: his name isn't even on the picture. All through the ambiguousness and gloom of *Ice*, Kramer seems to be saying that the movement is doomed and maybe the movie isn't worth doing; his pessimism is a deeply offensive form of face-saving sentimentality, since it is used to justify everything from killing to taking pictures out of focus.

In *One Plus One*, Godard's alienation devices backfired. He put down intellectuals, but he did everything in the movie for intellectual reasons; he used black actors as worker-guerrillas and had them recite political lessons inexpressively. Panthers, even when they sound programmed, convey the emotional basis for what they are saying, but in *One Plus One* there was no connection between the words and any revolutionary impulse. And since the words carried no emotional force—not even hate—audiences got bored and stopped listening. Without emotional charge, the revolutionary rituals were like parodies of what Godard himself apparently believes in. The black workers were just blank, and the demonstration-lecture style was so dehumanized that you couldn't even grasp why they'd get involved in a revolutionary struggle. But what you couldn't believe about his black workers you can believe about the educated young middle class. In *Ice*, the characters appear to get involved in guerrilla action *because* they are blank.

4

SCENES

WOODSTOCK

Hold On to Your Neighbor

JAY COCKS

It's happening all over again. Woodstock, the "three days of love and peace," has been re-created in a joyous, volcanic new film that will make those who missed the festival feel as if they were there. Those who actually were there will see it even more intimately. But *Woodstock* is far more than a sound-and-light souvenir of a long weekend concert. Purely as a piece of cinema, it is one of the finest documentaries ever made in the U.S.*

Making the movie was an enormous and sometimes haphazard undertaking. Director-cinematographer Michael Wadleigh organized a twenty-five-man crew on only a few days' notice, shot over one hundred and twenty hours of footage, then edited it all down in a frantic seven months. It is no small tribute to Wadleigh's dexterity that the film's three-hour running time passes with the mesmerizing speed of a Jimi Hendrix guitar solo. There could comfortably be even more. Using such intricate optical effects as split screen, overlapping, and double framing, Wadleigh has expanded and enriched the original musical performances so that, in many cases, they seem to be almost superhuman.

Woodstock's most obvious attraction is the music, and rock has

* Presumably because of some nudity and some rather raucous language, Jack Valenti's industry watchdogs have awarded *Woodstock* an R rating. Besides giving the whole thing a slightly salacious air, this means in effect that many young people who attended the festival cannot go to the movie without their parents.

117

never sounded—or looked—better than it does in the movie. "Hold on to your neighbor," says an onstage announcer at one point early in the proceedings, and moviegoers should be sure to take the same precautions. The sound track comes rushing out of a four-track stereo system that gives the exhilarating sensation of total immersion in sound. Joe Cocker delivers a gutsy, driving interpretation of the Beatles' *With a Little Help from My Friends*." Performing part of the rock opera *Tommy*, Peter Townshend of The Who tames his guitar like some wild electronic animal, while Santana makes the theater seats vibrate, and Alvin Lee of Ten Years After comes close to tearing down the movie screen. Crosby, Stills, Nash & Young sound slightly out of tune ("It's only our second gig," says Crosby, explaining the group's nervousness to the assembled 500,000) but Arlo Guthrie comes over with a sureness and command only intermittently evident in *Alice's Restaurant*. Sha Na Na offer a neat, affectionate, and very funny send-up of fifties rock with their strutting, snarling, pomaded version of "At the Hop."

Wadleigh is equally successful at conveying the sociological aspects of the event through concise interviews with townspeople, festival organizers, police, and members of the audience. Everyone from a chief of police to a maintenance man for the Port-O-San portable toilet corporation gets his say. *Woodstock*, however, is not an unrelieved celebration. For every shot of easy affection in the grass and innocent group bathing in the nude, there is a scene in the medical tent, or the ominous voice of the onstage announcers: "The word is that some of the brown acid being passed around is very bad stuff . . . Will Helen Savage please call her father at the Glory Motel in Woodridge?"

The technical expertise used to achieve *Woodstock*'s pulsating, visceral effects should stand as a model of nonfiction film making. Particularly outstanding are the sinuous color photography (a good deal of it done by Wadleigh himself) and the editing by T. Schoonmaker and Martin Scorsese—a masterly combination of taste, timing, and theatrics. There are sequences—such as one in which John Sebastian dedicates a song to a girl who has just given birth—of lilting simplicity. There is the hysteria of The Who and the pure rhythmic orgasm of Ten Years After. They all help to make *Woodstock* as unique on film as it was in fact, "the mind fucker," as John Sebastian puts it, "of all time."

Friendly Apocalypse

JOSEPH MORGENSTERN

Moms and Pops have their *Camelot*. Now the kids have their *Woodstock*, a romantic musical comedy about a 400,000-man rock group that plays a gig in the country and finds, or founds, Utopia.

For one brief shining (showering, downpouring) weekend the group renounces violence (except in its music), renounces capitalism (free admission to the biggest of the topless big tops), makes common cause with the Army (helicopter gunships as angels of mercy and nutrition), banishes hunger (free food for the needy), and dispels, by the simple act of survival, an apocalyptic menace which the group itself had summoned up by the simple act of coming together. Then, in a trice, the group is gone, leaving garbage, mud, and a legend of perfect friendship. It's a beautiful story with an exciting score, and on the amplifying strength of this movie it's a good bet that the legend has only begun to grow.

Director Michael Wadleigh and an adept crew of cameramen have shot and assembled a fascinating, overlong, earsplitting and screensplitting chronicle of the events that transpired on and around Max Yasgur's cow farm in August, 1969. The movie's attitude toward the event is predictably, commercially friendly, though not entirely uncritical; it tracks the movements of a drug snake in Eden and wisely declines to measure the snake's length. Wadleigh's sociology is slapdash, though occasionally acute. A blithely detached girl who lost her sister during Richie Havens' set thinks it would be nice to find her again because she's got to be back in the city on Monday morning for court. A pair of wandering middle-class waifs (the early scenes look like some Dayglo *Grapes of Wrath*) speak with moving generosity of the pain that exists on their parents' side of the generation gap, and the boy, trying to clarify his own status in the megagroup of youth, concludes that most kids trooped to Bethel for an Answer. "People," he says, "are very lost, I think."

They are indeed. We are indeed. But music is magnetic north for the kids, and *Woodstock* shows why on a wide screen with multiple images that split off, comment on each other, enhance each other, and provide at their best—the technique eventually gets tedious—a triptych in which mirror images on the outside panels play against the main attraction in the center.

Several attractions give a good show by any standards: Havens, with his Carborundum voice and ceaseless splay of guitar strums; Joan Baez, gulping in great gasps of air and letting them out as an exquisite "Swing Low, Sweet Chariot"; Crosby, Stills and Nash doing joyously right by "Judy Blue Eyes"; Alvin Lee and Ten Years After singing some old-fashioned blues; Jimi Hendrix wringing out of his guitar the most martial version imaginable of "The Star-Spangled Banner," complete with rockets' red glare, dive bombers, bugle calls, and the shrieks of women and children. Other performers are amazing for their mediocrity, insulting in their commercialized, institutionalized hysteria.

Good, bad or indifferent, the musicians are photographed brilliantly, probably better than they'll ever be photographed again in their lives. The night sequences are especially effective, faces and costumes shot against a background of black air, singers singing against an almost tangible pressure of unseen audience. Yet performances, as the movie makes clear, are not the content of an event such as Woodstock. The performers, true cyborgs whose thoughts are interconnected with guitars and sound systems, are only energizers. The content is emotion, pure groupification, and the operative process is amplification: first by amplifiers on the instruments, then by the kids, then by the news media, and then, in raging commercial feedback, by a movie replaying the original event. The power of this process itself is vast, and when it's amplifying something that was big to begin with . . .

GIMME SHELTER

Arthur Schlesinger, Jr.

Gimme Shelter, the Maysles brothers' "documentary" about the Altamont rock festival, is well worth seeing, even if one has never heard of Altamont and detests rock. But it falls short of its potential subject, and its failure, I think, is essentially analytical. To understand the deeper implications of Altamont, it is necessary to read the long piece in *Rolling Stone* of January 21, 1970, as well as the fascinating testimonies edited by Jonathan Eisen and published as an Avon paperback called *Altamont: Death of Innocence in the Woodstock Nation.*

What emerges from these reports is the traumatic impact Altamont has had on the American counterculture. Woodstock had produced euphoria among the young—a confirmation of powers, a surging belief in the omnipotence of inherent goodness and spontaneous brotherhood. The free concert offered by the Rolling Stones at Altamont was devised on the Woodstock theory and held only four months later. But it was marked by manipulation, fear, violence, and killing. It meant the collapse of a millennial dream and set off intense self-reassessment within the dropout society.

Too little of this is evident in the film. The Maysles brothers, with their colleague Charlotte Zwerin, are gifted practioners of what is misleadingly called *cinema-vérité*. This means trailing around after real people and recording their unpremeditated words and actions. The term is misleading because (like the word "documentary") it implies that here is the raw truth as against the hoked-up fictions of theatrical films. But obviously all we see on the screen is a small amount culled from a vast amount shot; selection requires choice; choice means interpretation. *Cinema-vérité* is no less subjective than theatrical films and may be more deceptive because of the pretense of authenticity.

Gimme Shelter is aurally and visually an exciting film. At the beginning the Stones are watching, in perplexity and perhaps in guilt, the rushes of Altamont, trying to figure out what went wrong. Then a series of bold images condenses their American tour before Altamont. Soon we see the preparations for Altamont; the ominous introduction of the Hell's Angels, the motorcycle thugs hired to keep order; the Angels doing their own thing—i.e., beating other people up; Mick Jagger pleading for control, "Please, you people, stop hurting each other"; finally, a sharp scuffle in the crowd, soon disclosed in slow motion as murder.

But despite the dazzle of technique the dramatic content could hardly be more old-fashioned. The conflict is perceived as between the Stones (good) and the Angels .(bad) with the crowd as innocent victims. Is it all that simple? The *Rolling Stone* article and the Eisen book give a far more ambiguous account.

They are highly critical of the Stones—for their money games and ego trips; for the sloppiness of the Altamont planning; for hiring the Angels as security guards; for delaying their own appearance until they could make a sufficiently dramatic entry after sunset. And they are critical too of the hip movement itself—for its faith in redemption by life-style; for its resort to festivals as substitutes for counterinstitutions; for failing to see how much the Stones, and the audience, resembled the society they pretended to reject. "It wasn't just the Angels. It was everybody. In 24 hours we created all the problems of our society in one place: congestion, violence, dehumanization." (*Altamont*, p. 215)

The Maysleses are unduly protective, not just of the Stones but of the Woodstock myth of the tribal innocence of the young. This reduces *Gimme Shelter* to an exercise in sentimentality. The Woodstock myth makes us all feel good, which may be why this film is loath to abandon it. But the young themselves have evidently learned a good deal more than this from Altamont and seem much less sure that the greening of America will necessarily yield milk and honey. The images of *Gimme Shelter* convey something of this sense of dislocation and panic, but its dramatic form suggests that the makers of the film did not really understand what they so lovingly recorded.

PERFORMANCE

Jay Cocks

Pop stars continue to have bad luck in films. Musical showcases like *Woodstock* display them to good musical advantage, but when called upon to act, react or recite a line, they generally perform like stumbling automatons. The Beatles—thanks to the brilliance of director Richard Lester—managed to escape. But it happened to Elvis, it happened to Sinatra at first, and it is happening now to Mick Jagger, rock's reigning Rolling Stone, who is currently on view in a couple of hapless films.

Performance casts Mick as a freaky rock singer who has given it all up and lives in a cavernous house in Notting Hill with two handmaidens, a little girl, some draperies, a few pastel pillows, and a lot of dope. Into this heady atmosphere comes a hood on the lam (James Fox) who rents the downstairs room as a hideout. The hood corrupts the singer, the singer corrupts the hood, and the two handmaidens (Anita Pallenberg and Michele Breton) just hang around, giggling a lot and getting into bed and king-size bathtubs with anyone available. The film, which pretends to have something more or less profound to say about exchanges of identity and loosening of the moral fiber, alternates between incomprehensible chichi and flatulent boredom.

Donald Cammell, the writer and co-director, edits his film elliptically and achieves a suffocating sense of baroque paranoia, but seemingly endless clichés overcome all the subliminal imagery. When someone talks about a pyramid, there is a flash cut of an erect nipple; when the hoodlum dyes his hair, there is a cut to the single spray-painting a wall. James Fox manages nevertheless to be excellent as the gangster, and Jagger seems to be having a lark. Few others will share his somewhat campy pleasure.

5

MASCULINE FEMININE

MY NIGHT AT MAUD'S

A Good Night

Penelope Gilliatt

A long view of a youngish man in a dark coat. Black-and-white photography; silence, as after a fall of snow. The first noise is the bang of his car door. Then Jean-Louis Trintignant, the wittily blah-faced engineer who is the hero of Eric Rohmer's marvelous *My Night at Maud's*, goes to Mass in Clermont-Ferrand. A glance passes in church, twice, between him and a fair-haired girl. There is a shot of him at home, reading a book of calculations, drinking coffee. Morning alarm clock. Arm out to turn on radio music. Bookshop. Attraction to a title: *Calcul des Probabilités*. He runs into an old friend (Antoine Vitez), a Marxist professor, who tots up the chances against their having met after all this time. They sit and talk. The friend holds you. A thin, comic man, very bright, amused by his sex muddles. He has a pleasant, speculative voice and a nose like a pen nib. His name is Vidal. The Trintignant character is called Jean-Louis. It is plain that they have known each other for ages. Rohmer has made a rare sort of film: his intimates really seem intimates. They talk their own thoughts instead of speaking lines, they react to the moment before last, they chat by laminating two monologues, they hang fire wondering about the next thing to say. The intelligence his characters are allowed to have is gentle and true. So is their attention to each other. The two men talk about choice and chance, Marxism, Jansenism. Jean-Louis is a Catholic who has placed his bet. Now he is waiting with his

124

own kind of quizzicality for the outcome of the game. He has no girl, for instance. He wants the blonde from church. Vidal has gambled on "Hypothesis B, the ten-percent possibility that history has a meaning," because if he gambled on the ninety-percent chance of Hypothesis A—that history has no meaning—his life would be lost. "Someone—Lenin, Gorky, or Mayakovsky—said that after the Russian Revolution they were forced to take one chance in a thousand, and that it was worth it," he says, speaking touchingly about himself, really, while he and Jean-Louis are apparently discussing Pascal abstractions. Clermont-Ferrand was Pascal's birthplace. Like Maud, whom the two friends go to see that evening, Vidal and Jean-Louis are steeped in the ideas of the thinker who proposed the famous wager about believing in God: the notion that if you win you win everything, and that if you lose you lose nothing; the argument that since you are obliged to play the game anyway, you renounce reason if you hoard your life for the sake of a calculable, finite stake rather than risk it for an incalculable, infinite gain.

Maud (Françoise Fabian), a great beauty, meeting Jean-Louis for the first time, watches and cooks and smokes. His determinism is not for her, nor his rigor, but she likes him. She tells him that her ex-husband had a mistress, a blonde with a character "rather like yours." She herself had a lover, killed in a car crash. Her nature makes her hate Pascal's lottery, but she listens carefully—to the cheerful professor, who is having an affair with her, and to this interesting friend, with his cordial intractability and his poor assessment of himself, who speaks rather solemnly about his mediocrity, about his incomprehension of unfaithfulness, and about his longing for the right girl. "The classified ads?" suggests Maud softly to this last problem. " 'Seeks blonde practicing Catholic . . .' " It is said with droll affection by this brown-haired, non-Catholic dish, whose habit of sleeping naked under a white fur rug in her living room ("I hate bedrooms") scares Jean-Louis nearly to flight once Vidal has left them together to go home because of the weather. Lust's hour is about to strike, you can see him thinking nervously. He looks at the unforeseeable freethinker wriggling about under her fur rug. "You both reek of holy water," she was saying to the men earlier. He wraps himself safely in another rug. She goes on smoking and talking to him. It occurs to you, as they go chastely to sleep, that this night with Maud confronts Jean-Louis with a problem vexingly Pascalian as well as voluptuous beyond his wits, since the oppressive possibility of making love to her represents a bet in which there is nothing to be lost and maybe a kingdom to be won.

Next day, intact, he finds the girl he saw in church. "I know I should think of something clever to say," he says urgently, "but how can I get to know you?" The courtship proceeds, clubfooted. Caught in the snow with her that night, he makes tea for her in her place. He does it with exquisite pedantry. Apart from some of the actors in the great Russian companies, Trintignant in this film is better than anyone else I have seen at playing a man amused at himself for being humorless. "No good being more Papist than the Pope," he mutters to himself at some point.

The script is Rohmer's own, one of six "Moral Tales." Two were made for French television. Another, a feature film, is called *La Collectionneuse.* Two to go. Sometimes this screenplay is in a literary class near Renoir's for *Rules of the Game.* And oh, the pleasure of a film that looks at people for long takes instead of going chop-chop-chop, like television; that so often finds a listener's face more interesting than a speaker's; that lets people *talk,* instead of yielding to the cant that talk isn't "visual." A lot of the producers and directors who intone this particular slogan now aren't very talented. Would-be classy cinema has acquired in them a new sort of middlebrow. They are people so fogged by tenthhand regard for the camera-stylo theory, and yet so far from kin to the *writers* who historically directed camera-stylo films, that they misunderstand the theory to mean throwing words out in favor of shock-cuts and zooms. Why is the sight of someone speaking necessarily less "visual" than the sight of someone walking? The word is one of the more inanely used elements in the cinema. You imagine that one day, off camera, your truly filmic hero is going to have to leap out of his chair and say to his girl friend, "Let's go out and do something visual." Like careering around Paris with a bevy of balloons, or eating frankfurters extremely fast on speeded-up film. Well, not many people could have done what Rohmer has. It is a very delicate triumph for the talkies, and the ending of his picture hangs there like the close of a great short story.

DIARY OF A MAD HOUSEWIFE

Harrowing Voyage

Paul D. Zimmerman

Her life is a nightmare that begins when she awakens. And it is on this moment that *Diary of a Mad Housewife* opens, as a young housewife arises to a reveille of criticism from her husband, her eyes a mirror of mental cruelty, her body worn thin by the demands of her existence.

Viewed from the outside, her nightmare looks more like the American dream. At twenty-nine, Tina is pretty and still young, the mother of two bright, presentable girls and wife of an ambitious, attractive young lawyer. He has sacked the legal profession and brought back as booty a spacious Central Park West apartment, entree to New York's swinging parties and a supply of vintage wines.

But even before we have gotten past the credits, producer-director Frank Perry and his wife, Eleanor, who wrote the screenplay, have shown us in fluid images the noisy, laundry-filled, floor-polishing, kitchen-anchored, handyman-harassed, vodka-soothed reality of Tina's struggle to survive as a New York City housewife.

Carrie Snodgress, who brings the husky gravel voice of a latter-day June Allyson to her film debut here as Tina, mopes around the house like a mournful cocker spaniel but she still has lines that bite as well as the resilience of a mistreated pet. Richard Benjamin, as the husband, Jonathan, ranges through a catalogue of small cruelties at his wife's expense. His pompous morality is as overdone as the omelets at his disastrous party to impress the "beautiful people."

In comic terms, the rooster-strutting husband is a masterly portrait, a stiff-necked monument to the superficial. He worships all labels, from those on suits and wine bottles to those on people, and fancies himself "creative" on the strength of his Caesar salads. At the same time, like some animal trainer, he remembers to ridicule his wife in front of their children, to criticize everything she does or wears, to whip her like his lead horse in a race for social status.

Jonathan infantilizes their sex life. And Tina takes a lover. It is the film's crowning comic truth and saving fall from grace that the lover mistreats Tina as badly as her husband does. Frank Langella, a young off-Broadway veteran with lanky sex appeal, plays the lover with a sensuality of undetermined gender, intent on hiding his own fear of feeling. In one brilliant moment, he juggles a gift he has bought Tina like a hot potato as though the affection it represents is too hot to handle.

Of course the affair ends, and Tina must return resigned to her unredeemable husband. The Perrys have stacked their cards too heavily against reconciliation, although they almost pull it off in a midnight kitchen scene in which Jonathan confesses to Tina how every pillar holding up his life has collapsed. It is, however, too late, and Tina's response—"I'm just a human being"—is a plea that follows the verdict of marital failure.

With its letter-perfect exchanges, its flawlessly observed urban setting, and its beautifully tightroped walk between realism and satire, this relentless, harrowing psychic voyage has uncovered enough small truths to justify the prevailing optimism that the independent American film represents the next *nouvelle vague*.

JOHN SIMON

Diary of a Mad Housewife is the updated version of the "woman's picture," in which the trials and tribulations of a misunderstood wife who turns into a misunderstood mistress no longer soak the female audience's handkerchieves as they did in the days when Joan Crawford and Joan Fontaine were being misunderstood. As Carrie Snodgress is misjudged and mistreated by her pompous, social-climbing lawyer-husband and clever but destructive novelist-lover, the matter is one for sophisticated nods, knowing snickers, and condescending chuckles. But, either way, the sensitive little woman at the apex is a cliché—once a heroic-pathetic cliché, now a wryly patronizing one—and the men at the vertices are oversimplifications of *machismo* or muttonheadedness, of one kind of immaturity or another, above whom our heroine rises, melodramatically or comically, to self-realization.

Why is this such a formula? Isn't achievement of self-awareness a valid topic for art; isn't transcendence of the fickle lover by the noble beloved one of the great themes in literature? Think of Rilke's mighty Beloveds, *"die gewaltigen Liebenden,"* who "while they called out to him, jutted over the lover; who shot up above his head when he did not come back to them." But in the "woman's picture," old or new style, the woman is always seen complacently as basically superior to the men—by some female scriptwriter; or, patronizingly, as the helpless victim of her passions—by some male scenarist or director. There is no contest between different but equal partners, and the greatness of the little woman has to be taken on faith—the movies' bad faith.

I have not read, nor wished to read, the Sue Kaufman novel on which this film, written by Eleanor Perry and directed by her husband, Frank, is based. But, I learn, the autobiographically tinged housewife of the book's title was really mad: angry, exasperated, in psychotherapy throughout. In the movie, Tina Balser is a perfectly normal little upper-bourgeois housewife who has the bad luck of being married to a fatuous young man, a lawyer intent on climbing all scales—social, financial, intellectual—and who finds that, try as she may, she cannot please him, being too direct, unassuming, and authentic. This housewife is not only not mad, she is a paragon of sanity, functioning despite her husband's nagging, needling, bullying, and humiliating her; despite his tyrannical demands on her time, attention, energy; despite his being the kind of domineering yet also whining ass from whom any judge would grant her a divorce on sight. But she puts up, shuts up, waits on him hand and foot. Sanity? Hell, it's sanctity.

Or is the point that she is a masochist? No, because she is clearly shown not enjoying playing Psyche to her oafish Cupid, even being mildly horrified by it. Carrie Snodgress is good at reacting painedly, with an expression half reproachfulness, half disbelief that anyone could be as beastly as her spouse. Yet even that does not make sense: she has been married to him long enough (their daughters are aged, roughly, eight and six) to have long since left him, murdered him, or acquiesced.

If, as in the book, we were given the first-person narrative of a heroine in psychiatric treatment, the film might make sense as Tina's distorted view of the situation. But early in the film we have evidence to the contrary. In the elevator, Jonathan Balser is telling his wife what to pack for him for a short business trip: the plaid suit from Sills; two voile oxford and two Sea Island cotton shirts; the robe from Turnbull & Asser; the shoes—not the new ones—from Peal's; socks—provenience unspecified; all into the oxblood suitcase from T. Anthony. As they leave, the elevator operator stares after them in dismay.

Incredulity is our reaction, too, from the very first scene. There is Jonathan upbraiding his wife, who is not really awake yet, for everything: for not being awake yet, for smoking, for not having enough vitality, for not shaping up, for being too skinny, for having straight hair, for—I can't remember what else. And she endures and endures, virtually without protest. It is preposterous. Meanwhile Jonathan is full of self-praise, and Tina doesn't demur at that either. Doubly preposterous. And as Richard Benjamin acts the part—and as Frank Perry directs it, and Eleanor Perry wrote it—it exudes exaggeration through every pore. Yet everything is played for laughs, so that Tina's suffering loses all dignity: the tenor is both more pseudosophisticated and genuinely callous than when Olivia de Havilland or Bette Davis had to suffer for the three-handkerchief trade.

Of course, Tina's little girls are obvious changelings, imps of the perverse; she has every kind of servant and household trouble; Jonathan gets beastlier; and then—then!—she meets this famous writer, George Prager. Now in the novel, I gather, he is a tough sort of writer in his early middle age, a Mailer or Styron, all bumptious sexuality and hypermasculine aggressiveness. But Perry casts in this part Frank Langella, an actor of not inconsiderable talent but inconsiderable virility, with a rosebud mouth that Betty Boop might have envied. He woos Tina with "Tell me, does screwing appeal to you?" and similar well-turned phrases, not to mention an erection which, right in the middle of a party, he rubs against her groin. He finally gets her, partly out of fascination with his unvarnished caddishness, but mostly out of pique against her husband, to come to his fabulous apartment overlooking the East River from her fabulous apartment overlooking Central Park.

Here the churlish wooing continues, e.g., "Please don't start that la-di-da stuff with me, it makes me want to puke." Swept off her feet by this love talk, Tina falls into George's bed. After the act, George resumes the courtship: "Baby, you are a terrific piece of arse; are you always that good?" "No." "Well, so much for the compliments, but now what do we do?" "What do you mean?" "I thought you were good for a couple of screws, but this may get out of hand." And he explains: "The thing it all hangs on is: can you have a straight sex thing or not?" (The way Langella enacts him, one doubts that *George* could.) Well, such words are irresistible and Tina falls in love with George, and spends her afternoons with him whenever he deigns to have her. So now she is getting it both from an egomaniacal, exploitative husband and an egomaniacal, sadistic lover, with whom she has—again in his brilliantly writerly words—"pure and incredible sex," a line Langella delivers like a slightly overripe mango.

Rather than go on summarizing this glamorized soap opera for illiterate sophisticates, let us get to the point. Mrs. Perry's writing (and, most likely, Sue Kaufman's) simply will not do. It is obvious and heavy-handed enough when she deals with children (*David and Lisa, Ladybug Ladybug, Last Summer*), but when she undertakes adults who are meant to be devious or pompous or crude, she hits us over the head. A mediocre writer's attempt at satire may well be the least digestible kind of writing there is. I have already cited the absurd catalogue of items Tina was to pack for her husband: absurdist humor (which was not intended, anyway) zooms around more fancifully; but even heightened realism cannot walk on such fallen arches. It is ineptly derived from Mary McCarthy's *The Group*, although there at least the boring brand names were an attempt at reconstructing a bygone era.

When Tina, angry at last, yells at George, "Save that for your bloody awful books!" the casual amorist runs after her enraged, suddenly hurt where he is most sensitive. He shakes her furiously and shouts, "Hey, wait a minute! Take that back!" That, you see, is the best a distinguished writer can come up with when wounded to the quick. And Tina obliges: "You're good. So good it doesn't bear thinking about." Now what is this? *The Sun Also Rises* filtered through *The Wind in the Willows*? One has the feeling that Mrs. Perry wants to switch here to a moment of seriousness, but her seriousness is indistinguishable from her satire, and both are kitsch. (If the dialogue is Miss Kaufman's, ditto for her.)

Now comes the obligatory intellectual superiority bit. We've had other kinds of superiority before: dinner at Elaine's, an opening at the Feigen Gallery (always with the real names loudly dropped) of a pop sculpture show by Allen Jones, about whose quality Mrs. Perry is careful not to commit herself. When Tina compares her innate gift for pleasing a man in bed to the gift Proust ascribes to Albertine, George bursts into a fit of immoderate laughter and informs his "poor baby" that Proust was a homosexual and Albertine really a boy. This comes as news to the poor baby, who was not taught it at Smith, though everyone in the audience who is going to get the point at all is presumably familiar with what the late Stanley Edgar Hyman called the Albertine Strategy. So it is one-upmanship for the half-baked, or half-upmanship. Then Perry cuts to the next scene (big laugh!): Tina in her conjugal bed trying to get at the bottom of this by reading *The Past Recaptured*. Since Albertine no longer appears in the final volume of Proust's work, we may assume that the Perrys' literary development stopped somewhere along *Swann's Way*.

Finally, after George has tormented Tina in much the same manner Jonathan has ("You have a pimple on your arse. You're getting too damned skinny . . .") and been unfaithful to boot, she erupts, "You're sick, sick! You've got to put on this big virile act because you're really a fag!" Incensed, George pushes her around a bit—rather gently for the sadist he is supposed to be—and turns her out for good. She goes back to her husband, who confesses that he has lost all their money in a socially prestigious but financially ruinous investment, that he is in trouble with his bosses at the law firm, and that he has been having an affair with a girl named Margo. Tina, guilty herself, takes it all in her stride, whereupon Jonathan exclaims gratefully and platitudinously (once again, we do not know whether this is satire or just bad writing): "Oh, Tina, you're wonderful. So patient and understanding. You're a fine human being, Tina. Do you think we can pick up the pieces and maybe have a better marriage than we ever had?" I guess it's both: satire and bad writing.

The last scene shows Tina in group therapy, being upheld by a couple of fellow patients and savaged by several others. How dare she complain, one of them shrills at her, when she has a husband, a lover, and an eight-room apartment? The audience laughs heartily at this, and the dishonest film ends with a predictable cop-out as Tina's eyes stare at us in mysterious close-up. Is she going to change, or is she just going to pieces?

And how has husband Frank directed *Diary of a Mad Housewife?* Modishly enough, with nervous camera movements in confined spaces, ironically commenting cuts ("Why don't you go to bed?" says Jonathan to Tina, and, pronto, we see her in bed with George), gratuitously nasty details that don't shed light on anything (a department-store Santa Claus picking his nose, followed promptly by two women wrangling over a taxi, only to have an insolent man steal it in front of their noses), a fair amount of arty lovemaking (e.g., underneath blue bedcovers, with arms and moans protruding), and many exposures of Miss Snodgress' vestigial breasts—quantity over quality, the perennial Perry formula for everything. Again the cinematographer is Gerald Hirschfeld, and, as in *The Swimmer,* he gives us his typically savvy but uninspired fashion-magazine color photography.

But where the director truly errs—over and above the casting of Langella as Prager, which makes the supposedly shocking revelation about him come as the slowest anticlimax this side of the New Haven Railroad—is in the consistent overstressing of what needs to be merely shown, omission of what might be of interest, and attempts at making something out of nothing. One example of each: a disappointing omelet is eaten by guests at a party with insulting contempt spelled out and underlined on every face; Jonathan's mistress, Margo, though not unimportant to the plot and listed in the credits, cannot be detected among the walk-ons by the most aquiline eye; and frequent training of the camera on a large Franz Kline painting on George's wall, though apparently meant to tell us something, remains as uncommunicative as Kline's work itself.

And there are the performances, also in part the work of the director. Richard Benjamin is allowed to turn Jonathan's priggishness into piggishness, and give one of the least restrained performances even in a Perry film. Carrie Snodgress has charmingly bewildered or ironic gazes at her command, and a voice that harbors not just one frog but a whole family of batrachians to delicious effect, though it is a little weak when fortissimos are called for. She has a nice ephebic figure and extraordinary eyes, but decision on her acting must await further exposure. The little daughters are two cuts below the Katzenjammer Kids, and minor characters like a Bronx baby-sitter and a bitchy, aging actress are overdone to a turn of the stomach.

THE OWL AND THE PUSSYCAT

GARY ARNOLD

"It's amazing," a film company executive told me recently, apropos of the box-office grosses on Mike Nichols' *Catch-22*: "People come out feeling miserable—you can see it any night if you stand in the lobby and watch 'em—but the long lines are still there. My teen-age boy was the same way: he just had to see it. Came home feeling lousy, just like he'd heard, but he had to see it."

This is a curious phenomenon even if one rationalizes it as, say, the spirit of the art house moving into the popular market in an inevitable and perhaps decisive way. The most viewed foreign film of recent years is probably *I Am Curious (Yellow)*, one of the most tedious ever made. And, after all, what arty foreign imports of the past year have surpassed a *Catch-22* or a *Five Easy Pieces* at being assiduously, self-consciously "artistic" and "ambiguous"?

In *Harper's* a critic writes, "More people than are conscious of it go to *Catch-22* half-hoping that it will spoil the rest of the day." I'm not so sure. Most people probably go expecting something both funny and illuminating and get depressed when they discover much more that's solemn and confusing.

Somehow it's difficult to believe that the expectation of a really bad time has become a major motive for going to the movies. It's easier to believe that too many unsolicited bad times and unfulfilled expectations have been depressing business in general. Misery may love company, but vice versa is debatable.

Moviegoers looking for a bad time should steer clear of *The Owl and the Pussycat*. This inconsequential and unself-serious romantic comedy, adapted by Buck Henry (ironically, the screenwriter on *Catch-22*) from Bill Manhoff's Broadway play and cleverly, transparently designed to capitalize on the talents of Barbra Streisand and George Segal, is more likely to make your day than spoil it.

With a bit more fine tuning here and there—the opening scenes are a trifle frantic, the closing ones a trifle flat—*Owl and the Pussycat* might be a perfect pick-me-up. As it stands, it's just one of the year's most enjoyable and invigorating pictures. One comes out of the theater feeling pleased and animated and convivial, with the conviction that the night is still young, that one has time and energy to burn.

The principal source of this conviction is Streisand, perhaps the single most powerful and valuable source of energy currently at work in American movies. Her presence is terrifically enlivening: physically, she's as vibrant and busy as Clara Bow in her prime, and vocally, she's as agile and inventive with comedy lines as Lee Tracy in his prime. One recalls Sydney Greenstreet's compliment to Bogart as Sam Spade in *The Maltese Falcon:* "Wonderful, truly wonderful, sir. One can never tell what you'll do or say next—except that it's bound to be astonishing."

Streisand's animation charges more than the film itself: it carries over into the real world, so that hours later one is conscious of reflecting her influence in peculiar ways—perhaps talking and gesturing more emphatically than usual or slipping into her idiom or simply feeling an excess of energy. Although she's playing the "pussycat," she does not pussyfoot around. This nervy, forthright quality reaches a sublime, crowd-pleasing perfection in the scene where she responds to the obscene suggestions of three guys cruising by in a car. Moreover, her verbal instincts get better and better: even when we know, as in this case, that she's about to deliver an explosively obscene rejoinder, one is surprised and amused by the exquisite way in which she has timed its final, resounding inflection and release. You're prepared for the zinger, but she zings it harder and higher than you expected.

In this film Streisand is being astonishing in a nonsinging role. She's Doris Wadsworth/Wellington/Waverly/Washington/Winters (nee Wilgus), a voluble and assertive big-city girl who describes herself as an "actress and model." Until the demand for her acting-modeling talent increases, Doris is trying out names and turning occasional tricks.

George Segal has been one of our most intelligent and attractive actors for several years now, but he's usually good in such a pleasant and/or unobtrusive way that we take his skill, like Gene Hackman's or Robert Redford's (before *Little Fauss and Big Halsy*, that is), for granted. The role of the "owl," Felix (nee Fred) Sherman, the timid and somewhat stuffy book clerk who's writing a bad experimental novel called *Scream* and inadvertently hooks up with Doris the hooker, gives Segal probably his best opportunity yet to use his comic gifts, which he spent four years training as one of the Premise Players.

He's the first leading man who isn't intimidated or diminished by playing opposite Streisand. As a matter of fact, their styles and roles dovetail beautifully, with his reactability complementing her forcefulness, his snide or skeptical asides countering her outrageous or opinionated assertions. Both performers know how to make fun of themselves, to get off their dignity, and this self-humor happens to be important to the romantic moral of the story, in which opposites attract and then adhere because they kid one another's pretensions and decide they're happier with themselves as they are— i.e., as rather singular commoners.

Segal has perfected looks of frustration and shocked sensibility that are as poignant and funny as any perpetrated by silent comedians, and he gets off one extended flight of improvisational fancy —a one-man re-enactment of late-night television shows, performed behind an aquarium for the benefit of Doris, who claims she can't sleep without TV—that's really charming.

I mean it as a tribute to Herbert Ross's direction when I say that most of the time I wasn't aware of it. The film has a good professional finish: one is caught up in the comic performances, occasionally delighted by an adroit bit of punctuation in the editing, rarely betrayed by the camera being in the wrong place at the wrong time. The effects are highly calculated and commercial, but no one spoils the effects, and it's a pleasure to watch comedy teamwork that pays off.

LOVE STORY

GARY ARNOLD

When it comes to a movie like *Love Story*, criticism and immunology necessarily overlap. It was quite apparent from the clearing of throats and muffling of sobs and blowing of noses going on at the preview showing that if one resists *Love Story*, one probably resists it in vain. Many people—perhaps a clear majority of the human race—are not just willing to be sapped by this sappy material; they're also willing to grab the emotional blackjack out of the hands of writer Erich Segal, director Arthur Hiller, composer Francis Lai and friends and happily sap themselves. Indeed, I'm not sure the material would work unless people were predisposed to swallow it whole and helped wash it down with lots of self-pity.

For the record, one notes that *Love Story* has been grossly successful in print both here and abroad and that the film version should be more grossly successful yet. Curiously, the story began as a movie scenario and was then recast as a wafer-thin, best-selling novel. This genesis may cause problems of categorization for the Motion Picture Academy, unless screenwriters have enough self-respect to decline blessing the script with an Oscar nomination at all.

Once one has conceded *Love Story* its popularity and profits, however, the diagnosis is gloomy. I found this one of the most thoroughly resistible sentimental movies I'd ever seen. And I mean resistible on commonplace grounds. There is scarcely a character or situation or line in the story that rings true, that suggests real simplicity or generosity of feeling, a sentiment or emotion honestly experienced and expressed. Moreover, the film simply compares poorly with countless decently or indecently sentimental movies one recalls with affection.

Having been susceptible to *Camille* or *Dark Victory* or *Jezebel* or *Goodbye, Mr. Chips* or *Lassie Come Home* or *The Rainmaker* or *Tiger Bay* or *Breakfast at Tiffany's* and heaven knows what else doesn't necessarily make one ready for *Love Story*. In fact, really vivid memories may be a hindrance, since they'd illustrate how elementary Segal & Co. are at the tearjerker game, how dependent they are upon our capacity for self-hypnosis.

What this means, of course, is that in rejecting *Love Story* one is essentially rejecting the side of people that makes them fall for it, or even *want* to fall for it. But, under the circumstances, what else can one do? This material tries to establish a very unhealthy relationship with our most morbid apprehensions and regrets, then flatters us for feeling susceptible. It's a smug tearjerker, worth resisting on principle, because it's been so deliberately designed as a mass-cultural bromide, a reactionary bridge over all the troubled political and artistic waters of the last few years, leading backward and going nowhere.

There is Dick Shawn on the *Tonight* show, subbing for Johnny Carson and congratulating Erich Segal on the success of his pint-sized powerhouse of a scenario-novella. Shawn remarks how refreshing he found the book to be and hopes, like thousands of others, no doubt, that it's a great trend-turner and trend-setter, the sort of entertainment we'll all be "getting back to." Segal accepts the accolades humbly but declines to make any far-reaching speculations about the drift of American morals and letters.

The situation would be laughable if it didn't have such pernicious implications. The book was, of course, widely promoted as an antidote to the "sort of thing" that "went too far," particularly Philip Roth's *Portnoy's Complaint*. Even if one were prepared to disapprove of Roth, the maudlin thing Segal is getting back to has never been a vital or wholesome part of American literature. *Love Story* is economy-sized Fannie Hurst written in economy-sized Ernest Hemingwayese. Ironically, college romance is a Roth specialty, and his accounts of it—in both *Goodbye, Columbus* and *Portnoy*—expose the shallowness of Segal's material.

One can imagine a new Rip Van Winkle, asleep for the past generation, waking and entering a theater playing *Love Story*. Except for details—clothes, hairstyles, the fact that Jennifer Jones and Robert Walker didn't quite look like themselves and that Ray Milland had somehow gone old and bald—he would probably feel right at home.

Segal himself must have mixed feelings about getting away with this smarmy, anachronistic piece of idealization. There's something rather anomalous and tragicomic about a professor of classical literature becoming a mass-cultural hero, adored for that book that doesn't take any effort to read and doesn't assault you with sex, sex, sex. Surely it's occurred to him that Plautus would have gone for *Portnoy's Complaint*.

One infers the ambivalence from the writing, which is surprisingly awkward. It was a chore to get beyond the following sentence on page 2: "I ambled over to the reserve desk to get one of the tomes that would bail me out on the morrow." Huh?

Segal drops this unwieldy sportive—if that's what it is—diction for his first-person narrator after a while, but the falsely snappy note remains in the dialogue:

"What the hell makes you so smart?" I asked.

"I wouldn't go for coffee with you," she answered.

"Listen—I wouldn't ask you."

"That," she replied, "is what makes you stupid."

To put it mildly, this is not particularly witty or winning repartee, and characters who speak it sound rather subhuman. "Listen—I wouldn't ask you" also sounds a bit *echt* Jewish for the hero, a Harvard WASP named Oliver Barrett IV, and the heroine, an Italian-Catholic Radcliffe girl, often repeats this locution. Is it intentional, accidental, mistaken, gratuitous? Who knows? I doubt if Segal himself does. What he's probably done is simply indulge an indiscriminate personal taste in kitsch, schmaltz, and whimsical-whamsical banter. He doesn't get it quite right, but if the rest of us are similar softies it won't matter. Finally, even the lousy emotional punch lines, like the heroine's great, dubious platitude, "Love means not ever having to say you're sorry," will touch the heart while they insult the ear and the brain.

The story's basic sentimental notion is derived from *Goodbye, Mr. Chips*. Ollie Barrett, the emotionally buttoned-up rich boy, is humanized by his marriage to Jenny Cavilleri, the warm, gay, magnanimous poor girl. The denouement partakes a little more of *Camille*. Jenny dies of leukemia, but her death results in the reconciliation of Ollie and his estranged Brahmin father.

At least this was the way it was supposed to work in print. There were stumbling blocks—the synthetic nature of the writing, the bathos, and, largest of all, a nauseating proportion of masochism. It was extremely distasteful to hear the smart little heroine getting the last aphoristic-shrewish word on her husband from first acquaintance to last gasp. Much of the book's appeal depends upon our sharing the hero's unattractive and life-denying notion that he was unworthy of this brave, noble, beautiful, understanding creature. Scenes like the following inspire one to question her divinity:

"It's nobody's fault, you preppie bastard," she was saying. "Would you please *stop* blaming yourself!"

I wanted to keep looking at her because I wanted to never take my eyes from her, but still I had to lower my eyes. I was so ashamed that even now Jenny was reading my mind so perfectly.

"Screw Paris," she said suddenly.

"Huh?"

"Screw Paris and music and all the crap you think you stole from me. I don't care, you sonovabitch. Can't you believe that?"

"No," I answered truthfully.

"Then get the hell out of here," she said. "I don't want you at my goddamn deathbed."

The Camille you love to hate?

The movie, as one would expect, is virtually word for word from the original "book," and Arthur Hiller's direction—now clumsy, now obvious—is syntactically faithful to the author's prose. However, there are some new stumbling blocks, which will require redoubled efforts at ignoring reality and surrendering to fantasy on the part of customers who want their money's worth.

To get away with a role like Jenny on screen, an actress doesn't need great talent. It will be enough if she simply looks beautiful and warm. For some reason, Ali MacGraw has been allowed to "interpret" the role, and she *plays* it as superciliously as the heroine's worst lines *read*. It's a performance that only makes sense if one decides that it's satirical—maybe a Wellesley girl's revenge on snotty-superior Radcliffe girls.

Miss MacGraw wears a permanently smug expression and fails to temper the vain, emotionally bullying tone of the dialogue. I realize there are people who still find her adorable, but I thought it one of the most effectively hateful characterizations I'd ever seen. When this little angel breathed her last, remorse and I were light-years apart. The performance is so wrongheaded that the emotional balance of the material turns upside-down: one prefers Oliver, in the amiable, steady presence of Ryan O'Neal, to Jenny.

Because Miss MacGraw is coming on shallow and disagreeable, viewers will almost have to substitute real loved ones or themselves for "the beautiful girl now dead." The film's one stroke of genius is to make this imaginative substitution more likely by building in *longeurs*.

There are lots and lots of *longeurs* in the final reel. Ryan O'Neal, stricken by the news of his beloved's incurable illness, is discovered sleepwalking his way along Fifth Avenue, while Francis Lai's somberly schmaltzy, fake-Chopin piano score encourages us to get way down in the mopey spirit of things. If you're sufficiently detached, you may feel a bit cheated: why not *real* Chopin, or *real* Rachmaninoff, instead of these cheesy imitations? Still, this is beside the point: people do begin to snivel in precisely the way the movie begs them to.

It's interesting to note, finally, that the movie drops the reconciliation scene between Oliver and his father (played by Milland—and it's quite disconcerting to see him aged and baldish). Instead, Oliver leaves poor old Dad with the same morally superior egg-on-the-face that Jenny used to dish out to *him*. One is compelled to conclude that this truly stupefying lack of generosity is the Great Lesson of Their Love. Real sweeties, these two.

Presumably, the new ending is intended to feed the resentments and moral vanity of the young audience. In a work this flagrant to begin with, maybe anything goes, but if I were the film makers I'd shoot the original conciliatory ending and give audiences a choice. Ideally, one would have a twin theater and get the kids for the version where Oliver is a snob and parents for the version where Oliver cries in his father's arms. It's one of the few messy but profitable possibilities the men responsible for this jerker seem to neglect.

ARTHUR KNIGHT

In these days when the old movie formula seems to have been reduced to boy meets girl, boy gets girl, period, there is something not only refreshing but downright exhilarating about *Love*

Story, a frankly sentimental, frankly tear-jerking, four-handkerchief picture. It reminds us, suddenly, of what movies once were all about: the kind of unabashed emotional involvement with beautiful, admirable characters whose triumphs and woes we shared so completely that we laughed and wept and cowered helplessly in our chairs, then left the theater still in the thrall of a catharsis that was all the more joyous because it reaffirmed our essential humanity. If we could respond so readily to those shadows, perhaps we could also respond to real people.

Since Erich Segal's brief novel (developed, incidentally, from his screenplay, and not, as is customary, the other way around) has been a runaway best seller since publication, presumably just about everyone in America knows that it is a combination of Cinderella and Horatio Alger, transplanted to Radcliffe and Harvard, and given the twist of an unhappy ending. Cinderella dies of an unspecified but incurable disease, and nobody lives happily ever after. What even the most ardent devotee of the novel will be unprepared for, however, is the emotional intensity achieved by its young stars, Ali MacGraw and Ryan O'Neal, by Francis Lai's affecting and often inventive score, and by Arthur Hiller's unobtrusive yet probing direction.

While Miss MacGraw and the engagingly handsome O'Neal could probably carry the picture on their charm alone, Hiller never makes this necessary. He lets their relationship—he the scion of a wealthy Boston family, she the daughter of a humble Italian baker —unfold and enfold through innumerable small, affecting details. There is O'Neal's original hostility to a "Radcliffe bitch," and the girl's self-protective scoffing despite her obvious attraction to the young man. There is a delightful sequence of horseplay in the snow and, for once, a serious premarital discussion of how marriage might affect their respective careers. The visits to the prospective in-laws are beautifully managed, particularly in the choice of flashbacks to highlight the girl's reception into the chilly bosom of the Brahmin family.

Best of all is a quarrel that flares up between the newlyweds when the girl tries vainly to effect a reconciliation between her husband and his estranged father. The crosscurrent of emotions in each of them is extraordinarily visible with a minimum of words;

when she runs out of the apartment, it leads to a prolonged search through the corridors of a music conservatory (she was a music student) ingeniously orchestrated by Lai as O'Neal dashes from one rehearsal room to the next. When he at last finds her, shivering on the porch of their apartment building, he is abject with apologies. "Love," she tells him, "means never having to say you're sorry." It is a small enough nugget of wisdom to carry away from a picture, but it is embedded in such a flow of emotion that one grasps at it as at a profound truth.

For Ali MacGraw, *Love Story* merely confirms what *Goodbye, Columbus* earlier suggested—that, properly handled, she is one of the most attractive and capable young actresses around. For Ryan O'Neal, who has been floundering in a succession of second-rate pictures, this film should mean instant stardom. No less impressive are John Marley and Ray Milland in the relatively minor roles of the two fathers. But when an entire cast is as consistently good as this one is, it is generally because of the director, and Arthur Hiller, who demonstrated that he could tap the emotions in last year's *Popi*, here has struck the mother lode. I predict that, like *Airport*, *Love Story* is going to bring back to the theaters large sections of that "lost audience" that hasn't gone to a movie in years.

PHILIP T. HARTUNG

Not having read Erich Segal's novel, *Love Story*, I came on the movie cold. In spite of the tears one is supposed to shed at this contrived film, I left it—still cold. Since the picture opens with the girl's funeral and then consists of a long flashback showing the boy and girl meeting, dating, falling in love, sleeping together, getting married (in a sort of do-it-yourself ceremony), enjoying life in an elegant New York apartment, it comes as no surprise that the girl dies. What did surprise me, however, is the girl's continued use of foul language, particularly the popular four-letter word for ordure. It seems to me that if scriptwriter Segal wanted to indicate how mod this girl is, he could have let her use the word once or twice. But Ali MacGraw uses it again and again—even in the classroom where she is teaching youngsters. So, long before this Jenny dies, I was tired of her aggressive modishness. As the young man from the very wealthy Boston family, Ryan O'Neal is fine. So are the music and good photography.

6

EUROPEAN POLITICS

BURN!

Mythmaking

PAULINE KAEL

Gillo Pontecorvo's *Burn!* is an attempt to tell the story of a mid-nineteenth-century slave uprising on a fictitious Caribbean island from a neo-Marxist, Frantz Fanonian point of view, so that it will become *the* story of black revolution and a call to action. No one, with the possible exception of Eisenstein, has ever before attempted a political interpretation of history on this epic scale, or attempted to plant an insurrectionary fuse within a historical adventure film. The 1952 V*iva Zapata!*, which also starred Marlon Brando, and which *Burn!* somewhat resembles, merely imposed the then current American liberalism on the Mexican revolutionaries. If Pontecorvo's film is flawed throughout, it is nevertheless an amazing film, intensely controversial even in its failures. The audience seems to be grooving to the emotionally charged imagery (which has some of that quality that Buffy Sainte-Marie and the Missa Luba and classic blues have of hurting while giving pleasure) and yet, at times, arguing about political points, and I think this mixed reaction is a valid one. *Burn!* is primarily a celebration not of Black Is Beautiful but of Black Is Strong, and the strength Pontecorvo celebrates has a far deeper beauty than we are accustomed to at the movies. Nevertheless, the movie goes wrong. Maybe it was one of those ambitious ideas that look great until you try to carry them out; if there was a way to make it work, Pontecorvo didn't find it.

145

Pontecorvo can show brutality without giving the audience cheap shocks, and he doesn't arrange suffering in pretty composi- tions. He has a true gift for epic film making: he can keep masses of people in movement on the screen so that we care about what happens to them. They're not just crowds of extras; they're the protagonist. And *Burn!* is perhaps the least condescending film that has ever dealt with slavery. No doubt the dignity of the slave vic- tims is ideological, but, clearly, Pontecorvo is not distorting his vi- sion to fit his ideology; when he endows them with nobility, it rings esthetically true.

The film is large-spirited, and sometimes it really soars with the imaginative force of art. Movie imagery rarely overwhelms us with such a mixture of sorrow and anger as the sequence near the open- ing in which the widow of an executed insurgent pulls a cart bear- ing her husband's decapitated body. The film, though political, is by no means Spartan; it's luxuriant and ecstatic. When black rebels ride white horses that prance to what sounds like a syncopated Gregorian chant, the sequence is so shimmering and showy that one knows that Pontecorvo and his cinematographer, Marcello Gatti, couldn't resist it. Wasn't it this kind of thing that drew the director to the theme? *Burn!* shows the violation of rapturous beauty, and this is the emotional basis for whites to believe that blacks should destroy white civilization. (It may be a tragedy for whites that their culture and traditions are not so photogenic.) In his feeling for crowds and battles, for color and imagery, and for visual rhythms, Pontecorvo is a sensuous, intoxicating director, and he gives his island (which has been synthesized from locations in Colombia, Africa, and the Caribbean) physical unity and, by the use of moving figures in the background of the compositions, a volatile, teeming population. In the last two years, Pontecorvo's *The Battle of Algiers*, a reconstruction of the violent death of a colonial regime, has become known as the black militants' training film. Pontecorvo appears fully committed to the idea of killing and being killed for your principles; in *Burn!*, however, the whites have no principles. *Burn!* is unquestionably intended to arouse revolu- tionary passions, but the racist-Marxist plot is too schematic to structure the heroic fall and rise of a people.

Some of the flaws in the film are not the director's fault. *Burn!* was originally called *Quemada*, which means "burned" in Spanish, and which was the name that Pontecorvo and his scriptwriters (Franco Solinas and Georgio Arlorio) gave to their sugar-producing island. They also gave it a history of having been burned by the Spaniards in the sixteenth century, because the Indians were rebellious, and then repopulated with African slaves. The movie was to show how, in the 1840s, the English fomented a new rebellion to wrest power from the Spanish. However, the current Spanish government, sensitive about Spaniards' being cast as heavies even in a period piece, applied severe economic pressures against the producers, who, remembering what the Spanish government had done when it was displeased by Fred Zinnemann's *Behold a Pale Horse* (the losses from the Spanish boycott of Columbia Pictures ran to several millions), capitulated. Parts of the film were deleted, others reshot, and the Spaniards who had historically dominated the Antilles were replaced by the Portuguese, who hadn't, but aren't a big movie market. The European title was changed to *Queimada*—the Portuguese for "burned." After the delays and extra expenses, the picture has still not been released widely; United Artists, which has probably been financially burned in the deal, has rather touchingly altered the American title to the opportunistic *Burn!* In addition, the American version has lost twenty-odd minutes at the hands of a New York "film doctor" whose previous experience was in editing movie trailers. These cuts are, I assume, responsible for some of the non sequiturs in the action and some of the lacunae. Finally, the movie was "dumped"—opened without the usual publicity and advance screenings. This ordinarily means that a company doesn't expect a movie to do well, and such a lack of faith usually insures that it won't do well, because magazine reviews will come out two or three months late, and even reviewers who might have been enthusiastic have their spirits dampened by the general feeling that it's a bomb and will close before they get into print. I'm reasonably certain that this film has been dumped not because of its incendiary potential but because of the company's evaluation of its box-office potential. I think that the company miscalculated and that *Burn!* could have been a hit, because it plays right into the current feelings of the young movie audience. But now we'll never know, though the picture may do well in revivals. Such are the business conditions in the background of a revolutionary movie, but the larger irony is that white men made this movie that says black men should never trust white men.

Despite its visual sophistication, *Burn!* has an unmistakable tang of the old heart-stirring swashbucklers in which Errol Flynn risked all for liberty, or Tyrone Power (*Son of Fury*) abandoned the corrupt life of the English nobility for an island, a dream, and a native girl (Gene Tierney). Although Pontecorvo's feeling for the slaves is that of an artist, his treatment of the vacillating, cowardly white colonial officials and their mulatto accomplices is exactly that of the more conventional seafaring adventure films. In scenes involving these officials, one might as well be at *Anthony Adverse,* and Marlon Brando's cynical, daredevil Sir William Walker seems a direct development from his foppish Fletcher Christian in *Mutiny on the Bounty.*

Considered politically (rather than dramatically), the plot is an ingenious synthesis. (You don't appreciate *how* ingenious until you think over what has been left out.) Sir William is an *agent-provocateur* sent by the British Admiralty to instigate a revolt of the slaves against their Portuguese masters. He tricks a band of slaves into committing a robbery in order to make them outlaws, arms them, turns them into killers, and trains a black leader, José Dolores (Evaristo Marquez), who defeats the Portuguese and tries to seize power for the slaves. Sir William is reluctantly preparing to eliminate him when José Dolores, unable to run the government without advisers, relinquishes power to the British and their mulatto puppet ruler. Having accomplished his mission and obtained sugar for a nation of tea drinkers, Sir William leaves the island. So far, he appears to be a super-cool C.I.A.-type mastermind crossed with Lawrence of Arabia. Brando's impersonation of a languid British gentleman is amusing and decorated with linguistic conceits, and since Sir William helped to liberate the slaves and tried to convince the businessmen of the economic advantages of free workers, one assumes he is personally on the slaves' side, and so does José Dolores, still his friend, who accompanies him to the ship to say goodbye. When José asks him where he's going, he replies, "I don't suppose you've ever heard of a place called Indo-China? Well, they're sending me there."

Ten years pass offscreen. José Dolores has been fighting the British all these years, and he has organized a new rebellion. Sir William has left the Admiralty and (like Lawrence?) has sought obscurity. The sugar company's agents go to look for Sir William in London, find him brawling in a cheap dive, and report that he is "like another man," but they make him a lucrative offer to return to Queimada to deal with José Dolores, and he accepts. His hopes are gone, he says, and the ten years have revealed the century's contradictions. He tries to establish contact with José Dolores but is rebuffed. Then, although he gives evidence of believing in what the rebels are doing and despising the whites, he organizes the slaughter of the blacks, burns native villages that help the guerrillas hiding in the mountains, and, when the puppet tries to regain control in order to end the suffering, has him executed. Sir William explains why the blacks will eventually win—a guerrilla can do fifty times as much as an ordinary soldier, because the guerrilla "has nothing to lose," and so on. Yet Sir William brings in British troops and destroys the island. It is shelled and shelled and then burned again, so that the British businessmen are left asking what good his actions have done them, since now there's no sugar for anybody. He says that he doesn't really know what he's doing but that he must do it. And so he comes to represent the murderous, self-destructive folly of colonialism—the whites' irrational determination to destroy everything rather than share with the blacks—and when he's killed there's a happy heavenly choir.

There's a contradiction between Brando's role as the personification of colonial manipulative policies (as well as, by implication, of the American involvement in Vietnam) and Brando's style, because, the way he plays his role, he's the comic relief in a tragedy. The oppressor as cynical clown is an entertaining idea, and perhaps the audience needs his foppish foolery, the contempt with which he addresses the English businessmen, his sophistic explanation that he's merely an instrument of government policy and if he didn't carry it out the Admiralty would send someone else, but he seems to have wandered into the wrong movie. He causes starvation and death, yet he's also slapping his horse and drawling, "Giddyap, you fool." If Sir William were played impersonally as a historical force, the movie would be heavy and didactic; a more conventionally villainous interpretation would probably turn it into Grade B melodrama. But when the role is played with Brando's bravura, so that Sir William becomes a daring white loner who loved and betrayed the blacks, it's a muddle, because we simply don't understand his motives or why he is so zealous in crushing the rebellion, or why no one else understands anything.

When you personify a deterministic theory of history and don't stylize it but, rather, do it in natural settings, the leaders seem to be all that matter, so the method distorts the theory. It seems as if history were a melodrama made solely by heroes and adventurers. This movie really becomes a swashbuckler—a romantic, glamorized view of black struggle—but a swashbuckler engaged in a cute game of slipping in historical parallels and of scoring textbook points. Almost every line jogs us to fit it into the scheme. "Ah, yes," we say to ourselves, "Sir William is a liberator of the blacks only when the English interests and theirs coincide," and so on. When Brando warns the English of the danger of making José Dolores a martyr— "Think of his ghost running through the Antilles!"—we see it as another point racked up, and when Brando thinks it's madness for José Dolores to sacrifice his life, we know we're being prodded to see that whites are incapable of understanding the blacks' true passion for freedom, and we're being prodded to see that it is this passion that makes the blacks superior, and will make them win.

The end is clearly meant to be only the beginning. The spirit of the film is one of triumph, for José Dolores, who preferred death to compromise, has set an example for the survivors and for the slaves on other islands. "Ideas travel," Sir William has explained, and dead heroes become myths. The message of the film is that freedom is worth all the suffering it takes. After we have seen the blacks tricked and maneuvered and crushed over and over again, this simplistic encouragement to die for your principles seems rather cavalier, as if the film had been made by a new incarnation of Sir William, who still doesn't know what he's doing. José Dolores' visionary speeches about lighting the flames for whites to burn in are fashionably modern, and his last words are "Civilization belongs to whites. But what civilization? Until when?"

There's something painful and disturbing about movies that fail on as high a level as *Burn!*, but mixing art and politics has always had its difficulties. Still, if you can't force human suffering into an ideological diagram without having it all look phony, that could be a blessing.

THE CONFESSION and INVESTIGATION OF A CITIZEN ABOVE SUSPICION

Robert Hatch

Quite far along in the fabrication of his confession, Artur London's interrogator explains to him that for the moment they are just putting together the objective facts; later, they can move on to the subjective considerations. Of course, they never do, and much the same thing may be said of Costa-Gavras' *The Confession,* in which Yves Montand enacts the horrifying experiences of London, a man high in the Czechoslovak Communist bureaucracy who was one of the defendants in the 1951 Slansky trials.

It is an exquisite film, constructed with a sensitivity to the texture of the jerry-built hell in which the victims of Stalin's death throes are confined. It never falters as to light or sound or the appalling detail that make this nightmare inescapably credible. I cite one example: London and his co-defendants are kept, when they are not being questioned, in rough wooden cells that resemble cattle pens in a slaughter yard. But the building in which they are held was evidently once a palace or elegant residence, and here and there the carpenters have taken advantage of the original walls. The contrast between fragments of elegantly wallpapered salon and the rough pine boards chills the heart with the realization that this is something remembered; that it is unlikely to have been invented.

And so with the process of preparing the confession, London is a tough and experienced Communist bureaucrat with a history of important party activity dating to the Spanish Civil War. He is also utterly innocent of any crime against the state. Yet he signs, memorizes, and recites in court a confession of treachery that stretches back for years. It doesn't seem possible until one sees the method, and then it seems inevitable.

London's inquisitors do not use torture, if by that one means racks and thumbscrews and the later electrical refinements. They need a seemingly intact London to display eventually at the show trial, and in any case such devices are not necessary. They half-starve the man, deprive him of sleep, exhaust him with enforced pacing of his cell. But these are done less to cause him direct pain than to confuse his mind and weaken his resolution. The process starts even before he is seized. For days, cars full of political police ostentatiously follow wherever he goes. This naturally alarms him, causes him to scurry about for conferences with colleagues (who are also marked for investigation). Such actions can later be cited as symptoms of guilt; more important, they make London feel guilty, though of what he cannot say.

His enemies were greatly assisted by the fact that London was (and as far as I know still is) a faithful Communist. He persists in thinking some terrible error has been made and that, between them, he and his tormentors can set it straight. He can even swallow the notion that he should confess because the party needs his confession. Of course, by then he is not thinking very clearly—he has reached the point of signing fragments of statements in exchange for a moment's sleep or a mouthful of food; such statements are "factually" true but they will be put together into paragraphs that are utterly false. But even years later, when he is free and resting among friends somewhere on the French Mediterranean, London still looks back on the horror as something done by bad men in a bad time. It is not just that he still believes in the theories of communism; he still adheres to the practice of totalitarianism, and cannot wait to get back to Prague to be reunited with the good totalitarians who have "corrected the situation." He arrives on the day when the Soviet tanks roll into the city, and the picture ends with Montand's face in close-up, frozen against a montage of the people's derisive but impotent resistance to a further "correction of the situation." Does he finally realize that his months of torment corrected an earlier situation and that under totalitarianism such correction will always be the procedure? The film doesn't say, but a fair guess is that London is a "believer," and such men do not learn.

I submit that Yves Montand is not the actor to play that man. He says the words of blind dedication, but coming from his lips they have no reality. He cannot look like a "believer"; he looks, moves, speaks like a sophisticated Frenchman of independent mind, logical acuity, and quick humor. That a man of that sort could have been forced into a confession is believable (indeed, it is obvious, since the method will work with any man); but that he could have been a loyal functionary of the regime for years both before and even after his ordeal passes belief.

This, it may be said, is a mere matter of personal style, but style is what a man principally tells you about himself. All through *The Confession* the audience identifies with the person Montand so powerfully projects, but at the end it is forced to admit that that was not the person about whom the story was being told. It is the same with London's wife. I suppose it is true that, after the trial, she wrote a letter to the authorities denouncing her husband; but if so, she is not the woman whom Simone Signoret plays throughout the film. The objective facts are all there, but the subjective meaning—which is what matters—is blank.

Much the same thing happened with Z, in which Costa-Gavras also directed Montand. I don't think it is entirely an accident. The purpose of these films is to supply the public with cat-and-mouse adventures that offer the added fillip of historical documentation. For that to work, the audience must identify strongly with the protagonist, and it isn't easy for most Western audiences to identify with underlings who go along for years not realizing that their state is a trap, who fall eventually into its jaws, and who escape without ever realizing what nature of trap it was. So the solution is to cast Yves Montand in the role, and never mind that it makes no sense. There were others in the cast, among the co-defendants, who looked exactly like "true believers"; unfortunately, one would need to be drugged to identify with them. If one could show how such men come to be, and what sustains them, it would be a revealing tragedy. But *The Confession* is not that; it is a romance that in the closing footage papers over the discrepancy between character and event with newsreel clips of a people's heroic defeat.

Investigation of a Citizen Above Suspicion reads like one of those titles that intend to call attention to the product by their very awkwardness. But Elio Petri, the director, was probably only stating the subject literally when he named his picture; he has created a fantasy on the entirely germane text that the exercise of power induces madness (Lord Acton raised one quantum jump), and needs no gimmickry to salt the box office.

The citizen in question is the chief of the homicide squad, presently elevated to chief investigator of political subversion. The city, I believe, is Rome of today or tomorrow, but with the oddity that Mussolini, or at least his ideals, appears to have prevailed. Policewise, it is a very tight town.

The homicide chief (Gian Maria Volonte) enjoys a somewhat daft mistress (Florinda Bolkan) whose pleasure is to pose as the body of the victim of each sex murder her lover investigates (he appears to investigate about one a day) while he assaults her with a candid camera. On their final meeting, she greets him with the question: "How are you going to kill me this time?" To this he replies: "I'm going to cut your throat." They then go to bed, and during intercourse he does just that, later retrieving the razor blade from among the bloodied sheets. He also tracks blood through the apartment, placing his feet carefully on absorbent surfaces, leaves his fingerprints on every polished surface and, after phoning his office to report the murder anonymously, has a pointed encounter with a young tenant of the building, who will certainly remember him if the question of his presence should be raised.

His point is to prove that a man in his position *cannot* be suspected of murder, and indeed he is right. When he and his staff speed to the scene of the crime (he has meanwhile returned to the office, bringing bottles of champagne from the girl's refrigerator to celebrate his promotion), his colleagues josh him gently about the clues pointing in his direction. They fear him, as well they might: he is a crude bully when he is not being a crude hail fellow. The inspector preens himself that his thesis is so neatly proved, but there is gall in his self-satisfaction. It begins to occur to him that he is being grossly overlooked by his industrious former staff; it is all very well to be untouchable, but it also takes on the exasperating quality of being invisible. The inspector keeps slipping away from his new job of rounding up every non-Establishment type in the city to invent additional clues for the dolts at homicide. It won't work; he gets some long looks, but no firm grip on his shoulder; and at the end he is revolving in what seems to be a compulsively repeated confrontation scene that repeatedly aborts. Quite mad.

As fable, this strikes me as very good. It illustrates by exaggeration what everyone has noticed: that people who wield power—little power, or big power, but in any case power that is not checked—develop before long traits of personality that suggest derangement. It isn't just arrogance; it passes over into fantasy. To be sure, this works some advantage to the holders of power, since other men, kept prudent by sanity, are less likely to challenge them. But it is unfair to ask anyone to take a job that will addle his wits; we no longer have mad hatters, reformers having taken mercury out of the felting process. Perhaps we should also detoxify the power process, starting at the level of the prowl car and ending, say, on Pennsylvania Avenue.

Of course, good fables should also be good stories. One remembers "The Fox and the Grapes" and "The Frogs and King Log" because La Fontaine made such faultless dramas in miniature out of them. On that score, Petri has not succeeded as well. He is extremely well served by Volonte, who knows how to twitch enough to seem unhinged without becoming overtly silly, and whose almost instantaneous shifts from one repellent mood to another are disconcertingly effective. But the details of the supporting narrative are rather slack and ragged, the mechanics of the action is inefficient and repetitious and the characters of those surrounding the inspector are not sufficiently developed to give him leverage. They seem as like as geese, which is perhaps how he saw them, but I did not take it that we were meant to be looking out through his eyes. I became a little restive, but I find the picture sticks with me. The screen doesn't often supply allegory as true as this, or as foreboding.

WINTER WIND

STANLEY KAUFFMANN

Winter Wind is confusing, and I left the theater disappointed in this new film by a director I admire, Miklós Jancsó. But then it began to work, retroactively. The confusions are not clarified now, but a rationale for the confusions becomes clear, an esthetic rationale.

This is Jancsó's third film since *The Red and the White* (1968); the two intervening films—*Silence and Cry* and *Ah! Ça Ira*—have not yet been shown here, so it is impossible to discuss his development in an orderly way. But some connections are evident even on the other side of this jump. His theme is once again power, the power of some men over other men's lives and the desire of the other men to reverse that power structure, and the way that the contest gets transmuted into statements of ideals. Once again he is concerned with the record of those contests, called political history. Once again he uses sex—not love, but sex, nakedly represented by female nudity—as a chemical in the compound. Once again violent death is treated, both by killer and killed, as an event whose time has come; once again fear is never shown, not because all these people are brave but because the characters have accepted their destinies in life, as the actors have accepted playing those characters.

The opening consists of clips from a famous newsreel of political assassination, the shooting of King Alexander of Yugoslavia at Marseilles in 1934 (and also of Barthou, the French Foreign Minister, who was welcoming him to France). This is shown silently, accompanied only by slow gong strokes. Then we are told that the story we are about to see deals with events leading up to this assassination, which was planned by the Ustashi. The latter were a group of Croatian fascist terrorists, trying to wrest Croatia from Serbian domination.

The first sequence that follows is the first of the unexplained incidents, an assassination attempt by a Ustashi band. We never know where the attempt takes place or who is in the carriage coming along the snowy road. All we know is that the sequence is filmed beautifully, almost idly—all we hear are hooves and shots, and the cawing of crows, as the camera circles continuously; following the men as they ride and walk across the snow-covered fields, take their places, then fire and are fired upon, and fall or flee, in a waking dream of killing. When Jacques Charrier, as the leader of the band, is waiting behind a tree for the carriage and crosses himself with a hand that holds a pistol, he epitomizes the film's atmosphere.

All the rest takes place on an estate in southern Hungary near the Croatian border, where the Ustashi are hiding while they plan the assassination of the King. The materials of the picture are the suspicions bred among conspirators by the very act of conspiracy, the corruption of small loyalties within the outlines of a large loyalty, the masquerades of ego and sadism under the name of fervor for freedom. The action centers on the leader, Charrier. At the end his followers form an agreement of cooperation with their Hungarian hosts. He refuses to abide by this agreement, refuses to commit suicide, expects to be shot, and is promptly shot. Then he is made into a martyr; the last scene is an oath of fealty to the movement in his name.

That much is clear. But dozens of details in the film are unexplained, abruptly introduced and dropped. Some examples: Why, when the spy is discovered, is he taken out and made to lie down in the snow, then ordered to get up again, and only much later shot? Who is the tall mustached man who brings the teen-age girl with him? Why does he make the two other women in the house undress? Why does he make the girl take a bath with one of them? I have no idea. (There are also anomalies of language: for example, they all speak French—this is a Franco-Hungarian co-production—yet sing their anthem in Croatian.) Trying to follow the story of this picture, as story, is an exercise in frustration. Yet, incredibly, after the film is over, a feeling begins to seep through the accumulated frustration: that the bafflement was expected by Jancsó; that it is the *choice* of an obviously skilled and accomplished artist.

Subsequently I read a recent interview with Jancsó, conducted by Jean-Louis Comolli and Michael Delahaye, in which they asked him why he refuses to give explanations and shows only unmotivated acts. He replied that it was because of conditions in Hungary where "we cannot put our message across as clearly and directly as we would like. . . . Since all of us want to say something, and at the same time are not forthright enough to do so, we count a great deal on the form of the film to make a statement. . . . Perhaps that is the reason why situations and acts are the most important things in my films. What interests me most is form."

He says that for several centuries, because of continually changing internal conditions, Hungarians have had to speak obliquely, using shape to suggest substance. We might cite exceptions, but perhaps Jancsó has found a rationale in the present authoritarian Hungarian state for a "private" method that he really has arrived at out of his own psychology and esthetics. At any rate, his film does find its life through its form.

This form has two principal aspects. First, the visible statement of unexplained acts in order to reach the unstated. The aim seems to be to make a film with the *aftereffect* principally in mind. Second, the use of continuous, generally circular camera movement. There are fewer than fifteen cuts in this film: which means that the entire eighty minutes were photographed on fewer than fifteen pieces of film. Compare that with, for instance, *Rashomon* which runs eight-eight minutes and is composed of four hundred and seven bits of film. Jancsó literally *follows* the action. Kurosawa has said that he photographs in order to have something to edit. Jancsó is photographing in such a way that editing is superfluous: which means that a good deal of his creative process takes place at an earlier stage in the making of his film.

Also, he has said that he shoots his films silent, or with a sound track merely for purposes of record, so that he can direct his actors while the camera is rolling and moving. (The final sound track is added later, usually with the actors who have played the roles.) This gives him the chance to keep some sequences running more than ten minutes and, although he has rehearsed them before he shoots, enables him to "conduct" the actors, à la silent-film days— or just as a conductor leads musicians whom he has already rehearsed. These long sequences, without cuts and with the flow of the camera's movement, are, I think, Jancsó's effort to capture some of the long, relentless, and cyclical swell of history, thus re-enforcing his theme with the look and feel of his film.

Theory is theory: and some excellent theories, excellently articulated—like Brecht's theory of epic theater—simply do not function as well as they read. But I am haunted by a feeling that Jancsó is on to something fascinating, imperfectly though he has accomplished it here: an attempt to record the subliminal; not with the by-now trite method of splattering in bits of nonsequential or non-"present" material, but by trying to capture a mystery beneath the surfaces of facts. A chief power of film has been its ability to make facts magical; Jancsó is trying to ignore that magic, is trying to catch the invisible *sum* of the facts, which is like the solid wheel that is made by spinning individual spokes. His inquiry is both thoroughly cinematic and quite revolutionary, but in a sophisticated and difficult way—much more daring than the Now editing that has been diluted by Now hacks out of Godard and Lester.

But, as noted, *Winter Wind* is unsatisfactory—possibly because it does not dare quite enough. A ballet is a ballet: we do not expect character dossiers or precise explications of this glide or that leap. But Jancsó has paused at a mid-point between veristic drama and nonprogrammatic ballet. A film on the *idea* of politics that, out of all history, specifies the Ustashi and then does not tell us why, has one foot in realism and the other in abstraction. Was Jancsó trying to say something about Hungary's dictatorial government of the time and its support of fascists? Was he trying to show us ironically that fascists are as pure in their revolutionary zeal as other zealots? These are only some of the foreground questions that he himself raises, then ignores as he concentrates on abstract matters of form and movement.

Charrier, in past films, has been an unremarkable good-looking young man. Here he manages more gravity than I would have expected but not quite enough broodiness and concealed fire. Marina Vlady suggests some sexual secrecies, as a woman assigned to the hideout. Zoltan Farkas, who has edited much of Jancsó's past work, is again his editor here, but, outside of possible help on planning the shape of sequences, could not have had much to do. The wide-screen color photography is by Janos Kende.

The matters I noted in *The Red and the White*—the constant shifts of power, the strings of footling commands—have now grown almost into *raisons d'être*, combined with longer and longer camera sweeps, and the result is an irritating, unsatisfactory picture, but it is by a unique and complex cinematic mind.

II:

TRIUMPHS AND TRIALS
OF THE MASTERS

THE PASSION OF ANNA

Bergman

PENELOPE GILLIATT

Ingmar Bergman's *The Passion of Anna*, which is a masterpiece, is one of the most specifically modern films I have ever seen, yet there is barely a modern object in sight. No traffic, no frozen food, no push-button sophisticated speech. It is the characters' plight that seems so modern. The people in the film live on an island off the Swedish coast. Bergman presents their world as theologically created, but the Theos is mute about what to do next. Blunders have the weight of heresy; idle errors have barbarous consequences.

I am not religious, but I can see how much our atheist epoch may have impoverished Western art by formulating no substitute order of good and evil. The flower children are about the only people poetic enough to have tried. The reign of black comedy, satanic comedy, has diminished literature, on the whole; it is very easy to write about evil, very hard to write about good and evil. The reason why so many rollicking antiwar films are nothing very much, the reason why they offer no convincing account of the diabolical, is that they present war as a given and uncontrollable condition outside any system of cause and effect, and therefore morally as banal as awful weather. They show within that condition no one who makes you suppose that he and his like might have created it. The lack of religion in a nontheistic sense—of a bond between a man and his scruples—has led lately to many

163

rather absurd attempts to manufacture a plastic sort of heresy instead. We have had, for instance, our glum orgies of blue films, which represent a supremely comic effort to blaspheme, considering that the effort is instantly scuttled by its own liberal argument that there is nothing blasphemous about pornography. And in the amoral world of our new, "liberated," but really rather line-toeing wacky comedies that specialize in the far-out, where nothing in the presented world remotely works but where anything goes, one simply misses somewhere to put one's feet; it seems that there is no floor, only falling.

The Passion of Anna is Bergman's second feature film in color. We see Max von Sydow at the start as a withdrawn, droll-looking hermit called Andreas Winkelman, with reddish hair and beard. He is mending a roof. The sunlight comes and goes. He has few friends. There are brief reprieves, but his soul lives mostly in the cold. We hear that he is divorced, "in a way." Much later, when he is living with someone, he has a terrified daydream about an unidentified woman. The image mixes up lovemaking and hospitals, and he comes out of the daydream to say that he was thinking of cancer. So did he leave his wife when she was deathly ill? Is that a part of his own mortal unease? His ex-wife's pottery barn, where we then see him twirling the potter's wheel and getting as drunk as he can, is "left exactly as it always was," except that he is now boozed out of his mind in it. On sacrilege, he and Bergman's film are experts.

As time goes on, Andreas gets to know two women. One of them is Eva (Bibi Andersson), married to a bilious architect called Elis. She has a brief and pretty melancholy affair with Andreas. The other is Anna (Liv Ullman), lame after a car accident that occurred when she was driving and that killed both her child and her husband, who was also called Andreas. Anna and the visible Andreas start living together, more or less happily. "There was violent dissension," she later says of this period, "but we never infected each other with cruelty or suspicion." She says the same thing of her first marriage, and we believe every word of it for a while. In a technically amazing monologue at a dinner party, she turns her head swiftly to the offscreen Elis, Andreas, and Eva, and the camera, unlooked at, presses in on her, close up, like the stare of conscience, as she talks about her marriage and about "living in the truth." She looks transparently honest but she is really lying in her teeth, for her marriage was a bad one and she half-consciously meant to kill the husband and child whose deaths now genuinely make her suffer so much—just as she means, later on, to try to kill the present Andreas in the same accidental way.

The film has partly to do with the malign hold that the past can have. The people in it wreck the present by too much re-enacting. They can't escape. The past has a grip on their feet, like mud in dreams. They can't make a move, and past behavior consumes the possibility of present action, just as the old, unseen Andreas begins so to requisition the present Andreas that there is a moment when von Sydow actually goes out into the garden and shouts his name to himself to call back his swallowed soul. And the two women— Anna, an angel-faced liar who at first seems really anxious for the truth, and Eva, a girl who thinks herself shabby-natured but who talks miserably well of sorts of puniness that are beyond the first one's comprehension—actually fit together like the halves of a walnut. They are described as inseparables, and their personalities flow in and out of each other, like the psychic exchangings of the two women in *The Silence* and *Persona*. So do the temperaments of every other pair in the picture, which is sexually geometric. (It even emerges, when the architect is talking to Andreas, that Eva, the architect's wife, also slept with the Andreas whom Anna killed.) There are extraordinary close-up two-shots—again like the ones in *The Silence* and *Persona*—in which two faces will move across each other in talk and sometimes slightly hide each other. (The cameraman, as always, is Sven Nykvist.) The composition is a little like a Picasso Cubist painting, one face often in full front view and one in profile; it is also entirely theatrical—an image of power in flux between one person and another, like the theme of Strindberg's *The Stronger*, in which a silent woman slowly takes over the authority from a prattler. One of the more trite questions of modern art is whether one can be two different people at the same time. Bergman is more interested in the opposite: Can two people melt into one? And, if so, what about the simultaneous deadly combat to remain separated? He has made, again and again, films that are about people's terror of being eaten alive spiritually and about their mesmerized longing to risk it, all the same. In the old days, he often went into that notion in stories full of charades, magic shows, apparitions, and the occult. Now he does it simply. Alma, in *Hour of the Wolf*, typically pointed out that old people who have lived together all their lives begin to look like each other. In *Persona*, in the scene when the two women are picking over mushrooms and their sun hats tip across each other, the characters quietly hum tunes pitted against each other in contradiction of the merging image. Bergman makes films that are about girls half formed until they are with other, stronger women, about men's abiding terror that the women loved in their maturity are going to eat them up and return them to the immurement known before birth. In this film, Andreas tells us that he has claustrophobia and that he used to dream of falling down potholes.

Andreas has no perceptible job. Now and again, he writes at a desk. The hero of *Hour of the Wolf* was a painter, the hero of *Shame* a musician; like Andreas, both were not working and seemed obscurely stalemated. People sometimes assume that because Bergman so often makes films about artists he is being autobiographical and self-important about creativity, but I think the artists are there because they are the most natural examples of men who work on their own and who can easily hit rock, in a way that moves and interests Bergman about people in general. The universe in his films is God-made, the invention of a Being who keeps His own counsel about how to live in it, and the inmates are hard-pressed by that silence. It rings in their ears. There are moments of conviviality that break up the isolation. Friendship. Love (never very erotic, and always tinctured with some dread of departure). Great tenderness (Andreas gently looks after a puppy that some madman loose on the island has horribly strung up by the neck from a tree). But such warmth of the sun is fast gone, and Bergman's people are again left to cope for themselves on a loftily conceived planet where they feel perpetually humiliated. Lately, his heroes have often spoken of that—of a humiliation that he sees as the companion of modern humanity, and hard to bear. Our social system is based on it, he says: the law, the carrying out of sentences, the kind of education we have, the Christian religion. Andreas feels himself stifled and spat upon, but without an alternative. He has a police record, the punishment for minimal crimes of rebellion. "I am a whipped cur," he says quite proudly, rage his only weapon. Does he bite? We'll see. The God whom Bergman's characters now rather prefer not to believe in is implacable and unexplanatory, much like an artist who declines to interpret his work. This Creator will not be His own exegete, and there are no footnotes. He remains entirely mute, without the ghost of a smile. Meanwhile, the inhabitants of His order stumble around in it, aware that there are rules, damned for breaking them, and sometimes powerfully longing to be out of the game. Evald, in *Wild Strawberries*, said, "My need is to be dead. Absolutely, totally dead."

In this supreme new work, Anna is the character who has been closest to death, and who is therefore—as people are—the least enlightening about it to anyone else. She talks of the car crash distantly. She remembers herself walking away, and her child's head in "a funny position." She speaks of thinking, "What a ghastly accident," and of wondering "why someone wasn't coming to help those poor people," including herself. The alienation is complete and rather frightening. And then we see a dream of hers, in black and white, starting off in a boat that is like the boat in *Shame*. She runs up a road, longing greatly for company and knowing somehow that it has gone forever. There is nowhere to go. A woman on the road is hurrying; she might be someone to befriend, but she turns aside and says, "I've changed all the locks." Then Anna sees another woman, sitting dead silent with a face of stone. Someone says that the woman's son is going to be executed. Anna falls on her knees in front of her and says, out of nowhere, "Forgive me. Forgive me." One remembers then that she was at the wheel of the car that killed her own child, and remembers having been told that this dream "troubled her at Easter." The word "*Passion*" in Bergman's title is certainly theological as well as vernacular. Bergman has always been one of the most Christian of film makers, but his old and rather affected apparatus of symbolism has now been replaced by pure human behavior, both more direct and more truly mysterious. He is also pulling farther and farther away from orthodoxy. There can seldom have been a Christian artist who held out less hope of an afterlife. It is as though he felt that if people can already be so troubled and so barbarous when they are in the temporal world, eternity must be unthinkable. ("For if they do these things in a green tree, what shall be done in the dry?" St. Luke wrote. Bergman makes one dredge up verses from the

Gospels that one didn't know one remembered.) The un-Christian possibility of suicide also comes up, when the four main actors jump out of character and speak directly to the camera about what they think of the people they are playing. Bibi Andersson says that she thinks Eva might try to kill herself. "I hope they'll manage to save her," she says, and adds that she hopes Eva will look at her own old ego with affection. This is one of the warmths in Bergman —his wish for people to extend charity to themselves. He does something amazing at the end of the sequence, just after Bibi Andersson speaks about Eva's possibly someday becoming a teacher and feeling blessed: on the word "blessed" Bergman changes the exposure and floods the screen with light. There are other halcyon seconds in the film that make you catch your breath. In the middle of violence and carnage—sheep killed by the madman, a gentle peasant called Johan committing suicide because he can't bear being accused of the outbreak of animal slaughter on the island— Andreas and Anna suddenly look after a dying bird that threw itself with a thud against their window while they were watching war news on TV. The island is racked with "physical and psychical acts of violence": we keep seeing the words tapped out on a typewriter, part of a letter left by the first Andreas, which reveals a good deal of prescience and also a dangerous degree of truth about the marriage that his widow has coaxed herself into thinking ideal. Bergman now seems free of the dank respect for passivity and the gluttony for suffering that clung to his earlier films. We hear in this film, after a stable has been set on fire, of "a horse that ran around blazing" and "damned well wouldn't die." There is another line, spoken by Andreas, in the same spirit of admiration for mute refusal to give up in extremity: "Has it ever occurred to you that the worse off people are, the less they complain? At last, they are quite silent." Silence. Bergman's obdurate theme for many pictures now.

The Passion of Anna (called *A Passion* in Swedish) is a wonderful piece of work, even better than *The Silence* and *Persona*. Again and again, Bergman effortlessly tops some amazing piece of invention. The material is complex, but everything seems simple and lucid. The human details are often strange but always convincing, in a slightly shattering way. Andreas, for instance, lets out a terrific wordless roar when he is lying alone on a bed after the insufficient, saddened Eva has left his place to take the ferry. "It's not enough," the roar says. "None of it's enough." Andreas and Anna don't love each other enough; Eva is out of reach.

Eva talks hopelessly about her cynic architect husband, who is building a culture center in Italy. "Building a mausoleum over the meaninglessness of Milan," he has said earlier, at their dinner all together. The scene seems improvised. The actors look a little flushed with wine and with the fire behind them. Bergman is one of the very great directors of acting. When the commentary here suddenly goes into the present tense and talks about Andreas as feeling "a rush of affection for these people," the affection is really there—even for Elis, the alien. Eva's husband is a pagan in Bergman's world of unwilling agnostics, and a further element in the film's scheme of the devouring and the devoured: Eva talks about herself as "nothing but a small part of his sarcasm." (When she is alone with Andreas, playing some rather horrible old dance music, she suddenly says, "What is to become of us?" Of all of them, she seems to mean.) Her husband, more buoyant, cheerfully collects photographs of people in the midst of violent emotion, which is his study. He arranges the pictures neatly in indexed boxes. The subject disagreeably fascinates him. "You can't read people with any certainty. Not even physical pain gives a reaction," he says, showing Andreas a picture of Eva looking beautiful. "She was just starting a migraine," he goes on—this eerie esthete of pain, one of the jaded, the out-of-heart, dead from the neck up and trying to quicken himself with snapshots of other people's intensity.

The whole movie is pitched very high, and made by a man technically at the top of his powers. He catches people in fibs that ricochet: in a tiny stinginess about pretending to have asked a telephone operator what a call cost on someone else's phone, in a lie about not having had an affair, in a lie that everything is fine. The method of the film forces the characters into absolute clarity of intention. It is as if they were pressed up against some invisible wall, with the camera unremittingly on their faces. Few films can have had so many close-ups. Instead of flashbacks, people describe things; Bergman is loosening the traditional film links between sound track and image. The moments when the actors slip out of their parts to talk about their characters are not modish, not neo-Godard, but brilliantly necessary. They have much the same effect as the showing of film-stock breaking in *Persona*—it is as though the dramatic medium itself had for the moment snapped under stress. Like the work of Renoir, Beckett, Buñuel, and Satyajit Ray, Bergman's new film is religious in the sense that it restores a lost weight to the human act, and an essential existence to its characters that is more significant than their existence in the eyes of the people they are addressing. There is agony in the material, but the attentiveness and the talent of the film maker are altogether reviving.

Bergman at His Bleak Best

RICHARD SCHICKEL

With *The Passion of Anna* the art of Ingmar Bergman reaches its pinnacle. Though it is in color, it is in every important way his most austere and elliptical work. A thing of silences and enigmas, it nevertheless makes very clear the tragic vision of life that possesses its author.

Gone at last are all traces of the baroque symbolism that marked —and often marred—his early work. Gone, too, is the yearning for evidence of the presence of God in the world. Bergman has, I think, accepted His death and, indeed, seems to find that event no longer worthy of comment. His absence is now simply one of the terms of our existence. Darkness is now settling over the island to which Bergman has now retreated for four consecutive films, a darkness relieved by only the bleakest of winter lights.

That island is, of course, a psychological landscape as well as a physical one and Bergman has gone to that stark, spare place in the same spirit that his characters have—out of revulsion at the meaningless cruelty of the world. There is no escape from it here, as *The Passion of Anna* makes abundantly clear, but it is at least somewhat reduced to a manageable, noninstitutional, human scale. Or so they permit themselves to hope.

This time those gathered here to await the end include: the lady of the title, who yearns for a perfect, transcendent love and probably, before the film began, accidentally-on-purpose killed her husband and child for failing to provide same; a financial failure, once jailed for forgery, who takes up with Anna mostly because she is there and may assuage the terrible emptiness he feels; an architect, whose distinguished career seems a mockery to him and who takes (and endlessly catalogues) pictures which, one imagines, he intends to be a complete record of our increasing inhumanity; his wife, who has apparently not found even the transitory rewards that the others have savored in life.

Not a great deal "happens" to these people. The failure has a roll in the sack with the architect's wife, a year-long "relationship" with Anna that always remains distant and cool. The architect (possibly a surrogate for Bergman) watches; his wife simply slips out of focus entirely. A madman, who might be any of the above (except the failure) or none, runs loose on the island slaughtering animals. A man who has been accused, perhaps falsely, of this crime commits suicide. Anna tries to kill her lover, fails and drives off, and we are left with an image of him, an image that grows increasingly grainy until it looks like yet another modern horror photographed off a TV screen, running first this way, then that, in an agony of indecision. Should he follow her or not?

We do not care. It is not important. Any action will, we know, turn out to be without resolving meaning. It will end only in the passage of more time. It is, in its quiet way, a shattering ending, brilliant in both its economy and its clarity. Bergman has, in that concluding sequence, as well as in the rest of the picture, stripped his art bare of all that is nonessential, all that is potentially confusing, all that offers any promise of warmth. Such hope as he offers stands outside the frame of the film. Periodically, we see a clapstick with the name of one of the actors on it, after which he or she faces the camera and discusses (in what only seems an improvised manner) the motives, the possible future of his or her character. Actorlike, they entertain some optimism for them, implying art may be impossible without at least a shred of hope.

Maybe so. In any case, this art is of the highest order. The controlled brilliance of Bergman's favorite actors—Max von Sydow, Liv Ullmann, Bibi Andersson—must be mentioned. So must the psychological depth with which they—and Bergman—invest these people. They are never abstractions. They are, God help us, our brethren. To spend a couple of hours with them is to be in the presence of genius at its ripest, most mature moment. We may leave *The Passion of Anna* more dubious than ever about man's

fate, but we leave with our faith in the possibilities of screen art—
much tested in recent months—miraculously restored.

ZABRISKIE POINT

ARTHUR SCHLESINGER, JR.

In his last three films, Michelangelo Antonioni has been
preoccupied with the violation of personality by technology in industrial society. His attitude toward technology has been somewhat
equivocal: While his mind has stressed the threat to individuality,
his eye has discovered beauty in the new industrial structures. This
inner ambivalence, no doubt, accounts for the diversity of solutions
he has suggested to the conflict between man and the machine.

Thus in *Red Desert*, a much underrated movie, the setting was
Italy and, in the end, the intrusion of technology was evaded by
inducing in his heroine a mood of lyrical resignation. The birds of
Ravenna, we were told in the concluding shot, could survive the
contaminated yellow smoke of the factories by learning how to fly
through it—a lesson for humans. In *Blow-Up*, the setting was England. Here technology was transcended by making the hero a
photographer, i.e., a technologist himself but in a marginal technology; the machine became his instrument rather than his master,
and in a marginal land survival was possible. In *Zabriskie Point*, the
setting is America where technological society is horribly triumphant. Here, as Antonioni appears to see it, technology cannot be
evaded or transcended. It can only be destroyed.

The film opens with a meeting of student radicals in Los Angeles
planning a demonstration. There is trouble with the police; the
students go on strike; a cop is killed. The boy who drew his gun to
kill the policeman escapes, steals a plane, and lands near Death
Valley, California, where he meets a young secretary who has tem-
porarily abandoned her job in search of spiritual salvation in the
desert. They make love at Zabriskie Point. The boy takes the plane
back; policemen waiting at the airfield shoot him down. The girl,

going on to rejoin her employer (and lover?) at a business conference in a luxurious, overstocked desert house, hears the news. Devastated, she drives away; then looks back and in her mind sees the house and its goods exploding into flames, again and again and again.

Like other directors making their first American films, Antonioni is fascinated by the iconography of the American scene and perceives a sinister loveliness in the American landscape. But his brilliant visual feeling for American images is dominated and used by his fear of American impulses. His vision of America is of a land of nightmare. Nature, though beautiful, is dead, "A heap of broken images, where the sun beats,/And the dead tree gives no shelter. . . ." Everyone living is a victim or a monster. Even little children are so deformed by the corrupt society that, when nine-year-old kids encounter the heroine, their first thought is rape.

Symbolism has always been Antonioni's weakness. This time it is his disaster. It may be all right, for example, to blow up the desert mansion as a metaphor for revolution; repeating the explosion eight or ten times may even add to its emotional force. But the sight of the artifacts of American capitalism, including canned goods, suspended in the air for long moments of arrested motion drives the point home a little too simplistically. The spell is broken; one whispers to one's neighbor, "This is the film that should have been called *Blow-Up*." Then, believe it or not, Antonioni follows the explosion by showing the sun on the horizon. The dawn of a new day, perhaps? This is back to agitprop.

His use of billboards to provide "ironic" underlining of the action is equally heavy-handed. When the cops attack the students, Antonioni gives us a sign on a college building: "Liberal Arts." After the shooting, the hero sees a placard advertising a mortuary; when he is hungry, he is assailed by food billboards; when he is trying to escape, United Air Lines tells him, "Let's get away from it all."

As anger has eroded Antonioni's subtlety, it has also eroded his originality. The scene when a plane buzzes a person in an empty field was better done by Alfred Hitchcock in *North by Northwest*. It was faintly plausible in *Easy Rider* that two Southerners might gun down a couple of gentle hippies on a lonely country road. But, when Antonioni repeats the scene in *Zabriskie Point*, it is a good deal less plausible. Here policemen, under the eyes of the press, casually and unnecessarily murder a young man who had been signaling his lack of aggressive intent by flying the stolen plane, now painted in psychedelic colors and marked "Peace," back to the airfield from which he had taken it.

Antonioni's dislike of America extends even to those he affects to admire. His actors are all director's puppets, without scope or personality of their own. His hero acts out children's fantasies—shooting a cop (or does he? this is another of Antonioni's little mystifications, reminiscent of *Blow-Up*), stealing a plane (does Antonioni assume that all American boys know how to fly?), buzzing a girl on the desert, making love at Zabriskie Point. This last scene turns ludicrously into what Antonioni must regard as his obligatory orgy, and Death Valley suddenly becomes populated by dozens of couples copulating in twos, threes, and fours. If this represents Antonioni's idea of his hero's vision of the good society, it is only one more piece of condescension.

Or it may be that the childishness of the hero's fantasies is a deliberate effort to suggest the futility of romantic individual rebellion as against the steel will of the authoritarian revolutionaries portrayed in the opening scene. Premonitions of revolution have always lurked within Antonioni's explorations of contemporary decadence. "I think that, in the years to come," he said in his famous interview with Jean-Luc Godard in 1964 (for which I am indebted to Andrew Sarris' valuable volume, *Interviews With Film Directors*), "there are going to be very violent transformations, both in the world and in the individual's interior. Today's crisis comes from this spiritual confusion, from this confusion of conscience, of faith and of politics; there are so many symptoms of the transformations to come."

But if Antonioni's idea is to make a contrast between rebels and revolutionaries, the film hardly sustains this point. Only the most devoted can regard the opening scene as an expression of serious revolutionary purpose rather than as a satire on those who play in the theater of revolution. In any case, the young revolutionists, who include Kathleen Cleaver (would Lenin have acted a bit part in a czarist melodrama? "who whom," as the old master used to put it), are hardly seen thereafter, and the contrast, if any is intended, quickly fades away.

Every artist has a right to his own vision. The sadness of *Zabris-*

kie Point is that anger has led a notably subtle director to make an exceedingly simple-minded hymn to violence. His hatred of America has given him a vision without nuance or complexity and has thereby betrayed him as an artist. Life becomes good guys and bad guys. Evidently Antonioni, with his counterversion of *The Green Berets,* has been Americanized too.

Andrew Sarris

Michelangelo Antonioni's long-awaited *Zabriskie Point* had its first New York press screening at 8 P.M. on Thursday, February 5, 1970, at the Coronet Theatre. Audience reaction seemed to range from mixed to negative, but I didn't really want to talk about the movie until I had sorted out my immediate impressions, and so I ducked the opportunity to gather gut reactions in the lobby á la Nathalie Sarraute. My review deadline for *The Voice* is normally Friday afternoon for the following Thursday's issue, which is usually on the newsstands by Wednesday afternoon. But because I had to leave on Friday morning for a wedding in Virginia, I pushed my deadline forward to Monday morning.

It is now Sunday afternoon, February 8, 1970, as I sit staring at my docile typewriter keys. I have been thinking about *Zabriskie Point* all weekend, on the plane from New York to Richmond and on the plane back, in cars and in cabs, in the city and in the country, in fog and in smog, but particularly in the placid company town of Franklin, Virginia, the most prominent features of which are three towering chimneys (the kind that are always tilted expressionistically in industrial documentaries) belching black, white, and gray columns of smoke into the coughing clouds. I may never revisit Franklin, and hence, I may never be able to separate my impression of the town from the image of its smoke streams. Mine is an outsider's vision of Franklin, a superficial view for a novelist or a dramatist or an essayist, but not necessarily for a painter or a sculptor or a photographer. It would seem that there is one standard of experience (and research) for the arts of the mind and another for the arts of the senses. Film-making draws from both realms, and thus what bores the mind may please the eye, and what offends the eye may stimulate the mind.

Zabriskie Point, an outsider's view of America, is as much a delight to the eyes as it is a disappointment to the mind, or at least to that part of the mind that relishes complications and consummations in its dramatic entertainments. Antonioni is at his best in the first hour when nothing happens and in the last ten minutes when nothing matters. In between he gets bogged down with two callow, inexpressive protagonists (Mark Frechette and Daria Halprin) who make love not sense. Mark Frechette was reportedly discovered at a bus stop in Cambridge, Massachusetts, shouting at a man who had thrown a flowerpot at a quarreling couple. He is described in the program notes as a twenty-year-old sometime carpenter, an occupation that in this context resounds with a quasi-Biblical solemnity and foreboding. He is inertia itself, having mastered the nonactor's trick of masking thoughts and nonthoughts alike behind the slit-eyed mask of a poker face. He cannot read adequately even the few laconic lines dredged up from the desert sands of Death Valley by the collective efforts of Antonioni, Fred Gardner, Sam Shepard, Toniono Guerra, and Clare Peplo. Daria Halprin displays an interesting bodily frame for the camera to photograph, particularly across the shoulders, and there is a slight spark in her eyes and teeth, but her face is hopelessly uncoordinated for any expression of emotion beyond the most rudimentary, and she tends to walk like a camel on a cobblestone road, hardly a disgraceful deficiency for a nineteen-year-old anthropology student at Berkeley. Together Mark and Daria (for so also are they called in the film) fail to achieve even the rapport of their shared awkwardness. They are as dead psychologically as their desert decor is dead metaphorically, and Antonioni must have sensed their inadequacy at an early point in the production, or why else would he have gone to such unprecedented lengths to establish visual correlatives for the most basic human emotions? For Daria to simulate tears at Mark's death, it is thus necessary for Antonioni to drench her with the twisting drippings of a granite grotto. And when Mark himself is finally trapped by California police as he attempts to land the small plane he stole for a joy ride, Antonioni diverts the audience's attention from the human confrontation between nonconformism and police authority to an aerial view of police cars constricting the free movement of a grounded metal bird painted over with the psychedelia of peace and flowery passivity. Mark's spirit, such as it may have been, flows out of his clumsy body into the metal metaphor of his aerial/ Ariel aspiration. And that's all there is to his youthful, disorganized, ultimately impotent rebellion.

For her part, Daria can only stand idly by while Antonioni's camera passes through her for his final explosion of America's Pop canvas into the spiritual shrapnel of materialism. For Antonioni, *Zabriskie Point* is a different kind of blow-up, not the magnification of art into truth, but the disintegration of America into trash, and not just America, but indeed the increasing muchness of matter everywhere, and all kinds of matter, even, or perhaps especially, books.

Almost half a century ago Lev Kuleshov performed an experiment with a relatively expressionless close-up of the great Russian actor Ivan Mozhukhin. Kuleshov intercut this same close-up first with a shot of a plate of soup, then with a child playing with a teddy bear, and finally with an old woman lying dead in her coffin. (Some French film historians have garbled the experiment by substituting a shot of a nude woman for that of the child with the teddy bear in Kuleshov's montage series.) The point of the experiment was that audiences of that time were allegedly deluded into thinking that Mozhukhin had masterfully changed his expression from hunger to joy to grief in response to the three situations when actually it was merely the juxtaposition of shots that created the illusion of an actor's performance. This hoary anecdote (reported initially by Pudovkin) has been used by directors for decades as proof that they don't need actors, and Daria's mental explosions of an Arizona chalet are perhaps the most spectacular substitution of a director's vision for a player's persona in the history of the cinema. But it doesn't really work or satisfy once we get back, as we must, to the player herself. It is at that moment that we feel the fatal rupture in *Zabriskie Point* between a brilliant documentary and a bedraggled drama. If people have to be used at all, they have to be good. Bad people can be transcended, they can be sublimated, they can be overshadowed, but they still flaw every foot of film in which they appear.

Still, *Zabriskie Point* is a film not to be missed. And yet, of all of Antonioni's films, it is the only one that does not require a second viewing for the resolution of its ambiguities. The main trouble with *Zabriskie Point* is that there are not enough levels of signification. Even *The Red Desert*, hitherto the most esthetical of Antonioni's works, contains plot nuances that require repeated viewings to clarify. The anecdotal material in *Zabriskie Point* is too slight to hang together believably. We never believe that Daria could ever serve as a link between muddled Mark and Rod Taylor's Lee Allen, a genially omnivorous land speculator with more skyscraping and glass-partitioned camera angles than lines of dialogue or discernible human feelings. The opening sequence of white radicals rapping with Black Panthers, and subsequent intimations of pig-panther rituals of violence, extend the film without enriching it. The two main characters are so unencumbered by psychological development that we are always left free to peer at the background for Antonioni's choice of American Gothic with which to embellish his fable. Antonioni's viewpoint throughout is that of the interplanetary visitor descending on the American West with more curiosity than compassion, but with far more compassion than contempt.

Audiences may be somewhat let down from the lurid expectations inspired by rumors of right-wing repression. (Conspicuously absent from the film is the "Fuck You America" that Daria was supposed to have scrawled on the desert sands for Mark's aerial appraisal.) The scenes of communal lovemaking are there in some measure, but they operate merely on a symbolic level, that is to say, as imaginary sociological extensions of the coupling of Mark and Daria. The skin is all there, but not the dramatic certification or pseudo-documentary simulation of Today's Youth on the Rampage. And never has Antonioni's depiction of lovemaking been so arid and listless. From the biological orientation of sex in *La Notte* and the chemical orientation of sex in *The Red Desert*, Antonioni has descended to the geological orientation of sex in *Zabriskie Point*, gradually sanding over the fleshy substances into the deathlike mineral constituencies of the dust and rock of Antonioni's American landscape.

As an American, I am not offended by Antonioni's apocalyptic vision of our supermarket civilization. It is his misfortune, however, that he has not provided facile fantasy figures with which his art-house audience can identify in its voluptuous isolation from the Great Silent Majority. If only Dustin Hoffman or Jon Voight or Jack Nicholson or Arlo Guthrie or even Peter Fonda had been joy riding over the Mojave Desert in a flying bike, *Zabriskie Point* would be this year's box-office bonanza and next year's subject for sociological essays. Unfortunately, Mark Frechette is endowed with so little charisma that even Antonioni seems to spend most of his time avoiding him. When Mark passes a sandwich counter on his way to make a telephone call, Antonioni cuts away from the call to some luscious red tomatoes about to be seduced by a hero sandwich. Indeed, Antonioni's relentless estheticism dilutes his ideological impact at every turn. If he had photographed the Nazi death camps, he would have found the most beautiful compositions available for that sort of material. This absurd dilemma of a Vogue photographer with a Marxist overview is Antonioni's curse and glory. It makes me enjoy *Zabriskie Point* more than I really respect it, but I can't help thinking that I belong to a minority of a minority in the pleasure I derive from dynamic visual forms for their own sake. Without pleasing performances, zippy dialogue, and an unspoken complicity with the guilt-ridden but oh-so-comfortable affluence of America, Antonioni's art must carry *Zabriskie Point* singlehanded, and that may not be enough to pay the rent in Culver City. But no one who takes cinema seriously can afford to pass up this latest canvas from the palette of the Michelangelo for our own time and our own medium.

FELLINI SATYRICON

Rome, B.C., A.F.

STEFAN KANFER

> *If I had taken these fantasies of the unconscious as art, they would have carried no more conviction than visual perceptions, as if I were watching a movie.*
>
> —Carl Jung

There have been hundreds of Freudian Films; *Fellini Satyricon* is probably the first—and certainly the most important—Jungian one. In the course of two hours and seven minutes, images, totems, and archetypes rise and burst like hydrogen sulfide bubbles from the marsh of the collective unconscious. The unsynchronized sound track has the timbre of racial memory, echoing some eternal dream time. The film's devices are, in fact, so frenzied and eruptive that they tend to obscure an artlessness of thought or substance. Perhaps it is just as well; the *Fellini Satyricon* is manifestly made for the eye's mind, not the mind's eye. "Faces are my words," says the film maker, and he manages to make them speak an epic.

Cinema's greatest living satirist (*La Dolce Vita*, 8½, *Juliet of the Spirits*), director Federico Fellini has always been half in love with his main target: decadence. His favorite gallery is Rome, where the extravagances of the Via Veneto add daily calories to the Sweet Life. The Appian Way leads into the past, into the harsh, lurid revels of Petronius, who mocked Nero's ancient Sybarites with the first *Satyricon*. Although only fragments of that manuscript survive, they are enough to reveal a Homeric spoof. The hilariously ignoble hero, Encolpius (sometimes translated as "the Crotch"), is a randy homosexual. His wanderings lead him not to godlike beings but to all too human Romans.

The true *Satyricon* is shot through with fragments of poetry. The *Fellini Satyricon* finds visual equivalents—but often at the price of coherence. Scenes are shifted, new ones are added, characters are blunted or sharpened. Still, Fellini has left the Petronian framework intact. Like almost all his social satire, *Satyricon* is a picaresque journey through the beds and banquet halls of Rome. Now Encolpius skirmishes for the affections of the young invert Giton (Max Born); now impotent, he whimpers about his "blunted sword"; now he overstuffs his gullet at a vulgarian's feast; now he is a starveling captive aboard a slave ship.

Fellini calls his *Satyricon* a "science-fiction trip into the past instead of the future." It blasts off with a scene so brilliant that the whole picture shivers from the thrust. In a masque, a musically flatulent clown capers on a stage, mocking the audience with scatological jokes and gestures. A grinning idiot is carried onstage and led to a chopping block. A headsman mimes a blow with his weapon—then chops the victim's hand off to a chorus of cackles, while freshets of blood stain the scene. It is a savage fragment of the cinema of cruelty, a death-in-life image, like T.S. Eliot's perception of "the skull beneath the skin."

Viewers—and the *Satyricon's* satyrs—periodically struggle up-ward toward the light, as if trying to wake from the sleep of reason. Unhappily, the light fails, for almost all the main characters are inept performers whose unmarked faces cannot register more than satiety and fatigue. The fault lies partly with the director. In the Fellini version, the actors literally performed by saying the num-bers. "It was a multilingual cast," says the maestro. "So instead of having them speak dialogue, I often just had them count one, two, three." Hiram Keller, recruited from the Broadway production of *Hair* to play Encolpius' intimate, Ascyltus, was given instructions of equal subtlety: "You are evil and you lay everything in sight."

Yet in so plotless a pastiche, the population matters less than the imagination that propels it. That quality the film has in super-abundance. Fellini's style is less theatrical than amphitheatrical. Colossal grotesques leap from private fantasy to public mind. In a set daubed with indelible cerulean and blood red, an albino her-maphrodite possessed of occult powers is abducted—only to wither pitifully in the desert. A quadruple amputee somehow manages a deep bow.

The catalogue of images is not as unrelated as it seems. At its best, the scenario synthesizes art, moving like music, and spreading out like a suite of paintings. In this, *Fellini Satyricon* exceeds the original. Petronius could only describe the obscenity of the ban-quet staged by Trimalchio, the *nouveau riche*. Fellini could portray it as a vignette of Rome at the end of its parabola of grandeur, complete with elaborate jokes and hoaxes. It is an occasion as bi-zarre and funny as the film's conclusion—in which a lady leaves a fortune to friends, with the proviso that they dissect her corpse and eat it. As always, the maestro's greatest strength is anecdotal. His account of a patrician husband and wife who commit suicide rather than submit to imprisonment is as affecting as the short tales of *La Dolce Vita*. His story of the adventures of a woman and the corpse of her husband is neoclassic black comedy.

The mosaic of individual insights and adventures never unifies into a single, coherent vision. It is as if the director, sidetracked by the individuals, grew impatient with the crowd. Much of Fellini's extracurricular career is spent deflecting exegeses of his films, but he seems genuinely anxious to have audiences compare his ancient Rome with that of the Twentieth Centurians. "Rome in its decline was quite similar to our world today," he insists. "There was the same fury of enjoying life, the same lack of moral principles and ideologies, and the same complacency. Today we are finished with the Christian myth and await a new one. There is analogy in *Satyricon*." But history, unlike jurisprudence, is not always based on precedent. It is, in Valéry's term, "the science of what never happens twice."

The simple juxtaposition of contemporary *angst* with a spiritually exhausted Rome Before Christ (and After Fellini) is as facile as it is false. Below the rationale, Fellini seems to sense as much. Encolpius and his colleagues are too obviously fashioned after contemporary faggots; his mourning widow is ominously representative of Jackie Kennedy; his wall friezes seem copied less from Roman basements than department-store casements. The forced modernity denies complexity and does much to weaken the work's polished irony.

Still, no one else could have brought a tenth of the *Satyricon* to the screen without the customary lubricity and X-rated smirks. When, in a climactic scene, Encolpius recovers his potency at the thighs of a gigantic black Venus, the viewer feels less a voyeur than an observer of some elemental sexual ritual brought intact from the beginning of the world. To be sure, between such moments, the film proves so personal that it amounts to solipsism. "The pearl," as the director once modestly observed, "is only the oyster's autobiography." *Fellini Satyricon*, at the end, may even be considered no more than an orgy of self-indulgence. But what a self! And what indulgence!

ROBERT HATCH

The Satyricon, that masterpiece of tantalizing fragments, is promising material for a latter-day "collaborator" in film. Get the tone right, and Petronius has at hand the unfailingly seductive anecdotage of those scapegrace elegants, Encolpius and Ascyltus, squabbling along the perimeter of the Roman Empire for the love of Giton, their indescribably complacent Ganymede. The brilliant scraps of picaresque larceny, perverse self-indulgence, and sardonic observation can be fitted as particularly bright stones into a new mosaic that reinvents the past or implies a contemporary judgment.

But the original tone—that of a disapproving laughter—is not so easily caught. Petronius indulges his characters with no understanding forgiveness; he understands them well enough, but he wallops them. They are a bad lot, spending themselves on every vice save hypocrisy. But if their perverse and clamorous appetites sink them below the beasts, their vitality raises them toward the gods—at least, it has won them immortality.

It is a great opportunity, and *Fellini Satyricon* misses it. The original traveled light; this reconstruction labors under the ponderous baggage of a spectacular. It seems to be taking place, not along the Mediterranean rim of Nero's imperialism but on some extragalactic planet of science fiction. The sun's spectrum is hotter than earth light, the architecture comes, not from archeology but from the fantasy of some exotic technology, and the horizon is not where one expects it.

Worse, the high wit and low merriment are gone. This film cries "woe," "repent," like some Old Testament bluenose warning of the wrath to come. It never shows its teeth in a satiric grin and the possibility of laughter does not arise. Fellini makes wickedness seem leadenly repellent; that may be good doctrine, but it is no way to win laurels. Oddly enough, he has invented more than he has borrowed. Many of the great scenes lie idle, while he improvises from hints and holes in the text. He invents to some purpose, it is true, but with a proliferation of furniture that obscures the surgical finesse. Trimalchio's feast looks like a drunken chautauqua, attended by thousands, and the portrait of literature's first tycoon is lost in the swarming squalor. It is not that Fellini's seaminess is more extreme than Petronius'; just that he recoils from its excesses with more assertive emphasis. He lacks the quick line of his preceptor.

Encolpius, as played by Martin Potter, is a pretty young stud, but a blockhead. When he spoke for Petronius, this inexcusable rascal saw through everything, including himself; under Fellini's management, he couldn't see through a hole in the wall. Ascyltus (Hiram Keller) sneers—and sneers again. It is not enough, nor is the agility of these tumbling boys. Giton (Max Born) is inanimate, as recessive as the leading lady in a Japanese costume movie. To do

him justice, he must be played as the foremost male bitch in literature (at least, until Genet came along) and if he is not so played,
the wheels won't turn.

This is laborious, I'm afraid pretentious, work, and it's a pity.
The Satyricon has been waiting for the permissive moment when
someone could romp it—savage, shrewd, revolting, and roaring
with laughter—across the screen. Now instead we have an art film
with indelicate acrobatics.

THE DAMNED

ROBERT HATCH

You might suppose that an Italian director who addressed
himself to the moral inadequacies of the Third Reich would be-
stow a quality of objective irony on the subject. He need not assume, after all, that the corruption is in *his* heritage. But Luchino
Visconti (*Rocco and His Brothers*) takes a morose view of life that
is more typically Teutonic than Latin, and in *The Damned* he
seems to clutch guilt to his bosom. He has produced a *Bildungs-
roman* about—and almost entirely within—a Ruhr steel-owning
family named Essenbeck, whose cannibalistic designs on one another, and whose individual indulgences in gross appetites, might
have overwhelmed the graphic powers of George Grosz. It cannot
be maintained that the Nazis corrupt the Essenbecks; they are already so corrupt that the most one can say is that if the Essenbecks
did not exist Hitler would have had to invent them.

Nor should it be supposed that Visconti's lurid chronicle can be
viewed as a later *Buddenbrooks*; it is a family chronicle, but at the
hack level—crushed by a monotony of facts that do not inform,
sodden with greed, perversion, hatred, and treachery. For three
hours it goes on, demonstrating that Fascist Germany was hell,
stimulating Hilter's imps to torment the lost souls with the goads
of their own sins. It is the most explicit of films, both in its sluggish

factuality and in its drawn-out, insistent imagery (the orange inferno of the steelworks; the "New Germany" in the person of an SA youth, wearing garter belt and black silk stockings).

The characters are many and the plot is a cat's cradle of complexity, with wickedness outwitting wickedness in a circular chain. I am not going into all that, for I should never get out again. The principal characters are Friedrich Bruckmann (Dirk Bogarde), who murders reluctantly (he dresses and bears himself in the restrained British manner) and only because he sees no other avenue to the Essenbeck power and name; Baroness Sophie von Essenbeck (Ingrid Thulin), dowager princess of the family and a woman who enjoys dressing her son in drag; Martin von Essenbeck (Helmut Berger), who in consequence hates his mother, abuses small girls, determines to rule the clan that despises him (on a stand-in basis for the Nazis), and rapes his mother as a step to that goal.

Berger's performance is in a way typical of the film. It is a matter of excessive surface effect and almost no internal structure. His Martin minces and displays delicate fingers; his eyes are made up to resemble those of a cat, and when he is riding a manic high, they are presumably hypnotic; but a feather will knock him down from that perch and he then runs sobbing to mother. It is disagreeable to watch, but more than that it is not very interesting—a sort of cartoon simplification of a case history. Like everyone else in the piece, Martin seems less a pawn of the Nazis than of the director, and since it can be seen from the start that the director intends to grind his monsters between millstones, the waiting becomes onerous.

I respect Visconti's purpose: he is intent on composing a panorama of pure evil, and he chooses Hitler's Germany as the worst manifestation he can call to mind. But pure evil (there is one good Essenbeck; a sort of boy scout, outraged in Sodom) is as stultifying as pure virtue; one is reminded repeatedly during *The Damned* of Wagner, Shakespeare, Dante, and one smiles at the incongruity of the associations. The film is to tragedy what farce is to comedy, but there is no word for that because it is dramatically abortive.

The trouble may be that Visconti, though perhaps closer to Germans than most Italians, is still an Italian. He seems to forget that he is dealing with men and women, not with trolls out of the Black Forest. Their vileness so exceeds normal expectations that they become exhibits, to be shown in a menagerie, not on a stage. That may account for the masquelike progress of Visconti's controlled and heavily painted figures. It makes a kind of effect, but, aside from the fact that a three-hour processional is overlong for the screen, masques must depend on a concept of grandeur; they cannot achieve their spectacle from a basis of squalor.

I started to look for some contemporary relevance in the film, but gave up, realizing that this view of human behavior is too single-focused to be relevant to any era. One character may personify evil—say Iago, though even he was not all bad—but a whole cast of Satan's familiars suggests an unfamiliarity with the species under examination. I gather that the Germans astonish Visconti; I wonder how many he has known.

The best thing about the picture is the Essenbeck family sets. These heavy, impersonal rooms, rich without taste, luxurious without joy, tended by impeccable, silent, faceless servants, who seem nevertheless the only true possessors of the iron-cold surroundings, suggest what is meant by a commercial dynasty. They evoke the Germany that Hitler knew was ripe for him, whereas the characters that move through them are only travelers' tales of two-headed dwarfs beyond the mountains.

BRAD DARRACH

The Damned is a movie of towering hubris that sometimes seems gross but much more often great. It undertakes the reconstruction of *Macbeth* as the tragedy of an industrial dynasty in Hitler's Germany. There is inevitably a loss of lordly language and heroic altitude, but there is a gain in perverse intensity and political relevance. Shakespeare's story of one man's crime and conscience is framed in a Wagnerian phantasmagoria of power and augmented by this century's epic of evil.

The Damned was made by Luchino Visconti, a sixty-three-year-old leftist of noble lineage who is just as famous in Italy for the plays and operas he has staged as for the films (*Rocco and His Brothers, The Leopard*) he has directed. The film's tragic hero is an industrial manager (Dirk Bogarde) who in 1933 is urged by an SS captain to seize control of the munitions trust that employs him. "Do what you have to do. We will back you." So the manager plots with his mistress (Ingrid Thulin), the widowed daughter of the ancient magnate who founded the firm, and the night the Reichstag burns they murder the old man in his bed. The manager takes charge of the firm; but he has made a pact with the devil, and in the end the devil sadistically takes his due.

Visconti makes a few major mistakes—the role of Macbeth is slighted as the drama advances, and the incestuous climax is too little prepared—but the film is so strong it hardly matters. The acting is relentlessly forceful: Thulin plays Lady Macbeth as a fanged madonna, and Helmut Berger, as her son, seems to slough skin after skin until the final glistening evil of his character extrudes. The script is a lesson in dramatic structure: with one exception of satiric genius, a saturnalia of Storm Troopers that concludes with an SS bloodbath (the historic "Night of the Long Knives"), scenes are simple, spare, classic in shape and force. In an era hung up on free form and fresh approaches, Visconti imperturbably maintains and develops the grand style and the tragic tradition. I am tired of this tradition. I resent it. I suspect it has nothing new to say to us. Nevertheless, I am moved.

ZABRISKIE POINT, FELLINI SATYRICON, and THE DAMNED

Three Italians Obsessed with Decay
RICHARD SCHICKEL

In the numberless interviews Federico Fellini has given out in publicizing his new film, pretentiously known as *Fellini Satyricon* although it relies heavily on the *Satyricon* of Petronius for the incidents that trigger his imagery, he has seemed to want to have it two ways. On the one hand he has insisted that his film has no "meaning" in the conventional sense of the word; on the other, he has insisted that there is an analogy between the decaying society he

has placed onscreen and our own. He has also flung out a challenge: we must not bring to his movie any preconceptions about
what a film should or should not be. If we do, and if we insist on
them, we run the risk of being judged out of it, not with it. The
kids, he says, dig what he's doing, apparently because of their almost divine cultural innocence.

Maybe so. But in evaluating Fellini's film his unresolved contradiction about intent is more significant than the challenge to join
the youth culture (such challenges becoming, like patriotism, the
last refuge of scoundrels). In any case, the best films of the past
few years have forced us to abandon the conventional expectations
we used to take to the movies. We know, without Fellini's telling
us, that they are likely to be free-form voyages of self-discovery,
attempts to reveal, in public, the private preoccupations of their
makers. Which means that his *Satyricon* is hardly the radical departure Fellini thinks it is. Nor is his sensibility as he reveals it to
us here so profound or so disturbing as he thinks it is. Quite the
opposite; his is a mind of truly stupefying banality.

In form, the film is merely a series of incidents in which a
young decadent, Encolpius, journeys from one unspecified place to
another across a scenic, hellish imaginary landscape of Fellini's own
devising. Each turn in his path brings him face to face with some
spectacular new depravity. Very often these are revealed to us in
striking imagery—the wedding, on a slave ship, of a homosexual
pair; the abduction of an albino, hermaphrodite, and dwarfish
oracle from its grotto; an encounter with a mock minotaur in a
labyrinth. Equally often, however, the imagery is simply an attempt to wow us with spectacle, as in a visualization of Petronius'
most famous scene, Trimalchio's banquet. But striking or not,
none of the incidents may be said to advance our understanding of
plot or character—conventions Fellini has totally abandoned. Nor
can they be said to help us penetrate deeper and deeper into the
director's mind, which, given a mind worth penetrating, would
have been a valid rationale. In tone and development the incidents
turn out to be curiously repetitive (Fellini's preoccupation with
the homoerotic is, shall we say, a drag). We begin to feel we are
trapped in an ill-catalogued, but highly specialized, junkyard.

The work can only be understood, I think, as ritual, and in fairness I should note that on the night I saw it, many in the audience assumed attitudes of near-religious veneration.

Ritual, of course, implies celebration and so we must ask what Fellini is asking us to celebrate—his own virtuosity or his vision of decay? The first is impossible, for however powerful his images, they are not enough to sustain us for the length of his picture. That leaves us with his vision—and with the contradiction I have mentioned. If the film is no more than the dredging operation in his unconscious, then we are forced to the conclusion that he is a man without sufficient wit or intelligence to hold us long. If, on the other hand, we are to accept his insistence that there is an analogy between his imaginary world and our own, we are forced to the conclusion that his vision is severely limited, for there is more to the world than the repetitive nightmare he insists on showing us.

Of course, there is a measure of truth in his vision. But an artist is obliged to do something more with such a relatively simple proposition than persist in illustrating it with ever more baroque, ever more hysterical demonstrations of it. Obviously one cannot be "faithful" to Petronius, whose work survives only in fragments. But as a start, Fellini might have done well at least to emulate the Petronian style—cool, mocking, ironic—instead of assaulting us in the elephantine manner he has chosen.

One can, however, state that Fellini is not so impervious to outside influences as he would have us think. For his *Satyricon* comes shortly after the other two leading Italian directors, Luchino Visconti and Michelangelo Antonioni, have loosed similar visions upon the world. Some kind of communal sensibility seems to be operating along the Via Veneto, for their films are also studies of decay. Indeed, Visconti's *The Damned* may well be the most curious of them all. In some ways it is the most conventional, an intricately plotted attempt to examine, through the microcosm of a great, Krupp-like family, the conditions that gave rise to Nazism in Germany some forty years ago. But the microcosm turns out to be a distorting lens. One emerges from *The Damned* with the strong impression that the yeast causing the rise of the Third Reich was exotic depravity—transvestism, child molestation, incest. No one denies that the prewar German power elite was, to put it mildly, an

unhealthy organism. But to imply a cause-effect relationship between sexual perversion and political perversion is historically inac-
curate and socially irresponsible. It has an odd, insulating effect on
us, making us feel that totalitarianism is a rare bloom, one that can
flower only in very special soil. There are plenty of arguments
against the "banality of evil" explanation of fascism, but it does
have one great virtue: it makes us aware, banality being omnipres-
ent in human existence, that evil can happen here (or there or
anywhere) at any time. To render Nazism exotic, a once-in-a-
lifetime phenomenon, is to miss the point. Granted Visconti does
so in grand, operatic style (imagine Verdi trying to write a Wagnerian opera), granted that such an enterprise, by its very strangeness, will catch unforgettably in the mind. Even so, it is a dismal
movie.

Antonioni's *Zabriskie Point* shares some of the defects of its
competitors. Like Visconti, Antonioni is a stranger attempting to
make sense of a strange land, in this case, modern America. Like
Fellini, he is in this film (for the first time in his distinguished
career) primarily an imagist, untrammeled by any strong storytell-
ing compulsion. Nevertheless, he is artist enough to have overcome
these defects. But in telling such a story as he has to tell—about a
radical youth wrongly suspected of killing a cop in a campus riot
and about a hippie girl who is sort of, like, you know, drifting and
of how they meet in the wasteland and then part, he to be killed,
she to be radicalized by his needless death—he gets distracted. Like
many European visitors, he falls under the spell of the American
vastness, the enormous emptiness of our spaces. There is great
beauty in some of his visions, but there is also a familiarity about
many of them that is dismaying in the work of an artist of his
caliber. We are, I think, to understand that the empty land is the
objective correlative of an emptiness of spirit he found here. But
that too is a cliché and no better than a half-truth. There are moments, particularly in the early portions of the film, where I imagined Antonioni had satire on his mind, aimed not merely at the
established Establishment targets, but at our harebrained revolutionaries as well. Alas, he does not stick with it. Or with anything
very long. The tensions he has created in his best work (*L'Avventura, Blow-Up*) through the use of mystery stories with existential
overtones is missing. So is the psychological richness he is able to

create with wordless glances and gestures. Even the most striking images in *Zabriskie Point* lack the rich texture, the overtones of meaning, characteristic of him. I never felt compelled to engage with him, to wrest from him those meanings that he has, however stubbornly, yielded up in the past. The uniqueness of *Zabriskie Point* in his canon is not that we reject it as a failure. That is a disappointment which we are prepared for in the work of any artist. What is odd is the superficiality of the experience we undergo, the ease with which we escape it. I expect that with Fellini; I am amazed to find it in Antonioni.

MISSISSIPPI MERMAID

Gary Arnold

What with Visconti's *The Damned* and Antonioni's *Zabriskie Point* and Fellini's *Satyricon*, it's been a slightly trying season for the best Italian movie reputations. The French had been holding up: Costa-Gavras was in brilliant form in *Z*; Godard kept saying that he was junking art for the revolution, but his new movies indicated that he was synthesizing them, that it was temperamentally impossible for him to cease being an artist; Eric Rohmer, new to American art houses but suggestive of Joseph L. Mankiewicz with a higher French education, revived conversation and the comedy of manners in *My Night at Maud's* and refuted the current dogma that films are a "purely visual" medium.

Now, in a manner of speaking, François Truffaut has gone over to the Italians. Truffaut's art, like theirs, seems to have come to a standstill. He's groping around, repeating himself, working with formula material that doesn't suit his temperament, keeping his hand in until inspiration returns.

Mississippi Mermaid is such a simpering, negligible little movie, a tale of obsessive love derived from a Cornell Woolrich thriller, that one wants to forget it and wait for Truffaut's latest film, *L'Enfant*

Sauvage, which sounds more promising. Back in the early sixties I doubt if anyone could have imagined the day when Truffaut would be writing and Jean-Paul Belmondo would be speaking lines as agonizingly imbecilic as "Love is a misery and a joy" and "You are so beautiful it hurts me to look at you."

That day has arrived. Catherine Deneuve, the recipient of these sentiments (W. C. Fields had the expression for them—"sweet pretties"), has lines quite as awful. The worst would make sense if Mae West were saying it, but it's a howler in this movie: Belmondo asks Miss Deneuve how strong she likes her coffee, and she replies tenderly, "As strong as your arms." In general, one might characterize Truffaut's problem as the inability to get things in the proper context.

For example, this movie is dedicated to Jean Renoir and includes an excerpt from his 1937 film *La Marseillaise,* but the homage is misapplied. One could make a bad case for Renoir's 1938 *La Bête Humaine* as the inspiration, but *Mermaid* is actually imitation Hitchcock, with random echoes of James M. Cain and Godard's *Pierrot le Fou,* in which Belmondo played a similar masochistic role. Moreover, it's imitation Truffaut. In part the characters are diminutions of Jeanne Moreau and Oskar Werner in *Jules and Jim.* They've been stripped of intelligence and sensibility, leaving us with a dumb bitch and a dumb beau. The climax of the film is staged in the same Alpine setting used in *Shoot the Piano Player.* It's Truffaut's most regrettable idea, the artistic equivalent of profaning hallowed ground. He betrays us, using this locale to evoke feelings that his new film fails to evoke on its own terms.

The story itself is very simple. A colonial plantation owner (Belmondo) is awaiting a mail-order bride. The girl who arrives (Miss Deneuve) is not the girl in the snapshot he carries and doesn't match the impression he got through months of correspondence. But she is beautiful, and he accepts, marries and falls in love with her.

As soon as they establish a joint bank account, the girl takes off with all his money. Months later he sees her by accident in France. She's working in a dive, apparently abandoned by the male accomplice who planned the swindle and killed the real intended bride. (The ship all three were sailing on was called the *Mississippi.*) The hero loses his resolve to murder her, falls in love with her again and becomes a victim again.

The premise could be played for romantic comedy and would probably be more agreeable that way. Truffaut fails to make it effective as either a thriller or a tawdry love story. Both stars are thoroughly misused and unconvincing—Miss Deneuve as an imitation Tippi Hedren (a scene in which she has nightmares makes no sense at all unless you recall that there's a scene like it in Hitchcock's *Marnie*) and Belmondo as a sad sack, a poor, unworldly fall guy. It's a terrible waste of glamour and talent. Instead of slogging through a self-pitying, lachrymose love story, these two should be reviving one of those gratifying love stories about a girl with a past who turns out fine when she connects with an independent but dependable guy who's also been around.

It shouldn't be too hard to shape the material for honest sentimentality. Truffaut is a film nut and there are plenty of models: *The Docks of New York* and *Morocco* and *Shanghai Express* and *To Have and Have Not*. Maybe even a variation of *The African Queen*. The point is that Truffaut is getting nowhere copying Hitchcock, whose training and temperament are totally different. He gives us the worst of Hitchcock—the perversities without the wit, the plots that don't parse, the gimmicks that backfire—in the same way Jerry Lewis gives us the worst of Chaplin.

At present there's a rather startling illustration of how helpless Truffaut can look compared to an accomplished hack director. In *Mermaid* Belmondo is waiting at the dock for the intended bride he's never met. In Henri Verneuil's *The Sicilian Clan* Jean Gabin is waiting at the airport for a relative he hasn't seen in thirty years. Truffaut manages to bungle the situation, while Verneuil resolves it charmingly. There's no reason why Truffaut should blow such a simple interlude, but he does. Perhaps it's because his head is too full of references and models. One hopes that *L'Enfant Sauvage* will renew him, because imitation is making him absent-minded.

THE WILD CHILD

ROBERT HATCH

Truffaut's *The Wild Child* is about a boy of ten or twelve. *The 400 Blows*, which was the first film he directed, concerns a boy of similar age, and comparisons are being made, it being suggested that Truffaut has a particular rapport with childhood. There is probably something to this, and Truffaut calls attention to it by dedicating the current work to Jean-Pierre Léaud, who played the lead in the earlier one. It is also evident that these two films are peak achievements in a somewhat uneven career.

But aside from empathy with the young, which in fact is not so rare a trait, the pictures are more different than they are alike. *The 400 Blows*, at least suggested by Truffaut's own childhood, was a deeply subjective picture. *The Wild Child* is the meticulous dramatization of a case history set down by a Dr. Jean Itard in 1798 and for a few years thereafter. For all that Truffaut himself plays— admirably—one of the two leads (Itard), it is studiously objective; dispassionate, crystalline, deductive. The compassion, the humor, the somewhat rueful doubts must be supplied almost entirely by the spectator. That is part of what makes it so good a film.

Reason is the key. France at the end of the eighteenth century was a society enraptured by the magnificence of logic and fascinated by the dexterity with which the human mind performed it. Truffaut etches in this enthusiasm behind his narrative with well-tempered chamber music, spare and elegant interiors, sober propriety of dress, the distant courtesy of daily intercourse, and a view of man's place in creation which, if not smug, is certainly self-assured. Into this formality and pride of ascendancy over the natural order is catapulted *l'enfant sauvage*, the wild boy, found by a mushroom gatherer, captured by hunters with their dogs, leashed by one leg, raving and lunging for rustic entertainment.

Clearly he is of the human species, but can he reason? Paris senses a unique phenomenon and off to Paris the boy is shipped.

An older physician, after careful observation and long searching of his experience, says no, the boy is an idiot; that is why he was abandoned in the woods. Itard, young, ambitious, and fired by the experimental opportunity of a lifetime, makes bold to disagree. The boy is normal, and he does not reason because he has been deprived of the company of man, the only source of reason. He, Itard, will take the savage into his home—Madame Guerlin (Françoise Seigner), his housekeeper, will assist with the domestic necessities—and an attempt will be made to have this child reborn in human guise.

The picture then details Dr. Itard's methods, and irony begins to develop. On the one side is the doctor, with his measuring tools, his daily schedules, his ingenious instructional materials, his mild, evenhanded administration of rewards and punishments; and on the other, this passionate, inquisitive, impulsive, incontinent young creature who repeatedly astonishes his rather literal-minded guardian by cutting across the paths of a well-coordinated pedagogy, but who is distressingly slow to take his place as a cadet in the French bourgeoisie. To a modern audience, the boy (played astonishingly well by Jean-Pierre Cargol—Truffaut has a truly magic grasp of what children find worth their attention) is in many ways less strange than Itard, the Encyclopedist: we understand ferocity in confrontation with the rules, and we no longer lean with confidence on the syllogism.

There is in the film a suggestion, I think, that the boy might have progressed faster had he been left in the hands of an old peasant of the village who pitied the young being and who offered him only wonder and love. But it is no more than a suggestion, because one really cannot decide what to make of this boy. When he was found, he was ten or a little older; he could not speak, clothes were utterly unfamiliar to him, he showed no recognition of such familiar objects as bowls, shoes, door latches. How old was he, then, when he was exposed (among many scars, inflicted presumably by animals, there was a sinister straight slash across his throat)? How did he survive in a French winter (true, in Southern France, but that is not mild) at the age, say, of four? Had he really no memory of human contact; had no one in the village watched over his movements? We do not know—"wolf child" accounts are always unsatisfactory on this point—but it is possible that Dr.

Itard's austere study was for the boy more promising neutral ground than any peasant's cottage could have been.

In any case, the boy shows progress up to the point we take leave of him; evidence from later years is not available. The doctor, ever faithful to his muse of reason, is troubled that Victor (a name tried at hazard, and to which the boy responded with surprising alertness) shows no more than an increasing alacrity to perform by rote. Was he developing no sense of the human contract by which men deal responsibly and cooperatively with one another; no sense, in short, of justice? One final experiment: the boy will perform a task perfectly and the doctor will punish him as though he had obstinately failed. This is done and, eureka! the boy flies into an unprecedented spasm of hysteria and bites his patron's hand. Itard clasps his pupil to him—"welcome home, my child!"—and at last the love which the scientist has been so studiously disciplining to logic asserts its authority.

All this Truffaut details in the most chaste photography, flaring sometimes in the placid light like a daguerreotype. There is a stillness about the scenes, an expectancy, that endows each small development with almost stunning importance. The film is cool, and at the same time tense with these recurring minicrises; a shattered bowl can seem appalling. It is a film elevated by respect—respect for Itard's confidence in the triumph of order and for the boy's rebellious forays into freedom. And, finally, it takes notice of the poignant fact that it always seems a miracle when these two—order and freedom—are resolved; in the general run of men they come to terms.

Truffaut Contre La Mode

DAVID DENBY

François Truffaut's new movie, his strongest since *Jules and Jim* (1962), was the standout attraction of the eighth New York Film Festival in September and is the most beautiful picture I have seen in 1970. Yet there is reason to suspect that *L'Enfant Sauvage* (*The Wild Child*) will not be a hit in this country. The movie has been set in the past—an exquisite, slightly stylized version of the eighteenth century, perceived without condescension or anachronistic touches. Responding to its ideas and formal rhetoric may require a degree of historical imagination and sympathy that today's art-house audience—so harshly engaged with the crisis of the present—isn't willing to expend. Typically, this audience looks for confirmation of its own fears and desires; it won't find it in *L'Enfant Sauvage*.

Truffaut has structured his movie around some highly unfashionable themes, such as the humanity of science and pedagogy, the dignity of the student-teacher relationship, and the value of *learning* as the activity which above all allows us to become fully human. He dramatizes this material without much surface emotion and with a high degree of spare elegance. The great moments and revelations are there, but they don't grab you by the throat; the film requires an effort of emotional as well as intellectual projection. Its antecedents include the paintings of Chardin, the French engravings of the eighteenth century, and the great early films of Robert Bresson, such as *Diary of a Country Priest*.

Truffaut's true story is based on the journals of Dr. Jean Itard, *Memoire et rapport sur Victor de l'Aveyron*, published in Paris in 1806. In 1798 Itard took upon himself the stupendous task of educating a boy who had lived alone in the woods for eight or nine years after being abandoned as an infant. A naked howling animal of twelve years, the boy cannot speak and hears only natural sounds; one expert thinks he was abandoned because he was deaf and dumb. Itard's immediate aim is to prove that the boy's intelligence is simply dormant, undeveloped; his long-range intention is to bring this creature, whom he names Victor, to a state of fully developed humanity, which means to claim him for eighteenth-century civilization and order. Itard cannot for more than an instant entertain the fancy that Victor was better off in the woods, and it is obvious that Truffaut doesn't either—although he does show the savage as noble in his physical abilities. Perhaps most modern artists would be struck with the egotism inherent in Itard's project or even its foolishness or futility, but Truffaut presents it as a blessing for the boy and a valiant adventure for Itard.

The action of the movie is reinforced and discussed in excerpts from Itard's journals that are read onto the sound track, and these excerpts show why Truffaut treats Itard without critical irony: although Victor's unformed mind is a field for experiment, a test for pedagogical theory, Itard is anything but a tinkering, uninvolved scientist-observer. He soon learns to love the boy deeply, and every new method he tries with Victor is also a risk for himself: What if the boy should become upset and escape to the woods? Victor's lessons are painful for both of them; in a festival press conference, Truffaut compared Itard's emotions to those of a father taking a child to the dentist for the first time, hurting the child in order to help him. The journals also reveal Itard as a man quick to admit his own mistakes, as a masterly self-observer and self-critic. He is much too aware of this egotism to be threatened by it.

Truffaut plays Itard himself. The director is a darkly handsome, deft little man, but as a performer he's terribly buttoned-up and inexpressive. The fear of vulgarity seems to have choked him. Nevertheless, the performance claims our interest as a sign of how completely Truffaut admires and identifies with Itard. Perhaps he imagines his task as an artist to be something like Itard's as a scientist; for both, creation begins with a loving but rigorous observation of human nature. In the more immediate sense, they are both educating a boy; Itard's forming of an intelligence and personality that remains uncreated is paralleled by Truffaut's work with a twelve-year-old gypsy from the south of France, Jean-Pierre Cargol, who is unformed as a performer, and who has to be taught to move, listen, and react in a completely new way. Truffaut wanted to do this without an intermediary.

He has gotten a tremendous performance out of Cargol as Victor—a startling projection of the physical nature of man when he lived as an equal with the other animals. When we first see him, scrambling on all fours through the woods, or once captured, being led on a leash through a crowd of derisive villagers, he looks like an immense, maddened insect, struggling to find a safe spot on familiar ground. Truffaut keeps the camera back in long shot, and Cargol holds his head down, so we can't really make out what he looks like. Only later, in a sudden, stealthy camera movement toward the subject, do we see the human face, blinking and terrified, as it is wiped clean of grime. Even after Cargol has been taught to walk upright and sleep in a bed, the strangeness of his physical presence is often moving. At times he escapes from the house and rocks back and forth on his knees on the earth, in ecstatic, soundless serenades to the moon and the rain; we observe him at these moments from behind a window in the house, as if to preserve his privacy and separation from us. At other times, frustrated by Itard's constant lessons, he throws a furious and completely awkward tantrum, dropping to the ground abruptly, kicking wildly at nothing. Cargol conveys an extraordinary capacity for pleasure and pain that has been frozen into odd gestures and peculiar movements. Now that the wolf man has come out of the woods, he looks passing strange, but he doesn't frighten. Nothing could be further from Truffaut's intention than titillating us with a freak.

After Itard rescues Victor from an institute for the deaf and dumb, where he is considered an idiot and publicly displayed for the amusement of fashionable Parisians, he takes him home to the country and surrounds him, with the aid of his housekeeper (Françoise Seigner), in an atmosphere of loving order, cleanliness, and discipline. Victor's education proceeds in stages. First he is given a definite identity—a name, his own clothes, a room, and some privacy; later Itard tries to teach him the function of language, the relation of names to pictures and pictures to things; finally, he schools the emotions and the sense of justice, which become the principal element in Victor's moral development.

Itard's general method—with many experimental variations—is to punish Victor for not making an effort, force him to try again if he makes the wrong response, and reward him with a glass of water when some light breaks through. The inadequacies of this approach are completely obvious to him, and only a gross lack of historical perspective could fault his inventiveness in such an unprecedented job. Anyway, what is most reprehensible to modern educational practice—punishment in a dark closet—turns out to be crucial to Victor's developing sensibility. At first Victor has no sense of personal injury; it is only when his teacher puts him in the closet that he weeps. At the most exalted moment of the film, Itard tries to punish him unjustly to see if he rebels. It is a moment of great danger, for Itard risks destroying all the rapport he has built up with his student. When Victor does fight back, Itard concludes that the boy has been "elevated to the full stature of a civilized man"—even though Victor still cannot speak or read. Such a generous conception of civilization should be very attractive to today's audience, but Truffaut has too much pride or reticence to seek their favor by making it a big moment.

Anyone who remembers his first feature, *The 400 Blows*, with its deathly schoolroom and petty-bureaucratic teachers, knows that he doesn't have a shred of general sentimentality about the value of education or the nature of its effects on children; he simply won't treat this story from the past as a framework for plugging in contemporary attitudes and judgments in the manner of Tony Richardson (*Charge of the Light Brigade* and *Ned Kelly*) or Ralph Nelson (*Soldier Blue*).

Victor is the student *in extremis*; he resists at every moment what is being done for him and longs for the freedom of the woods. The beautiful room in which his painful lessons take place becomes a prison (from which, however, he is always free to escape), and Truffaut poses him characteristically at the window, staring out into the sunlight. The opposing claims of the natural world and of civilization hold the movie in tension, and Truffaut doesn't neglect the ambiguity in either. When Victor lived in the magnificent woods he could climb trees like a cat, and his time was his own, but he had to contend with the other animals for food and shelter—when he is captured his body is covered with scars. The civilized world included those sensation-seeking Parisians and parents who would abandon an infant in the wilderness, but also the ideal society of Itard, his housekeeper, his married friends nearby and their children, and their houses and properties which constitute ideal use of the natural environment. The claims don't balance out; the whole latter part of the movie attests to Truffaut's love of the organized social life of man. The movie almost becomes an idyll: Itard's house is without conflict or ugliness, poverty or ostentation, and the study room, with its plain wood furniture and wainscoting and broad, open windows flooding the interior with light, may be taken as an embodiment of the beauty and possible perfection of civilization.

To photograph it, Truffaut chose to avoid color film, which so often looks banal; instead, he and his director of photography, Nestor Almendros, rely on the elegance of black and white, with its exquisite capacity for recording the texture of light on solid materials. As Victor is introduced to the world of objects—bowls, utensils, tables, a heavy brass key, a book—we seem to be seeing them for the first time, too. Some of these shots may remind us of Chardin's *Kitchen Still Life,* and it's hard to remain unmoved by the plain beauty of these man-made artifacts, each so precious and singular in the period before mass production and superfluity. Everything is seen clearly, distinctly, in full possession of its exact function and shape.

Godard's old description of Truffaut's work—"rigorous and tender"—has never been more apt. By pulling us away from the characters with the recitations from Itard's loving but precise journal, Truffaut restrains the sentimentality inherent in the story. The constant use of medium distance shots has the same effect; they allow us to see the interactions between Itard and Victor without the effect of emotional underlining produced by cutting into close-up. Truffaut expects us to do a lot of careful listening and looking. He seems to have thrown off his famous charm and his recent obsession with Hitchcock's crowd-teasing and crowd-pleasing trickiness. The result is a great step forward for him as an artist.

THE RISE OF LOUIS XIV

Stanley Kauffmann

The photography for this film by Roberto Rossellini was done by Georges LeClerc, the costumes were designed by Christiane Coste, and I can describe the result only with the venerable phrase "a feast for the eyes": because I had the figurative sensation of devouring scene after scene. This is no case of imposed prettiness, like *Elvira Madigan,* no sentimentally spurious selection of decor to support a romantic concept. Here the exquisite fabrics, the richness of texture, the modeling of space by light, all are used to validate a complex reality. Artists have arranged matters, but there is no straining for arty effects. So they get the best possible result for a historical film: this is how the mid-seventeenth century must have looked when it was new.

Louis XIV was made for French television (which may give us a
hint about the high quality of the TV sets in French homes).
When you consider that it was finished in 1965 (it was shown in
the 1967 New York Film Festival), you recognize once again that
critical pronouncements, in any country, about the state of film art
don't reflect that state as accurately as they reflect the profit hopes
of distributors. Getting a picture made is only Money Problem
Number One for a film maker; Number Two is getting it distrib-
uted, in the country of origin and elsewhere. At any moment—at
this moment—there are films in existence in many countries that,
one way or another, would seriously affect anyone's estimate of the
current film situation, if he could see them. For the general public
in the U.S., Rossellini's film has not existed for the first five years
of its existence.

Rossellini, born in 1906, has had a long and influential career.
He was one of the pre-eminent postwar Italian neorealists (*Open
City* and *Paisan*), and he helped launch both Fellini and Antonioni,
among others. His work in the fifties, insofar as it was available
here, interested me less than it did other people. His last previous
picture that I saw—not the last one he made—was *General della
Rovere* (1959), which started slowly but became a fine idealistic
thriller.

The French title of the new film is more precise than the English: it translates as "The Seizure of Power by Louis XIV." Rossellini begins with the deathbed of Cardinal Mazarin in 1661. The
royal ministers then ask the young King to whom they should report, and Louis makes his famous surprising reply, "To me." The
film ends with the arrest of Fouquet, the establishment of Colbert
as chief adviser, and the relish of kingship realized, as Louis em-
barks on what turned out to be fifty-four years of rule.

The picture has been called a psychological study and a recreation of historical forces. In the usual senses, these terms seem
to me misleading. In the way that Eisenstein's *Ivan the Terrible* is
a psychological study, in the way that Jancsó's *The Red and the
White* exposes the nerves of political kinetics, *Louis XIV* only
glides on the surface. Rossellini creates his picture with pictures—
not quaint tableaux but the visualization of daily life in the great
houses by following details; the doctors bleeding Mazarin, the
maid sleeping on the floor outside the curtained four-poster where

the King and Queen repose, the dumpy progress of the little King plodding down the corridors, sentenced to immense journeys just in getting from one chamber to another. It's a species of naturalism, a reliance on surface fact to evoke inner truths, and is thus related to neorealism. In *Open City* the facts were those that Rossellini's contemporaries knew: which was the whole point of Italian neorealism—to show Italians recognizable Italy for a change. Here the factualism is in the past, but the artistic rationale is much the same. There is a scene in which Louis dines alone, with nobles (not servants) to serve him, with his brother on hand to provide the napkin, with dozens of courtiers standing below the dais to watch the King eat. The pace is natural, thus slow. The meal is a ceremony that reveals more about the evolution and power and responsibility of the institution of monarchy than most overt commentary or dramatization could provide. "Save the Surface and You Save All" is the slogan of a paint manufacturer; it is Rossellini's artistic credo here, and it works.

Music is also a strong element, in a unique way. At the start, we hear music of the period, and after it ceases, the picture seems to continue in the same stately tempo and sonority. From time to time, music rejoins the film, but always as if we had been hearing it all along.

The slow movement of the picture itself and of the characters within it has no relation to Eisenstein's tempo, where he often selects elements for Byzantine emphasis, nor to Antonioni's middle films, where he distends time for philosophic reasons. Rossellini is simply re-creating life—no, not simply, of course, but with the main intent of verisimilitude. And the rhythm and shape of that life are caught so well that the verism eventually takes on aspects of abstraction.

We get very few explanations of Louis' radical decisions. We never go "into" his head, and we see only a little of the exercise of shrewdness—in a scene with his mother. But all of his acts are credible, largely because of the performance of the role. Jean-Marie Patte, short and plump and plain, clumps his way to genuine regality with the full assurance of gracelessness. His very lack of stature and his disregard of that fact convince us that there must really be something in a man who has such assurance despite those physical odds. As Mazarin, an Italian actor called Silvagni and, as Colbert,

Raymond Jourdan fill solidly the spaces assigned to them in the composition. Rossellini casts a pretty actress (Joelle Laugeois) as the neglected Queen and a merely handsome actress (Françoise Ponty) as the King's adored mistress. Neat.

The script by Philippe Erlanger and Jean Gruault has its mechanical moments. The opening creaks with old fashions: peasants discuss their troubles—for our edification—outside the château at Vincennes, then two doctors ride by en route to the sick cardinal, then we follow the doctors into the sickroom. The authors put a stranger in the court to whom another courtier can explain some things that need explaining to us. Rossellini, too, has a few awkward moments: more than once, a character gets up from a chair, takes a few steps, and returns to the chair. This trope, which is supposed to add movement to a static scene, is only staginess.

But the picture is a serene, savory delight. To the French, this account of the Sun King's self-realization must be rich with reverberations. To other viewers, lots of other historical parallels are available. More important than such parallels is the beauty with which a certain portion of past time is made to flow through the glass once again. This is the work of a film maker calm and sure enough to relax without being lax: enjoying the fruit of long experience in the case and clarity with which he is now able to work.

BRUCE WILLIAMSON

Among a certain cult of film critics, the greatness of a movie is often measured in degrees of tedium. By this standard, Roberto Rossellini's *The Rise of Louis XIV* ranks as a masterwork. Ordinary moviegoers are supposed to suffer through it because they have been told the experience will be good for them. We say the hell with it, unless one is hooked on meticulous period reconstructions and dreary academic acting. Originally filmed for television in 1965 (in French, with English titles), *Louis XIV* plays like one hundred minutes of exposition for a behind-the-scenes human drama that never gets under way. The seventeenth-century costumes are perfect, the interiors sumptuous, the history conscientious to a fault in recounting how young Louis, at the age of twenty-two, asserted his personal power after the death of Cardinal Mazarin and began to build Versailles in order to keep the restive French nobility busy at court. But the actor chosen to play Louis XIV—the Sun King, one of the most colorful autocrats in European history—is a lumpish lad (Jean-Marie Patte) without a smidgen of charisma. Ringed around him are a host of secondary players who wear their costumes and recite their set pieces as if they had been asked to pose for a historical tableau. All in all, the movie comes off like a series of Famous Artists reproductions, adding little luster to the crown of Italy's reigning neorealist, the Rossellini of *Open City* and *Paisan*.

TWO OR THREE THINGS
I KNOW ABOUT HER

PENELOPE GILLIATT

Two or Three Things I Know About Her. It is one of Godard's most beautiful titles. Yes, you think, that's Godard—laconic, tentative, decorous. Not at all the savage tub thumper he used to be taken for, until we sensed his style. This is a truly speculative man, a passionate witness to an epoch that strikes him as both barbarous and majestic, a poet with a temperament of rage and urgency held in check, a dogmatist laying down no law, a learner hard-driven by the idea that we are ignorant and don't even know that we are ignorant. His films are often full of quotes, but he is the opposite of a show-off. He sometimes sounds, in fact, as though he were truly terrified that he might turn out to have been one of the last bookish men on earth. He can seem to be passing on for the record what moved him long ago—an impulse that his youth and politics make poignant. The world he creates is scaringly modern, but he speaks of it in his films almost as if he were a vestige of some other time, noting casual slaughters that the assimilated inhabitants take for granted. Godard's films would not carry such a charge of love and anger if he did not feel himself mysteriously supplanted. There is the same energy of the displaced in Shakespeare and in Swift. Some tribe has left the earth, say his films—*my tribe*—and taken away the dictionaries. But the memory of something lost goes with a furious connection with the present. If Godard characteristically seems nonchalant, I think it is only because the glare of the world he is attached to is too blinding for him to stare at it for long. And when he looks perfunctory about character, it is an act of courtesy, not of indifference: He wants to leave air around people. It is necessary to let them live their lives. He would not wish to scrutinize them out of existence. He allows infinite room for their stammering and their ambiguities. Some of them spout tenthhand dogma, learned by rote from pulp fiction about sex or from rabble-rousing books, some of them scrawl cant phrases on walls, but all of them know for certain only one thing—that they are not yet dead.

Two or Three Things I Know About Her expresses, to begin with, the consciousness of a lower-middle-class young wife in the outskirts of Paris who lives in a modern egg box and goes on the streets, respectably parking her children, to earn enough loose change to buy the clothes and the smokes of a bourgeoise. The social irony is a simple circle, perfectly and swiftly made in Godard's particular way, and the girl's consciousness of it is both bombarded and blithe. She takes it to be a fact of her city. The "her" of the title probably refers as much to Paris as to the heroine, who is played by Marina Vlady. The picture begins with the sound of a whisper—Godard's mind—nearly drowned by traffic. The whisper goes through the movie, worrying away at scraps of thought about existence and language through the racket of cars and building sites. As in most of Godard's work, the split between the subjective and the objective in the film is not simple. It hacks the picture down the middle, in fact, leaving it spilling some of the director's blood, though the blood is made to seem tomato ketchup, because a light self-mockery is his manner. It is a system of apathy that conceals violent feeling. The subjectivity is all in the whispers, barely audible, intermittent, quoting words from Wittgenstein, from the process of this film making, from Communist newspapers, whatever. The objectivity is about the enacted drama, the characters in the film, the visible. Godard is the most Brechtian of directors. Marina Vlady first appears as herself, named as herself, noted as being "of Russian extraction." She turns her head. Then she is introduced as the character. "Not of Russian extraction." She again turns her head, but now the other way, because the actress's point of view has switched to the audience's point of view. She speaks "as if she were quoting truths," which is the way Brecht always wanted actors to speak. In a wonderfully managed scene in a dress shop, she swivels from naturalistic behavior to direct talk to camera. Godard's contemplative moments are sometimes derided for literariness, as though they were doomed to pretension in any film, whereas they would do fine in a book. But this man, in the middle of meaning to kick away our sympathy, actually holds us in thrall by a technical mastery that razes to the ground most of the dumb received ideas about cinema. His technique serves exactly what he means. So when he says "The city of the future . . . will almost certainly lose part of its semantic wealth. Certainly . . . Probably . . ." it doesn't for a moment seem an assumed anxiety; it is his own, and a typical salute to dubiety. When he says, as the heroine has her pretty little red car washed, "Why do we take better care of objects than of people? Because they exist more than people do," it isn't one of our vapid cult-cynicisms, because we have already seen a good deal of the fugitive attention paid to this usual but particular girl. The gaps that have troubled linguistic philosophers trouble her without training. "The reason for my tears is not described in the streaks on my cheeks," she says to the camera, quite fiercely. Godard forswears the forces of sympathy and audience participation, which are perhaps forms of fear, but this does not keep him from a furious pity and expressiveness. There is a sight of an old man telling a story to a child who isn't allowed out of a modern apartment block to play. Once, the heroine runs around Paris, intoxicated: "I was the world," says the commentary for her, speaking about the present in a typical past tense, "and the world was me." In a café, covering a held close-up of a cup of swirling *café filtre*, there is a long voice-over monologue about the subjectivity that suffocates and the objectivity that alienates; only Godard, maybe, could make this amazing pole vault over the difficulties of getting us to pay heed in the cinema to pure talk, and only Godard would risk at the end of the monologue the beautiful acknowledgment of the epiphanic power of listening to the world as if it were a fellow creature. In spite of systems that make us "greatly evil without realizing it" this is the way Godard sees Paris. Raucous, avid, in straits, interesting. *"Mon semblable."*

SYMPATHY FOR THE DEVIL

Collision of Ideas

JAY COCKS

Jean-Luc Godard faces off with rock, drugs, and the black revolution in *Sympathy for the Devil*; the result is pretty much a stalemate. The film is fragmented, delirious, and didactic, sometimes to the point of stupor. But it displays the incontestable energy and stylistic daring that have made Godard the cinema's foremost Pop essayist.

*Sympathy for the Devil,** filmed in London in 1968, is rather formally divided into sections: Mick Jagger and the Rolling Stones performing the title tune over and over again in a recording studio; a group of black guerrillas bloodying white girls and reading excerpts from black writers in an auto graveyard; and a wraithlike creature named Eve Democracy (Anne Wiazemski) wandering through the woods, giving an interview to a pursuing film crew. A narrator intrudes from time to time to read selections from a mythical political-pornographic novel (" 'You're my kind of girl, Pepita,' said Pope Paul as he lay down on the grass") that are outrageous and very funny. The result of the separate episodes, however, is not a coherence of ideas or images, but merely a collision.

For years, Godard's films have been essentially free-association essays. Recently he has become less interested in culture than in politics. Films like *Le Gai Savoir*, for example, are basically director's monologues, with actors as mouthpieces and the audience made mute witness to sometimes incoherent polemics. *Sympathy for the Devil* is a kind of transitional work, an attempt, albeit un-

* A slightly different version is titled 1 + 1.

even, to blend esthetics and revolutionary politics. Unfortunately, Godard's symbolism is shopworn. The automobile graveyard as a symbol of Decadent Culture is as much a cliché of the New Cinema as riding off into the sunset was of the Old. Godard's constant use of acrostics, anagrams, and linguistic puns ("Cinemarxism," "Freudemocracy") reads like old issues of *Time*. The Stones' song, which through constant repetition becomes a raunchy liturgy, is musically outstanding but lyrically pretentious. "And I shouted out, 'Who killed the Kennedys?'/When after all it was you and me," typifies the level of political sophistication in much of the film.

As is usual with Godard, many of the images—like a climactic one of the bloody corpse of Eve Democracy being borne aloft on a camera crane—are crazily beautiful, and the photography is impeccable. Godard makes films quickly and cheaply. If they lack consistent intellectual quality, they possess a vigorous timeliness. Godard is like a manic eclectic, rebounding from issue to issue, composing a body of work that in years to come may look like nothing so much as a cracked mirror of our time.

LE GAI SAVOIR

Bruce Williamson

References to William Burroughs, Cohn-Bendit, Chairman Mao, Nanterre, Vietnam, Cuba, *Cahiers du Cinema*, and free Quebec litter the sound track of *Le Gai Savoir* (translated as "Joyful Wisdom") like the passwords for shock troops besieging a freshman dormitory. It should surprise no one that this new attempt to create a kind of abstract, stillborn anticinema is the baby of France's Jean-Luc Godard, who has apparently given up all semblance of form and decided to issue kinky philosophical tracts from time to time, as the spirit moves him. Which would be all very well if Godard were even a passably clear thinker. In *Le Gai Savoir*, he leaves his camera running on an incredibly tedious young couple (Juliette Bertho and Jean-Pierre Léaud) who sit, or stand, or shuffle, or strike poses in an inky-black limbo while they discuss the meaninglessness of language and the need for de-education. Occasionally, Godard cuts to cartoon strips, Pop posters, and street scenes, as if to illustrate—though not intentionally—that images can be pretty meaningless, too. Communication with his audience is minimal, to say the least, yet Godard would almost certainly scorn the suggestion that he ever intended to communicate anything in the language and pictures he deplores so passionately, and at such length. And why should he, when apologist critics stand ready to shed their blood justifying the movies he slaps together, often in a matter of days, with more cynicism than sweat? (The august *New York Times*, for example, went into somersaults of syntax to describe *Le Gai Savoir* as "one of Godard's most visually lucid films, even when the screen goes completely black." No wonder the erstwhile moviemaker begins to consider himself the natural successor to Nietzsche.) But as spokesman for a generation in revolt, the role he evidently savors above all, Godard is an intellectual washout—for he casts his net upon the contemporary world's troubled waters, drags in a few fashionable clichés of protest, and mounts them as if they were trophies honorably won, while the substance of every issue escapes him completely.

TRISTANA

Harold Clurman

With Luis Buñuel's *Tristana* one enters a shadowy realm, mysterious and possibly disturbing. Buñuel's nature is complex. Visually he is a superb artist. Every shot is rich with the feeling of place: the locale is probably Spanish Toledo in the twenties. The backgrounds are beautiful with an old beauty which bespeaks an experience of life of profound substrata articulated in grave splendor.

I do not cavil at the ambiguity in this film, if in fact it exists. What is puzzling in it does not arise from a partiality to obfuscation or to supposedly "modern" cinematic gimmicks. Buñuel never deliberately injects difficulty into his pictures as a warrant of sophistication or originality. What is dense is Buñuel's soul, and he can do no other than express it as he does, leaving others to interpret it as they may.

Tristana deals with the tragedy in desire. The film's central figure, Don Lope, is an elderly gentleman with an almost quixotic sense of honor. Though he comes of a wealthy family, his fortune has been rapidly declining, but toward the end of his days he recovers some of it through an inheritance. Don Lope has elevated moral standards in unusual combination. He is a rake, but he believes it wrong to seduce the wife of a friend or a pure girl. He scorns the Church, hates bigotry. He is against the police because it stands for power, while he is always on the side of its victims, the weak. He is a duelist, and something of a "Socialist." But the drive of his sensuality leads him to make love to his ward, Tristana, a beautiful young girl and a virgin. Yet he suffers very little sense of guilt because of this. He considers himself to be her "father" and her "husband," though he does not offer to marry her.

Tristana herself is hardly a simple person. She submits to Don Lope because she has been trained in obedience. When he kisses her for the first time in passionate embrace she does not resist but giggles in surprise. But, while submissive, she hates the old gent who, because of his intense sexuality, is menacingly jealous. She realizes the extent of her abhorrence when she meets Horacio, a young artist from Barcelona, to whom she gives herself. On this affair being discovered, she defies Don Lope who ineffectually challenges his rival to a duel. Tristana leaves Don Lope and goes off with Horacio to Barcelona.

Three years later the artist comes to tell Don Lope that Tristana is terribly ill and wants to come back to his house. Tristana has refused to marry her lover, perhaps because Don Lope has so often repeated that wedding ties are a bondage. It is to be noted that when Tristana is resting at Don Lope's place, she tells Horacio that

if he really loved her he would not have consented to bring her to
Don Lope's home—nor would Don Lope have acted in like manner under similar circumstances.

Tristana has to undergo the amputation of a leg. She occupies
herself by playing a piano Don Lope has bought her. She now
moves about on crutches or on an artificial leg. She has become
"correct" and hard. She finally agrees to marry Don Lope; when he
wishes to sleep with her on their wedding night she ridicules him
for it. Still she satisfies a deaf-mute boy's lust for her by exposing
her bosom to him—at a distance. When Don Lope has a heart
attack, he bids Tristana to call a doctor; she only pretends to do so
and the old man dies.

Why, one asks oneself, does Buñuel resort to the odd turn of the
story—the crippling of Tristana and the various distortions of her
later behavior? Must Tristana and the others suffer for their sins,
which result from the freedom of their natural but perhaps excessive concupiscence? One cannot tell, but I suspect that despite
Buñuel's intense anticlericalism, the residue of his original Catholi-
cism remains implanted in him.

Unabated desire, raw sexuality, though inevitable in nature, poi-
sons the blood. This is tragic because of the inexorability of the
impulse, the ineluctability of its consequences. We may deny or
dislike this pattern of conscience; it is extremely Spanish and, contrary to the power of his own rationalism, it seems to be very much
part of Buñuel.

What is important in this instance is that it is revealed without
preachment or explicit doctrine but with pictorial eloquence, emotional reserve, highborn dignity. And, don't be shocked at my saying this: there may be some truth, anyhow a truth in Buñuel's
view. We always pay a price, in disappointment or pain, for whatever is in us, even when it is not evil.

III:

ADAPTATIONS

WOMEN IN LOVE

Arthur Schlesinger, Jr.

Women in Love is one of those films of literary origin that, if you know the novel, seems inadequate and, if you don't know the novel, may well seem incomprehensible. In this case, one cannot altogether blame Larry Kramer, the writer and producer, and Ken Russell, the director. D. H. Lawrence's novel, a work of great complexity animated by an intensity sometimes bordering on hysteria, is itself a dark and mysterious document.

The ostensible story is of Ursula and Gudrun Brangwen, two sisters living in the Midlands just before World War I. Ursula falls in love with Rupert Birkin, the school inspector, who is already involved with Lady Hermione Roddice, an intellectual hostess of the neighborhood; Gudrun falls in love with Gerald Crich, the son of a local mineowner. Each girl pursues her fate. One relationship ends ironically, the other tragically.

But the story is more elusive than that; and, confronted with Lawrentian ambiguities, Kramer and Russell have chosen to resolve many of them in a single direction—to such an extent, indeed, that some may wonder why the film is not called Men in Love. This sharper homosexual emphasis in the film seems an obvious response to the preoccupations of our own time. Yet it is by no means clear that the film does injustice to unconscious tendencies in the book. Consider Lawrence's imagery:

"You seem to have a lurking desire to have your gizzard slit, and imagine every man has his knife up his sleeve for you," Birkin said.

215

"How do you make that out?" said Gerald.

"From you," said Birkin.

Birkin was based on Lawrence; and Alan Bates, made up like Lawrence, plays the part well in a generally subdued vein. Crich, whom the novel describes as "erect and taut with life, gleaming in his blondness," is acted by Oliver Reed, a dark, stocky man with an unfortunate resemblance to Jerry Colonna. Though Reed is a serviceable actor, a good deal of the contrast between the two men emphasized by Lawrence disappears in the film. Hermione, inspired by Lady Ottoline Morrell, receives something of a revue-skit performance from Eleanor Bron.

The two girls—suggested by Frieda Lawrence and Katherine Mansfield—are well played by Jennie Linden as Ursula and Glenda Jackson as Gudrun. Miss Jackson in particular conveys the repressed hysteria of the novel with great delicacy and force. The concluding scenes, when the lovers go to the Tyrol on a skiing holiday and Gudrun and Crich torment each other in savage quarrels, come off with immense power.

Yet motivation and behavior remain unclear, as of course they do in the original. Still, the novel, with its more highly charged complexity, preserves the impression that the mysteries have a solution—an impression that Russell, the director, does not quite produce in the film, where much of the action seems merely gratuitous and unintelligible. Where Russell succeeds marvelously, though, is in the evocation of the atmosphere of the time—the girls, their hats, dresses, gait; the sooty ugliness of the mining town; the flickering lights of a boating party at night; the comfortable simplicity of a Tyrolean mountain lodge. *Women in Love* cannot be claimed as a success; but it is a fascinating and intelligent try.

BRUCE WILLIAMSON

Male and female nudity are shown with complete frankness—but without a hint of exploitation—in the course of *Women in Love,* producer-adapter Larry Kramer's literate treatment of the fifty-year-old novel by D. H. Lawrence. Wearing a beard and mouthing the author's prophetic beliefs about men, women, marriage, and sex, Alan Bates could pass for Lawrence himself.

Women in Love has little to do with conventional ideas about romance; yet director Ken Russell, who indulges in a good deal of slow-motion camera work when he wants to wax romantic, deserves considerable credit for the fact that Bates and his gifted co-stars appear to know precisely what they are talking about at all times. As four English gentlefolk bedded for matched doubles during the early 1900's, they talk with Lawrence's own passionate intensity about the nature of love and friendship—between man and wife, man and mistress, man and man. That the discussions never become bookish is surprising, since the movie dotes on words and more words. Bates manages his brilliantly as Rupert, the articulate hero who achieves sexual fulfillment with the pretty schoolteacher he marries (Jennie Linden) yet craves the satisfaction of another deep, but unperverted, love relationship with his best friend (played with deliberate stolidity by Oliver Reed). His wife doesn't understand, and neither does the friend, who dies a very novelish death after an unhappy affair with Rupert's sister-in-law teaches him that he probably can't love anyone. Playing the sister-in-law, Glenda Jackson (of London's Royal Shakespeare company) delivers a strikingly offbeat performance as one of those brainy New Women who tended to express themselves in impulsive bursts of interpretive dancing. The compromises people make and the complex emotional drives that force them to choose one way or another are the issues here. In a film created with keen intelligence, integrity, and meticulous period flavor, Lawrence's ideas about life and love retain remarkable potency.

THE VIRGIN AND THE GYPSY

This England, This Past

PENELOPE GILLIATT

Sunday matins, the Sunday roast. Oh, England. How D. H. Lawrence loved the place and hated its suffocating rituals.

Christopher Miles's film of Lawrence's *The Virgin and the Gypsy* begins in the grip of the English middle-class Sabbath at full strength. In the dour light of Derbyshire, twenty miles away from industrialism, a rector played by Maurice Denham avidly intro- duces one of the Church of England's most metrically depressing hymns. His two grown daughters are coming back from school for good; we see them at the station, and then they go straight into the hell of the family Sunday lunch. The meal is nearly as allegorical about bourgeois England between the wars as the one in *Budden- brooks* about rising Germany. It nails a certain characteristic gluttony for the dismal, a certain kind of roughness without much fun or ease, and a certain contradictory sense of a pitiful privation that has no tongue. The vicar, full of skulking self-love, carves the joint and makes brittle small jokes. Aunt Cissie, gray-faced, so but- toned up that food strikes her as some sort of licentious outrage, grimly eats a single boiled potato. Granny—played by Fay Comp- ton, and therefore a less gross figure than the prognathous monster in the book—plants her old bulk firmly on her chair and begins before the others. The girls get the giggles, through terror, and famine of any other impulse. In this stone vicarage, in this indus- trial Midland county where no one is ever entirely well, in this house of proscription and sarcasm, where the air has the stagnancy of a crypt and where Granny rules the pious table with a pagan and lewd form of majesty that turns the girls' stomachs, Lawrence's two virgins are waiting to be wakened into sensual life. The story of Yvette (Joanna Shimkus) is one of his Sleeping Beauty parables; it directly foreshadows *Lady Chatterley's Lover*, which he began in the same year (1926). The girl is wonderfully well played. Hidden somewhere in the ethereal romantic is the hint of a peculiar insula- tion and self-will, like her grandmother's. She belongs to the bour- geois freemasonry, however charming and wayward she is for the moment, with her straying detachment from heavy Midland things, and her insistence on wearing a red dress that the family calls fast, and her growing passion for a gypsy whom you know she will drop as soon as he has wakened her from this stone sleep. Franco Nero plays the gypsy. The character is one of Lawrence's risky ones: melodramatic, not without romantic bathos, yet some- how also commanding and natural. There are fine scenes for him in the film (which has been well adapted by Alan Plater). He emits a mysterious force of endurance that is very Lawrentian. It is the endurance of the primitive man who survives by opposition but without an idea of victory. The unlocking of the virgin's soul is no particular triumph for him. There is no feeling that he has magicked her. In fact, in the last scene, freighted with symbolism, when he at last makes love to her in her own house while it is being flooded with racing brown mill water, there is an interlude shot when he comes out onto the stairs to look at the water in a mood of terror about what he is going to do. Stir up middle-class England and you unleash a good deal. The character of the girl comes out in the film as having terrific dewy stubbornness. She hates her family. She hates this house, where her hypocrite father snipes at the bad blood that his children inherited from their mother, who ran away with another man. She loathes her greedy grandmother and the terrorized maids and the bedrooms where women sleep two by two in rather repulsive, testy surrogate communion. She develops a crush on a racy divorcée (Honor Blackman) who has eloped with a Major Eastwood to live with him in a very twentyish kind of brazenness that is actually too hysterical to be at all free. But, all the same, the girl belongs obstinately to her class. She would like to pull the temple down, but she would prefer to keep the prestige of picking away at the columns from within.

If you care for Lawrence—and though the draft of the novel was never revised, some of it is magnificently written—the film is likely to strike you as truthfully done and satisfying. Some of the lines sound prosy, some of the camera work is busy and rubs your nose in its points, but the picture is an intelligent piece of work, with Lawrence's strength and a passing silent humor of its own. There are scenes one doesn't forget: the tyranny of the old lady about a crossword puzzle, choosing to be deaf so as to extract the maximum attention, although she can hear like a weasel when no one wants her to; a naked bathing sequence, with the characters full of a perfectly in-period jolliness about free love; the vicar telling a fearful joke about the pearly gates; the more timid sister sobbing over coming from "half-depraved stock" after one of her father's outbursts about his ex-wife, whom he would surely like to rub out from sight altogether, except that his daughters keep reprinting her image in his head. Lawrence, tarred and feathered in his time for his longing to free instinct and language, fills even his lesser books with the nobility of a man out on his own.

STANLEY KAUFFMANN

The Virgin and the Gypsy is fairly faithful to the D. H. Lawrence original and is therefore fairly silly. This posthumous short novel, unrevised by the author, simplifies foolishly some of the themes used better in, among others, *Lady Chatterley's Lover* and *Women in Love*. The recent film of the latter was unsuccessful, but at least it had some complexities to dally with. Here Lawrence uses the same opposition of warm blood and cold climate, the "poetic" urge battering at the cabbage-and-potato proprieties that still pertained in England after the First War: but with what baldness and mechanics. And, as filmed, *The V. and the G.*, directed by Christopher Miles, is a color-me-passionate primer, full of italicized symbols: the fumed-oak rectory imprisoning the repressed clergyman's daughter, the black stallion on which the handsome gypsy rides the countryside, the girl's first view of the dam as a crack in it is being repaired, the bursting of the dam that floods the v. into the g.'s arms, and so ludicrously on.

Still, putting the symbols aside, if that were possible, this faded story of life-hungry revolt might have made a tolerable period piece if the heroine had been well played. Joanna Shimkus is an Anglo-French Candice Bergen: a pretty girl who, by trying to act and failing, makes herself unpretty. Miss Shimkus pouts, or doesn't pout, and has a thin, vapid voice that disintegrates if she has two consecutive sentences to speak. (And some of the things she has to say are horrendous. To a friend: "It's as you were saying the other day—life can be very difficult.") Franco Nero, the gypsy, has the asinine job of being the Male Principle incarnate; he tries earnestly, but sinks into repeated ruts.

In 1964 I saw a half-hour film in London called *The Six-sided Triangle*, made by Christopher Miles with his sister Sarah—six comic versions of a love story, an old revue idea and not very well done. Miles was being highly touted as a new talent; yet it took six years for us to get his first (as far as I know) feature. It has all the latest cinema lingo: lush color (as photographed by Bob Huke), dream and reveries sequences in slow motion without sound, exaggerated lyricism (why was the brief trip across the lake so dazzling?), lopping off scenes before they actually end to hurry things along. As is now customary with directors of British films set in the country—particularly in the past—Miles gets the most out of stone bridges and old artifacts (a wooden coal scuttle, for instance), and their beauty has gone a long way to gain him credit for making a beautiful picture, which it is not. Young American directors have developed their own anonymous, interchangeable filmic patter; young British directors are developing their equivalent, equally interchangeable among them. In both countries they represent the most deplorable aspects of the new film consciousness: linguistic cleverness and novelty as a substitute for flavor and commitment. How can you say I'm not an artist when I've just shown you this ingenious shot in the bedroom mirrror?

At the end the ex-virgin goes off with a free-living lady named Mrs. Fawcett and the latter's lover, which the girl does not do in the book, thus cheering up Lawrence's tale of Anglican doom. In the film Mrs. Fawcett is not Jewish, which omits not only Lawrence's persistent anti-Semitism (he refers to her throughout the book as "the little Jewess") but his fascination with her as the outsider who can better afford to Dare.

THE GREAT WHITE HOPE: I

ANDREW SARRIS

The Great White Hope was considerably overpraised as a play, partly as a reflex reaction to its roaring out against racism in America, and partly as a testimonial to the alleged vitality of so-called regional theater, a largely mystical entity which double-domed theater pundits were pushing last year as a form of cultural decentralization to purify bad old Broadway. For whatever reason,

Howard Sackler's drama managed to garner the Pulitzer Prize and the New York Drama Critics and Antoinette Perry Awards for 1969. Sackler himself wrote the screenplay, and Martin Ritt directed the movie with what, at times, amounts to Famous Players fidelity to the stage production.

But suddenly the spell seems to have been broken. No longer do masochistic movie reviewers diagnose their own discomfort as another instance of Hollywood hacks betraying the divine drahma. No indeed. They go right back to the source of the trouble, and to hell with the Pulitzer Prize and the New York Drama Critics and the Antoinette Perry puffs. Howard Sackler wrote a bad play, which was badly performed, and almost everyone was taken in by it, or at least pretended to be taken in by it.

Why? Well, when James Earl Jones as Joe Jefferson alias Jack Johnson beats his chest like a tom-tom and rumbles out his basso profundo challenge to a guilt-ridden white liberal audience, it is admittedly difficult for that audience to avoid looking with glazed eyes beyond the stage to the ugly realities outside. The old problem of extracting the ethics from esthetics bedevils the brashest reviewer whenever the race problem is raised. It is so easy to be misunderstood. So easy and so dangerous. Hence, any reasoned judgment of *The Great White Hope* becomes almost impossible in the wild oscillation between extreme critical caution (racism is always relevant) and extreme critical bravado (racism is the last refuge of thesis drama).

Howard Sackler's tactics in treating the shameful story of Jack Johnson's ordeal as World Heavyweight Champion from 1908 to 1915 may be rationalized as Marxist and/or Brechtian, but even so, the treatment of the central character and his milieu is neither coherent nor consistent. I don't go along with the current criticism of Sackler and Ritt for not letting the movie tell it exactly like it was (the time-honored realism argument). *The Great White Hope* is much more a race movie than a fight movie, and sobeit. The trouble is that Sackler and Ritt move from an overly explicit exposition of the basic problem to an increasingly vague development of that problem's effect on the black champion and his white mistress. Dramatic psychology is sacrificed, almost absentmindedly, to racial mythology. And thus as I have watched both play and film, I have found my attention wandering from the awkward histrionics in front of me to the more complex historical presences lurking behind stage and screen.

The best writing I have ever read on the subject is the late John Lardner's two-part article in *The New Yorker* of June 25 and July 2, 1949, entitled "The White Hopes." Earlier that year Joe Louis had retired from the heavyweight championship in an atmosphere of relative good will, racially speaking. Indeed, Lardner pegged his articles on the contrast between the Johnson years and the Louis years. Whereas Louis proposed and effected a match between the two men, both black, whom he considered best qualified to fight for his title, Johnson was subjected to a steady stream of white hopes without ever being consulted. Lardner was very careful, however, to qualify the contrast in periods with the observation that Louis might have had less trouble in Johnson's time than Johnson did, and Johnson more trouble in Louis' time than Louis did. And it is well that Lardner provided this qualification, for with the advent and misadventures of Cassius Clay—Muhammad Ali, the relevance of Jack Johnson becomes more painfully pointed. Ali, like Johnson, has been everything that Louis was not in his championship years—arrogant, proud, boastful, stubborn, ostentatious, even a bit sadistic beyond the functional demands of his profession.

But there are crucial differences as well between Ali and Johnson. Ali is more overtly political, even factionally political, than Johnson ever dreamed of being. Johnson's greatest offense against public opinion in the early 1900's was his open preference for white women. Lardner even quoted Johnson firsthand on the subject: " 'I didn't court white women because I thought I was too good for the others, like they said,' he told me one day in the 1930's, when he was working as a sideshow attraction at Hubert's Museum, on West 42nd Street, a few years before he died in an automobile accident. 'It was just that they treated me better. I never had a colored girl that didn't two-time me.' "

Sackler's script glosses over the multiple connotations of Johnson's self-professed womanizing by caricaturing the villainous faithlessness of Joe Jefferson's black wife while idealizing the crusading fidelity of his white mistress. (Johnson was actually married three times, his second wife, white like his third, having committed suicide.) By making Johnson more relentlessly monogamous, Sack ler deflects the audience's attention from the internal feelings of the characters most concerned to the external pressures of a racist society. But all around the edges of the drama there are dissenting murmurs—a black power prophet here (Moses Gunn), a massah-dear mammy there (Beah Richards), little dribs and drabs of racial dialectics which evoke more complexities than they explain. With one eye on the black theoreticians and the other on the theater parties, Sackler balances off the bloated rhetoric about white devils with an Odetsian Jewish fight manager called with endearing condescension "Goldie" (Lou Gilbert).

James Earl Jones acts Joe Jefferson with the loftily liberal knowingness with which Paul Robeson once played the Emperor Jones. On stage, Jones acted by fits and starts, and his voice lacked expressive resonance. He lurched about more with the inexorability of a golem than with the grace of a fighter. So much so that he had made me completely forget the interestingly disciplined performance he gave as the bombardier in *Dr. Strangelove*. But I remembered that performance when I saw him go into the malignantly self-mocking rendition of Uncle Tom in the movie version of *The Great White Hope*. The effect is still too broad, too theatrical, in fact, but it is the kind of theatricality that belongs more on the screen than on the stage. Jones is at this point more a stirring presence than an accomplished actor, and he is not up to the kind of Brechtian role playing and commenting that the Sackler script calls for, and, besides, the great contribution of D. W. Griffith to the cinema was not montage (and certainly not race relations), but rather the development of a privileged sanctuary for the actor to express his most intimate feelings with the most delicate gestures. *The Great White Hope* represents a long step backward to the days of Italian divas like Lydia Borelli who waved their arms frantically in a show of emoting. But I think Duse herself would have asked her director for a more oblique camera treatment of the dreadful scene in which James Earl Jones is asked to heave with Herculean sorrow over the soggy corpse of Jane Alexander.

THE GREAT WHITE HOPE: II

The Great White Hope does not exaggerate the rampant racism of American life between 1908 and 1915, a period in which Jack Johnson was both persecuted and prosecuted for being too uppity. Indeed, the evidence of racism is so overwhelming that Howard Sackler's play and screenplay run the risk of incurring the intellectual sin of obviousness. Some subjects, in and of themselves, are too morally one-sided for the dialectical demands of drama. What is one to say on the most literal level about the Nazi death camps or apartheid in South Africa beyond cease and desist we pray you or lest we forget.

Unfortunately, Sackler's attempt to avoid the curse of cant results only in psychological obfuscation and ideological confusion. All the sound and fury of James Earl Jones's performance, and all the whimpering and whining of Jane Alexander's, never gets us any closer into the core of their drama together as a doomed couple. Martin Ritt's Philco Playhouse staging of the indoor scenes is so unimaginatively three-wallish that we never feel either privacy or intimacy.

Ultimately, Sackler's politicalization of the subject subordinates the sensuality of a fact to the rhetoric of a right. A self-mocking joke about sunburn across the color line is boomed beyond the bed and across the footlights so that we can all laugh too comfortably about the absurdity of discrimination. And all the time the character of Joe Jefferson is kept in the limbo of innocence betrayed. By the time the white devils of the fight game, our shameful surrogates historically and allegorically, have completed their conniving, Joe Jefferson has been battered into a bloody hulk beyond good and evil, beyond irony and ambiguity, beyond edification and catharsis.

However, *The Great White Hope* raises other questions that are never even considered, much less answered, in Sackler's one-issue presentation. Jack Johnson was a fighter, a man of violence, a professional inflicter of pain on other men. The spectacle of one man hurting another is, under any circumstances, morally ambiguous.

The enjoyment of this spectacle is even more dubious. I am happy that Ali vindicated himself after being wrongfully and hypocritically stripped of his title, but I cannot rejoice that Jerry Quarry required eleven stitches to close the cut over his eye. I have not reached that stage of ideological commitment that would enable me to regard Jerry Quarry as any less human than Muhammad Ali. (I wince even when I see old fight films of Max Schmeling being demolished by Joe Louis in their second fight.) No man is an island apart from me, and no man's pain can leave my own conscience painless. It is not that I wish to ban boxing or anything like that. It is simply that boxing, like all other sports and wars and competitions, is more fact than fable. Some people win and some people lose, and afterward the commentators draw the appropriately moralistic conclusions, which are, more often than not, the most rancid of rationalizations. If Joe Namath throws five touchdown passes, hurrah for the swinging singles, and if Fran Tarkenton throws five touchdown passes, hurrah for Sunday School and clean living.

The late John Lardner observed in his *New Yorker* articles that the four best fighters of Johnson's time, apart from Johnson himself, were Sam Langford, Joe Jeannette, Sam McVey, and Harry Wills, all blacks, and hence racially ineligible to qualify as white hopes and indeed challengers of any kind. Johnson himself rationalized his reluctance to take any of them on with the frank admission that the meager gate would not be worth the major risk. Langford, Jeannette, McVey, and Wills were so good, in fact, that they seldom received the opportunity to fight any white pugs, and on the rare occasions they did they were strongly urged by the all-powerful white promoters to avoid delivering knockout punches.

This extraordinarily unfair situation would seem to be a thing of the past. Whatever your politics, Ali and Frazier are both black, and it would seem that in the fight game we have come a long way in rewarding pugilistic talent regardless of race, but I say "seem" advisedly because it is quite clear that the white race has farmed out the heavyweight championship to what it considers the lowest orders.

For all the vaunted violence of American life, few parents above the subsistence level encourage their boys to dream of becoming heavyweight champions of the world anymore. The lower East

Side Odetsian sagas of the Jewish or Italian boy who must choose between his violin and fame and fortune no longer have the slightest sociological underpinning. Max Baer was the last of the credible Jewish heavyweights, Marciano the last of the Italians, and Quarry could be the last scrappy Irishman to be a contender. Middle America prefers the controlled violence of pro football, and there is where the crunch is still felt, not so much on the Johnson-Clay level of recognizably superlative talent, but on the Langford, Jeannette, McVey, Wills level of either intermediate or indeterminate talent.

Discrimination in the most invidious sense is now subtler and less conspicuous, and the thin line between persecution and paranoia seems to vanish almost entirely under the varnish of antiracist rhetoric so relentlessly applied as to make the black seem unreasonably suspicious. But facts are facts. The black schoolyard basketball players on the Atlanta Hawks know that they have a vested interest in subsidizing Pete Maravich's inflated salary in order to pacify the rampant racism of their potential fans. All the players, that is, except Jumping Joe Caldwell, who knows that right now he is an infinitely better pro player than Maravich, and wants to be paid accordingly. And then there is the tantalizing question of racial balance on the Knicks with Reed, Frazier, Debuscherre, and Barnett belonging on the starting team through sheer talent, and Bill Bradley and Cazzie Russell fighting it out for the fifth spot, and neither able to prove a consistent superiority to the other, but the suspicion still lingering that Bradley is currently preferred so as to provide better racial balance for the Buckley fans from Mineola.

The rumblings of black revolt on high school, college, and professional teams across the country are matters of record, but the prospects for black athletes are even bleaker vis-à-vis their white counterparts once they have hung up their jock straps for good. I saw a sad picture the other day of Marion Motley coaching a girl's football team in Cleveland, and whatever happened to Marion Motley, the bulldozing fullback and pass blocker who helped Otto Graham make the Cleveland Browns so omnipotent in the old All American Conference days. Graham has had top-flight coaching jobs galore whereas Motley has to scrounge around on a semipro level. There has been exactly one black pro basketball coach (Bill Russell), and he had to contribute his superlative playing services to make the grade. There have been no black pro football or base-ball coaches, and no one is holding his breath till the first black breakthrough occurs. (For that matter, there have been patheti-cally few black film critics employed on a regular basis beyond the obligatory black power article.) Yes, we whites are all still guilty of racial discrimination even though our practice of prejudice has be-come more refined and, hence, more shrewdly self-serving than ever before.

But by being too stark and too abstract and too allegorical, *The Great White Hope* actually distracts us from the refinements of current cruelties by wailing too loudly about the rawer brutalities of another time. In this one respect, however, the film improves on the play by substituting the late Chester Morris' quietly manipu-lative fight promoter as a reasonably realistic white presence for the blustering, bellowing, bigoted poet laureate of white supremacy embodied by George Matthews on the stage. Morris reminds us as Matthews did not that reasonableness is the most pernicious as-pect of and attitude to racism. Still, Lardner's oblique treatment of the racism in the Johnson years is more persuasively critical of White America than all of Sackler's flat-footed forensics.

For one thing, Lardner contoured his articles around the crooked contortions of the fight racket, and thus provided a left-handed parody of capitalistic exploitation. As it was, the white hopes themselves were so many lambs led to the slaughter, some-times literally as well as figuratively. Maimed, mangled, and muti-lated to the roar of the crowd, they took on the role not so much of the glorious matador as of the gored bull. And for all their suffer-ings, they usually ended up being swindled by the system. Jack Johnson was part of that system, and he was accustomed to the fast shuffle and the double cross. On one occasion, according to Lard-ner, Johnson was fighting Stanley Ketchel, a much lighter man, both skinwise and weightwise, under a gentleman's agreement that no knockout punches would be attempted. When Ketchel rared back and floored Johnson with a fully swung white hand, the champion, in Lardner's words, "recognized the blow as sincere to the point of treachery. He was used to double crosses, and had had signal success in frustrating them. Rising, he hit Ketchel in the face so hard that the middleweight's lips were impaled on his teeth. He was unconscious for an hour."

The Johnson-Ketchel fight is not even fictionally referred to in *The Great White Hope*, even though it is this fight that persuaded Jack Jeffries to come out of retirement for the purpose of upholding the honor of White America. I did happen to see the Ketchel fight on film some years ago as part of a television series, and I was most struck by the period defensive style with which Johnson fought the fight. He seemed the last of the great classical fighters as Dempsey was the first of the great modern fighters. The point is I did feel the patina of pastness settling on his reputation and upon an era in which men thought nothing of fighting for twenty, thirty, and forty rounds.

As corrupt and brutal as boxing may be, it does have its own logic and nuance, and the James Earl Jones King Kong characterization of Johnson is somewhat unfaithful to the ironic fact that Johnson depended more on speed and guile than brute strength. And this adds a further complication to the problems Johnson (and Ali) have had with certain segments of the bloodthirsty public. Great defensive fighters simply do not bleed enough. They also don't take enough chances with their opponents, nor score as many clean pow! bam! knockouts. Thus, Jim Corbett was never really as popular as John L. Sullivan, nor Gene Tunney as Jack Dempsey; nor Ezzard Charles and Floyd Patterson as Jersey Joe Walcott and Rocky Marciano. By contrast, with Johnson and Ali, Joe Louis created in the ring the atmosphere of a jungle in which at any moment the hunter might be brought down by the hunted, and this is what fight fans all lust for, a sense of mystery, suspense, and danger, not a neat night's work accomplished with the monotonously rhythmic thrusts of a left jab on a slower man's skin tissue. Ali, like Johnson before him, does a neat night's work and is not about to let himself get marked up to satisfy the blood lust of the ringside ghouls.

The Great White Hope doesn't go into any of these questions possibly because to do so would mean raising moral questions of an absurdist order such as why do Mafia chieftains discriminate against blacks in the recruiting of gunmen. Hence, ring action is kept to a minimum so as to allow more time for the rhetoric of racism, and every time James Earl Jones blows up on stage or screen we are encouraged to believe the cause is invariably racial persecution untainted by any innate meanness of spirit. This overloading of sympathy I find incredibly naive. Indeed, a little more meanness would have made the character infinitely more believable and his plight infinitely more moving.

Curiously, the movie does finally venture out into a still disputed historical terrain that the play avoided like the plague. In short, did Jack Johnson actually throw the championship fight to Jess Willard in Havana in 1915 or was he legitimately defeated by a younger, stronger fighter? The play strongly implies, as Johnson did himself in what was described by Lardner as a somewhat fanciful autobiography, that the fight was indeed so much of a tank job that it splashed under the hot Havana sun. The movie is more ambiguous. Sackler suggests (in both versions) that some sort of deal was arranged on the Mann Act conviction. If so, Johnson was double-crossed again because he finally served out almost his entire sentence. Lardner suggested more plausibly that the deal entailed money and film rights to the tune of at least thirty thousand dollars.

Last year, a compilation of fight films entitled *The Legendary Champions* professed to prove that the controversial still photo of Johnson apparently shielding his eyes from the hot sun as he was being counted out created a misleading impression that was corrected by the motion picture footage of the fight long unavailable to the American public because of the fear of race riots. The motion picture footage shows Johnson's legs (drawn up in the still photograph) slowly sagging down till they were flush with the canvas. But it must be recorded that Lardner himself never considered the evidence of the still photograph conclusive evidence. We may never know what actually happened on that racist afternoon in Havana, but what little we do know is infinitely more interesting and complicated than Howard Sackler's shrill simplistics would indicate.

I NEVER SANG FOR MY FATHER

ARTHUR KNIGHT

I Never Sang for My Father, adapted to the screen by Robert Anderson from his own stage play, never gets quite far enough away from the original to ever make it as a first-rate movie. But the theme is so very pertinent, and the performances so very affecting, that one is more than willing to settle for less. At its center is the pill-produced world of the aged, an octogenarian who can still function as despot over his fully grown children. Tom Garrison (Melvyn Douglas) has long since retired from both the business world and politics; in fact, his mind wanders just a bit. But he is still a formidable character to his son (Gene Hackman), a writer and teacher; somewhat less so to his daughter (Estelle Parsons), whom he banished from the house for marrying a Jew. The death of the children's mother (Dorothy Stickney) precipitates the decisions from which the drama derives.

Admittedly, the theater is better for this sort of thing. It thrives upon the self-revelatory dialogues, the verbal flashbacks that bring each of the characters into focus. Indeed, it used to be fashionable to label these adaptations "uncinematic"—as if the lack of tricky camera work and snappy editing were enough to put seriously, intelligently conceived material beyond the pale. One can still regret that *I Never Sang for My Father* was not more completely "cinematized"; but the fact is that unless it had first been conceived for the stage, it would probably never have been made into a movie at all. For here is the kind of character revelation that keeps one going, hopefully, to the legitimate theater; it seems to happen in films only when those films have been adapted from a stage play.

But even in this instance things are done on screen that the theater could never accommodate. There is a beautiful sequence—photographed in a lovely wisteria garden in White Plains—during which the brother and sister reach some form of understanding. The maturity of the trees, the manicured lawns bespeak the whole life of the departed mother and throw into effective but unspoken contrast the life of the arrogant, unfeeling old man in the house beyond.

But there is compassion, too. There is no question but that, by his own lights, Tom Garrison was a fine, respectable, respected citizen. What makes the film hurt, what makes it ache for anyone at all empathic to its story, is the plight of the second generation, the tragedy of those who live in the shadow of a great—or not quite so great—man. They bear the burden and the guilt. A documentary-like sequence—again impossible on the stage—reveals old-age homes for what they are: places for dying. The son, understandably, is not able to consign his father to such a dismal, futureless future. But when he suggests to his father that he come and live with him in California, the father, no less understandably, is not willing nor able to abandon all the things that have given his life meaning.

I Never Sang for My Father, produced and directed by Gilbert Cates, may set no milestones in cinema. But it has truth, and heart, and a sensitivity to human relationships that lift it far beyond the more aggressively movie movies.

THE ANGEL LEVINE

It Suffers in the Translation

ARTHUR KNIGHT

All my life, it seems to me, I have been listening to long, complicated Jewish jokes with the tag line in Yiddish. Everybody laughs, applauds the speaker, and loves the whole thing. But if, timidly, I ask for a translation, I am invariably told that it's not quite the same in English. I had something of the same feeling after coming away from The Angel Levine, based on a short story by Bernard Malamud, and adapted by William Gunn and Ronald

Ribman. Just as the film reaches its climax, they switch to Yiddish. And while I'm sure that it was all very touching, tender, and tinged with humor—just as the rest of the film had been—nevertheless, I felt a little left out, a little cheated. At the very least, they could have provided subtitles.

On reflection, I suspect that the entire picture could have benefited from a bit more clarification. Why does the aged Morris Mishkin, searching through Harlem for the Negro Angel Levine, simply leave Levine's battered hat on a pew instead of asking the rabbi if he knows him? Does Mishkin, in the final shot, really think that the pigeon feather floating down from on high is from Levine? Has he suddenly come to believe in both angels and the God that this particular angel stands for? In his earlier film *The Shop on Main Street*, director Jan Kadar provided an apotheosis that told us, in a lovely, romantic, somewhat sentimental way, that his two main characters were reunited in death. In *The Angel Levine*, he leaves us dangling.

Though the inconclusive ending is no longer a novelty, it is disconcerting to find it attached to a movie that, in all other respects, is reminiscent of Frank Capra at his prime, with just a touch of *Here Comes Mr. Jordan* thrown in for good measure. Morris Mishkin, superbly played by Zero Mostel, is an elderly, defeated Jewish tailor with an ailing wife (Ida Kaminska, of *The Shop on Main Street*). While he rails against God's injustices, and she lies dying, Harry Belafonte introduces himself as a Jewish angel condemned—one gathers for previous, unnamed sins—to rekindle the flickering flames of Mishkin's belief in the Lord's goodness. There is an irony, not nearly sufficiently developed, in the fact that Mishkin, who has been a pious man, must accept Levine—who has been anything but—as an emissary of the Lord before the miracle that will save Fanny Mishkin's life can be wrought.

Kadar is beautiful and right in his treatment of the scenes between the elderly couple. There is a sense of ethnic awareness rarely encountered in American films; a sense, also, of an enduring relationship in which each is all too aware of the human weaknesses of the other. The core of the film, the sad acknowledgment that the death of a loved one is imminent, Kadar has realized with a tender compassion that is infinitely moving. It is the otherworldly aspects of his story that give him trouble, that cause him to fumble.

At the opening, when Mishkin inadvertently causes the death of a young sneak thief, the shots desaturate from color to black and white, then back to color again. Why? The real question is whether the dead young man is the Angel Levine who returns to haunt him, but this is never cleared up. And how do angels make assignations with former girl friends?

Such inconsistencies constantly undermine *The Angel Levine,* as does a camera style that went out of date with *Citizen Kane,* when cinematographers learned to keep both foreground heads and background heads in focus. And yet I am sure that I shall continue to be haunted by shots of Mostel puttering about a shabby kitchen, trying to read a Jewish newspaper while his wife watches TV, and exuding warmth and humanity as he seeks to dissuade the angel from committing suicide. *The Angel Levine* shows a side of the world that we rarely see on the screen, the world of the common man.

THE BOYS IN THE BAND

Harold's Birthday

HOLLIS ALPERT

A time-tested dramatic and comedic device is to give a party for someone, and, depending on what subsequently transpires, the course can be run toward either hilarity or pathos. In *The Boys in the Band,* taken directly and with little change from Mart Crowley's stage success, there are both hilarity and pathos, but the hilarity generally has a sour note, and the pathos seems forced. And, while the acting of a cast of eight ranges from good to superb, the filming under the direction of William Friedkin has a way of exposing the artifices of the play's construction.

This may have occurred because Mr. Crowley, who served both as adapter and producer of the film, understandably did not want to tamper with success. When first staged two years ago, the play

sss

was regarded as the frankest treatment of homosexuality to hit the boards. Not only did it deal with homosexuals somewhat sympathetically, it also, less sympathetically, took their pretensions for a campy ride. All that is in the film, and most of Mr. Crowley's witty and acerbic dialogue, some of which he has updated in line with current standards of frankness.

What one doesn't get is any real sense that a film has been created, although the beginning offers promise. We see several of those invited to a birthday party for Harold heading toward Michael's apartment, where the party will be held. Harold, according to his own definition of himself, is "a thirty-two-year-old, ugly, pock-marked Jew fairy," and it is rather a pity that he doesn't arrive earlier in the film, because when he does his impersonator, Leonard Frey, takes malevolent charge of the proceedings. In his high, whining, vaguely fatigued voice he further explains himself with: "and if I smoke a little grass before I can get up the nerve to show this face to the world, it's nobody's goddamn business but my own." Mr. Frey is priceless. He all but carries the film on his sagging shoulders.

But Mr. Friedkin, after proving that he can move his camera around effectively, all too quickly settles for the form of the play as originally written, which means that it is confined to a single setting—Michael's Manhattan apartment, with a terrace added, and, fortuitously, two telephones with separate numbers. Those telephones are clearly necessary so that the "truth game" may be played, an indulgence of truly extraordinary masochism and one which all too neatly reveals the various hang-ups and self-hatreds of the participants in the party. Guilt eventually undoes everyone but Harold, who walks off with his "gift," a young Texan hustler.

One other problem handicaps this literate exposé of what purports to be the homosexual milieu, and, for it, we have only the times to blame. So much frankness, nudity, obscenity, and what was once known as pornography has engulfed us in the mere two years since the play was presented that the tears shed by Michael over the awfulness of his love and sex life have a crocodilian tinge. In fact, the attitude of the film toward its characters—that they are more to be pitied than censured—seems rather unnecessary during these ultraliberated days.

IV:

MUSICALS

ON A CLEAR DAY, YOU CAN SEE FOREVER

Regressive Behavior

Joseph Morgenstern

In *On a Clear Day, You Can See Forever*, Barbra Streisand plays a wistful little drab from New York City who tries to cure her chain-smoking through hypnosis. Under the spell of psychiatrist Yves Montand, she regresses to a previous incarnation as a fiery beauty of a British social climber circa 1814. In point of fact, however, Miss Streisand progresses pretty remarkably as an actress while the movie around her keeps regressing, back through the Technicolored mists of time, to some of the dreariest, fustiest, mustiest habits of Hollywood's great musical-comedy era.

Putting Miss Streisand in the dual role of Daisy Gamble/Melinda Tentrees was the movie's first, best, and only inspiration. It's almost inspiration enough for a while. She's alive and at home in any period, any accent the movie requires of her: the haughty, throaty refinement of an English lady, the Cockney chirping of that lady's humble youth, the dejected plaints of a collegiate nicotine addict. She looks grand as Melinda, stroking her breast with a cool crystal goblet of white wine to arouse a man ogling her at dinner (the gambit would work equally well with red wine). She's a thoroughbred clotheshorse for Cecil Beaton's costumes. She flashes lightninglike between Melinda's airs and Daisy's earthiness, and when her Daisy admits to possession of various psychic powers —"I make flowers grow"—she does so ruefully, as if it were a curse and she were Mrs. Job.

If only she could make movies grow when she isn't onscreen.

239

Director Vincente Minnelli and his photographer, the late Harry Stradling, whip up some lovely old fluff in the regression sequences, which were shot in England at Brighton's Royal Pavilion. The decor is sumptuous, the extravagance justified, the tone lightly self-mocking. A flashback within the regression, to Melinda's childhood in an orphanage, suggests a witty parody of *Oliver!* But Minnelli and Stradling, custodians of a defunct tradition, bring a negligible sense of style or pacing or humor to those modern sequences which constitute, alas, most of the movie's running time. They, far more than poor Daisy Gamble, are haplessly trapped in the present.

Minnelli gets no help from Alan Jay Lerner's script, with its embarrassing pseudo-science, its atrocious dialogue and its inexplicable reluctance to modernize itself and capitalize on the growth of interest in psychic phenomena that's taken place in the United States since 1965, when the original show opened on Broadway. But Minnelli gives no help to Jack Nicholson, who seems to have forgotten how to act as he struggles with the small part of Miss Streisand's ex-stepbrother, and less than no help to Montand, whose performance as the amorous Dr. Chabot can only be described as indecent exposure.

Montand actually seems to have regressed since his unfortunate American movie debut in *Let's Make Love*. His English is so graceless and halting that you want to reach out and burp him. He's directed and photographed badly in almost every scene, every close-up, but really grotesquely in his first chorus of the title tune. It would be easy to conclude that Montand destroys the movie singlehandedly, and that's probably the conclusion most casual spectators will draw.

Most casual spectators, though, don't remember Montand's fine performances (in his native French) in *The Wages of Fear* and *La Guerre Est Finie*. Most casual spectators haven't been exposed to his awesome powers and devastating charm as a music-hall singer. Only those few spectators who've seen Chris Marker's delightful documentary *Letter From Siberia* will recall a song, seemingly an old Russian folk song at first, whose lyrics declare jubilantly that "when we hear Yves Montand's voice on short-wave radio, the boulevards of Paris reach all the way to Siberia." Miss Streisand's success in *On a Clear Day* is her own, while Montand's failure is partly his own, of course, but also that of the director, producer, writer, photographer, and executives of the financing company. It is the failure of established, enormously prosperous people who don't want to be bothered any more with what they once knew about casting, showmanship, craftsmanship. It is the failure of moviemakers who have themselves become the most casual of spectators.

SCROOGE and SONG OF NORWAY

Meanest Man in Town

PHILIP T. HARTUNG

I was surprised the other day when Charles Dickens was telling me how much he liked the musical movie called *Scrooge* which was based on his much-loved short novel, *A Christmas Carol*. When I protested that the music didn't amount to much, he admitted that the score and lyrics by Leslie Bricusse weren't particularly memorable, but, he insisted, the screenplay, also written by Bricusse, was fine. With this I had to agree—after pointing out that most of it was lifted right from the book. And then Charlie replied perhaps that's why he liked the script: most of the words were his.

Charlie should have given the cast some credit too—for putting over the good Dickens lines and for bringing the characters to life so well. Albert Finney is, no doubt, the youngest of the many actors I've seen portraying Scrooge. This does have one advantage however: in the scenes during which the Ghost of Christmas Past conducts Scrooge back into his youth, Finney looks good as a handsome young man. And he also looks appropriately mean and stingy and bitter when made up as the old Scrooge in the present. Finney plays the role well, often hamming it up to the hilt. But most of the movie Scrooges through the years, and there were many, saw fit to exaggerate the role. Certainly the last one (Alastair Sim in 1951) did.

Under Ronald Neame's direction, an excellent cast surrounds Finney as ghosts and characters from Scrooge's past, present, and future, all seemingly determined to make the miser mend his ways —or else. Alec Guinness is just right whooping it up as Marley's Ghost. Edith Evans, with her perfect diction, is elegant as the Ghost of Christmas Past. Kenneth More, looking exactly like the John Leech illustration in that first 1843 edition of the *Carol*, is properly jovial and serious as the Ghost of Christmas Present who wears holly and icicles in his hair. Paddy Stone is so swathed in black robes as the Ghost of Christmas Future that one can hardly tell what he looks like until we discover he is a skeleton.

Among the less ghastly characters, I particularly liked Laurence Naismith as Mr. Fezziwig and Kay Walsh as his wife, described by Dickens as "one vast substantial smile." Also good are Michael Medwin as Scrooge's nephew, David Collings as Bob Cratchit, Richard Beaumont as his son, Tiny Tim, who is played without any of the usual maudlin sentimentality.

Since most of *Scrooge* is so good (Robert H. Solo's production with those handsome costumes and mid-nineteenth-century sets in lovely color photography), I'm sorry that the music isn't better. And I wish that one episode in which Marley's Ghost conducts Scrooge to Hell had been omitted. It's a bit too grim for youngsters —but perhaps its moral serves a purpose (I'm not sure what purpose!). Most of *Scrooge* is on the fun side; and I'm sure any adults who take their kids to it will enjoy it as much as the kids. I understand why Charlie Dickens liked it.

Another old-fashioned musical film (even more old-fashioned than *Scrooge*) is *Song of Norway*. It purports to tell the story of the struggle of Edvard Grieg to gain recognition and success. The only good things to be said in favor of the film are its music, most of which stems from Grieg, and its gorgeous scenery, photographed in color in Norway and Denmark. Since Andrew L. Stone wrote and directed *Song*, the movie's faults and pleasures must be credited to him. The bad film making is his. The music is Grieg's. But only God can make a tree and a mountain and a waterfall.